OF SUGAR AND SNOW

CALIFORNIA STUDIES IN FOOD AND CULTURE

DARRA GOLDSTEIN, EDITOR

OF SUGAR AND SNOW
A History of Ice Cream Making

JERI QUINZIO

UNIVERSITY OF CALIFORNIA PRESS
BERKELEY   LOS ANGELES   LONDON

The publisher gratefully acknowledges the generous support of the General Endowment Fund of the University of California Press Foundation.

University of California Press, one of the most distinguished university presses in the United States, enriches lives around the world by advancing scholarship in the humanities, social sciences, and natural sciences. Its activities are supported by the UC Press Foundation and by philanthropic contributions from individuals and institutions. For more information, visit www.ucpress.edu.

University of California Press
Berkeley and Los Angeles, California

University of California Press, Ltd.
London, England

Library of Congress Cataloging-in-Publication Data
Quinzio, Jeri.
  Of sugar and snow : a history of ice cream making / Jeri
Quinzio.
    p. cm.
  Includes bibliographical references and index.
  ISBN 978-0-520-24861-8 (cloth : alk. paper)
  1. Ice cream, ices, etc.—History. I. Title.
TX795.Q59 2009
641.8′62—dc22   2008026041

Manufactured in the United States of America

18 17 16 15 14 13 12 11 10 09
10 9 8 7 6 5 4 3 2 1

This book is printed on Cascades Enviro 100, a 100% post consumer waste, recycled, de-inked fiber. FSC recycled certified and processed chlorine free. It is acid free, Ecologo certified, and manufactured by BioGas energy.

To Glen

CONTENTS

ILLUSTRATIONS FOLLOW PAGE 144.

PREFACE

During the past few years, whenever I told people I was working on a book about ice cream, they invariably smiled. Then they told me their ice cream stories. Some described how they struggled to turn the crank of an old-fashioned ice cream maker on a summer afternoon, just so they could lick the dasher when the ice cream was ready. Peach ice cream was a particular favorite. Some reminisced about waiting for the familiar jingle of the ice cream truck's bells when they were kids, and then having trouble deciding between a Popsicle and a Fudgsicle. The tales were predictably happy, except for the ones about a scoop of ice cream falling out of a cone onto the street.

People also told me stories they'd heard about the history of ice cream and its creation. One woman, a Philadelphia native, said that as a schoolgirl she was taught that ice cream was invented in her hometown. When I told her it wasn't, she said, "I didn't quite believe it even then." People spin all sorts of tales about ice cream's origins, and most of them are wrong. That's too bad, because its history is remarkable. It doesn't need embellishment.

I'd like to set the record straight.

One popular myth has it that Nero invented ice cream since he liked eating snow with honey poured over it. He may have enjoyed that particular treat; however, pouring honey over snow is not making ice cream.

Marco Polo may have tasted ices in China in the thirteenth century, as many believe, but he did not bring recipes or information about freezing techniques back to Italy. If he had, there would be references to them in the books, letters, and diaries of the time. If he had, Italian scientists would not have been experimenting with freezing techniques three centuries later.

The most enduring myth is that Catherine de Medici introduced ice cream to France from Italy when she married the future king Henry. However, nearly a century after Catherine's death, M. Audiger, a French confectioner, said he had to go to Italy to learn how to make ices. Surely that would not have been necessary if Catherine's Italian cooks had taught the French how to make them when she arrived in 1533.

Not only is there no documentary evidence of ice or ice cream making in Italy so early in the sixteenth century, but also, as Alberto Capatti and Massimo Montanari point out in *Italian Cuisine: A Cultural History*, culinary techniques and knowledge circulated widely between Italy and France as early as the thirteenth century.[1] There was no need to rely on Catherine de Medici for recipes.

Even if the Italians had known how to make ices at the time, Catherine was hardly in a position to influence French dining habits. She was a fourteen-year-old girl when she married Henry, Duke of Orléans, who was also fourteen. As the second son of King Francis I and Queen Claude, he was not expected to reach the throne, so he had little influence at court. Since Catherine was a foreigner and not considered a great beauty, she had even less. When Henry did become king, following the untimely deaths of his older brother and then his father, Henry's mistress, the beautiful Diane de Poitiers, actually wielded more power than Catherine.

Catherine came into her own after her husband died and the first of her three sons who would become kings of France took the throne. During the reign of her son Henry III (1560 to 1574), the French, like the Italians before them, became entranced with ice and snow. They began decorating their tables with carved ice sculptures, serving dishes atop piles of snow, and putting ice in their drinks. But there is no evidence that they ate ice cream.

Another tenacious ice cream myth is that King Charles I of England, who reigned from 1625 to 1649, had a French cook who made ice cream. The story is told two ways. One has it that King Charles was so enamored of the ice cream that he rewarded the cook with lifetime tenure. In the other version, he was so impressed that he threatened to have the cook killed if he revealed the recipe to anyone else. The English writer W. S. Stallings Jr. has laid both versions to rest. He wrote that the story "is undocumented and is first seen in print in the 19th century. The documentation of ice cream in England begins following the return of Charles II from his exile in France." That was not until 1660. In fact, the first known recorded English use of the words *ice cream* is from the Feast of St. George at Windsor in May 1671, when "One plate of Ice Cream" was served to the table of King Charles II.[2]

Stories of kings having cooks killed over an ice cream recipe are entertaining, but I find the facts more fascinating. Ice cream, like the Zelig character in Woody Allen's film, has been on the scene for some of the most dramatic events of the past. Sometimes it played a leading role; at other times, it was an extra walking through the background. Following ice cream's progress through time tells us a great deal both about ice cream and about the era in which it was made. It's a tale that takes us from palaces to playgrounds, from banqueting rooms gleaming with silver and crystal to city streets teaming with pushcart vendors. Along the way, it touches on nearly every important social, political, and economic development of the past four centuries.

In this book, I trace the history of ice cream from its early days in seventeenth-century Italy to the dawn of its industrialized production in America. My title—*Of Sugar and Snow*—is drawn from a phrase early confectioners used to describe the desired consistency of their ice cream. Throughout the book, I use comments and recipes to illustrate how the making—and the eating—of ice cream changed according to its circumstances and surroundings.

For example, medical opinion regarding ices and ice cream was and is ever-changing. In the seventeenth century, some believed its cold temperature would bring on paralysis. Others thought it was just the thing to cure scurvy, emaciation, and, yes, paralysis. In the nineteenth century, it was believed that eating ice cream chilled the stomach and stopped digestion. It was also considered a good, healthy treat for children. In the late twentieth century, Americans blamed ice cream for coronary artery disease. Yet in every era, praised or maligned, it has been a much-loved dessert.

Scientists and inventors have been as important to the development of ice cream as cooks and confectioners. Italian scientists experimenting with freezing in the sixteenth century inspired confectioners to create ices and ice creams in the seventeenth. In the nineteenth century, an American woman named Nancy Johnson invented an easier-to-use ice cream maker, and home cooks began making ice cream more often. Frederick Tudor, a Bostonian, developed the ice industry and made ice cream available to nearly all. Mechanized production methods, refrigeration, and railroads each changed commercial ice cream making and distribution.

Surprisingly, the democratization of ice cream was not met with universal approval. When peddling ice cream on the street became an entry-level job for nineteenth-century immigrants, fashionable confectioners and their customers were dismayed. Nevertheless, by the turn of the twentieth century, Americans were gobbling up five million gallons a year, and ice cream had become a mass-market product.

Many events that seemed to have nothing to do with ice cream had a huge impact on the business. During Prohibition, corner saloons were often transformed into soda fountains, and the ice cream business prospered. But repeal and the Great Depression of the 1930s hit it especially hard. Celebrated in songs, poems, and children's rhymes, ice cream was an early film star and a soda fountain favorite with the bobby-soxer generation. It took on a patriotic flavor in America during World War II and became more widespread than ever afterward, partly as a result of the development of the federal highway system. Now a Fourth of July tradition and the obligatory accompaniment to a birthday cake or a slice of apple pie, ice cream is a staple of supermarket freezers.

Today, commercial ice cream making is a sixty-billion-dollar global enterprise dominated by two companies: Nestlé and Unilever. They control more than a third of the market and own such famous brands as Ben & Jerry's, Häagen-Dazs, and Dreyer's. They're rapidly expanding in such markets as China, Brazil, the Philippines, and Indonesia. Their story is less about ice cream and more about global business, so I leave the telling of it to another author.

I close with a brief look at today's ice cream artisans, the women and men who are carrying on a tradition of quality and creativity by making and selling their own unique ice creams in small shops. No doubt their ice creams will be the stuff of the nostalgic stories of tomorrow.

ACKNOWLEDGMENTS

I am grateful to many individuals without whom, as the saying goes, this book could not have been written. They helped with translations, found books and illustrations for me, and read and corrected various drafts of my manuscript. They also played the important, if more subtle, role of offering cheer and encouragement along the way. I value each and every one.

They include Ken Albala, Gary Allen, Jackie and Parviz Amirhor, Rob and the late Alice Arndt, Ubaldo di Benedetto, Madonna Berry, Marilyn Brass, Sheila Brass, Joe Carlin, Kyri Claflin, Roz Cummins, Ivan Day, Anne Faulkner, Norma Gahl, Barbara Haber, Susan Jasse, Sheryl Julian, Rosemary Kafka, Janet Katz, Lynn Kay, Patricia Kelly, Daniel MacLeod, Douglas and Lola MacLeod, Ellen Messer, Doris Millan, Deb McDonald, Sandra Oliver, Beth Riely, Susan Rossi-Wilcox, Lynn Schweikart, Andrew Smith, Nancy Stutzman, Agni Thurner, Joyce Toomre, Barbara Ketcham Wheaton, Joan and Jay Wickersham, Winnie Williams, and of course, my husband, Daniel Coleman.

Librarians are special individuals. I am indebted to those at the Boston Athenaeum, the Boston Public Library, the New York Public Library, the Winterthur Library, the Library of Congress, Harvard's Botany and Houghton Libraries, and above all, everyone at the Schlesinger Library, most notably Marylène Altieri and Sarah Hutcheon.

I also thank the ice cream people who were so generous with their time and even their ice cream. Steve Herrell, founder of Steve's Ice Cream and now owner of Herrell's Ice Cream based in Northampton, Massachusetts; Gus Rancatore, owner of Toscanini's Ice Cream in Cambridge, Massachusetts;

Stephanie Reitano, of Capogiro in Philadelphia; Amy Miller, of Amy's Ice Cream shops in Texas; Torrance Kopfer, of Cold Fusion Gelato in Newport, Rhode Island; and Gabrielle Carbone, of the Bent Spoon in Princeton, New Jersey.

The members of my writers' workshop have meant more to me than I can express. They are Myrna Kaye, Roberta Leviton, Barbara Mende, Sabra Morton, Shirley Moskow, Beth Surdut, Molly Turner, Rose Yesu, and the late Doris Luck Pullen.

Everyone at the University of California Press—Randy Heyman, Kate Marshall, Laura Harger, Bonita Hurd, and Mari Coates—has been enormously helpful to me. Finally, I appreciate the guidance and support I received from Darra Goldstein and Sheila Levine. They are editors—and individuals—par excellence.

Thank you all.

ONE

Early Ices and Iced Creams

A royal dinner in seventeenth-century Naples was a dazzling spectacle. The splendor of the décor complemented the magnificence of the foods, to the delight of the guests. Confectioners seized the opportunity to demonstrate their considerable talents and turned tabletops into showcases of their art. They carved hams from ice and displayed them in baskets made of sugar paste; they shaped lions and bulls from butter and posed them in battle stance. They created fruit-and-flower-filled ice pyramids that glistened in the candlelight. They molded gods from marzipan to watch over the mortals at the table.

The foods that the diners actually ate were equally splendid. They feasted on a dozen or more courses, possibly spit-roasted pork topped with a crown of lemons, fresh strawberries bathed in wine and served atop a mound of snow, lasagna sprinkled with sugar and cinnamon, and dishes of fresh fennel, pears, grapes, and artichokes adorned with snow and flowers. Parmesan cheese was served with sage under it and laurel leaves painted silver and gold over it. There was an abundance of wine. The grand finale was an array of cookies, pastries, and the fashionable new dessert: *sorbetti*.

At the time, Naples was still part of the Spanish empire, and Charles II was its king. Although Spain's power and influence were declining, its nobles entertained as sumptuously as they had when Spain was the dominant power in Europe. They were in the vanguard of the dining changes sweeping through the continent. During the seventeenth century, wealthy Europeans were enjoying products from the New World, tasting tomatoes, chocolate, peppers, and other new foods. At the same time, changing theories of science were revolutionizing medical and nutritional doctrines, and new techniques and inventions were transforming culinary practices. Nowhere were the changes more pronounced than in fashionable Naples. It was the perfect setting for *sorbetti* to make their debut.

Turning to Ice

All the dining changes taking place were important to the development of ice cream, but first and foremost among them was the discovery of freezing techniques. Long before anyone made ices and ice creams, much less served them to kings, ice and snow were highly valued. They were hard to get, difficult to store, and expensive. In other words, they were perfect status symbols. Those who were able to acquire them flaunted them, using them to add elegance to tables, cool the air on hot summer nights, and crown foods. Athenaeus, the second-century Greek philosopher and author of *The Deipnosophists*, wrote that "in the island of Cimolos underground refrigerators are constructed in summer, where the people store jars full of warm water and draw them out again as cold as snow." Alexander the Great is said to have had pits constructed in which he stored snow and ice. A fourth-century emperor of Japan, Nintoku, was so pleased by a gift of ice that he designated the first of June as the Day of Ice. On that day each year, he gave chips of ice to palace guests in a ceremony called the Imperial Gift of Ice.[1]

By the fifteenth century, the elites of Spain and Italy could send their servants or slaves to nearby mountains, where they gathered snow, packed it down, wrapped it in straw, and carried it home, sometimes on mules' backs, sometimes on their own. They stored the snow in pits dug for the purpose on their masters' estates. Those who lived in areas where shallow ponds froze in winter harvested the ice and stored it in pits. Initially, the storage pits were simply holes in the ground filled with alternating layers of snow and straw and covered with straw or wooden planks. Over time, Europeans built larger and more elaborate pits and lined them with bricks or wooden slats. The pits were located in dry, cool spots, often on a slope so they would drain well. Later, the well-to-do constructed large, aboveground icehouses, often of brick. Some of the icehouses were so well constructed that water in them could be frozen into ice, cream could be chilled, and meltwater channeled to cool wine in a nearby cellar. In England during the eighteenth and nineteenth centuries, icehouses became architectural whimsies: they masqueraded as Greek temples or Chinese pagodas.[2]

But an icehouse allows only storage. The key to making ices was in finding out how to make ice or snow freeze other substances. That happened in the mid-sixteenth century, when Italian scientists learned that immersing a container of water in a bucket of snow that was mixed with potassium nitrate, or saltpeter, would freeze the water. Giambattista della Porta described the theory in his *Natural Magick,* published in 1558 and soon translated and disseminated throughout Europe.

Wine may freeze in Glasses.

Because of the chief thing desired at feasts, is that Wine cold as ice may be drunk, especially in summer. I will teach you how Wine shall presently, not only grow cold, but freeze, that you cannot drink it but by sucking, and drawing in of your breath. Put Wine into a Vial, and put a little water to it, that it may turn to ice the sooner. Then cast snow into a wooden vessel, and strew into it Saltpeter, powdered, or the cleansing of Saltpeter, called vulgarly Salazzo. Turn the Vial in the snow, and it will congeal by degrees. Some keep snow all the summer. Let water boil in Brass kettles, and pour it into great bowls, and set them in the frosty cold air. It will freeze, and grow harder than snow, and last longer.[3]

Eventually, scientists and then cooks learned that common salt would work as well as saltpeter. For centuries, the combination of ice and salt was used for freezing. Even today, some home cooks use the method when they're making ice cream. Mixing salt with ice lowers the ice's freezing point, causing it to melt. As it does, heat is transferred away from the ice cream mixture and it freezes.

When Della Porta filled his vial with wine diluted with water and turned it in the salted snow, the result was a semifrozen, slushy wine that was a hit at banquets. Illustrations of vials or flasks being turned in their tubs look uncannily like later illustrations of ice cream freezers being turned in their ice-filled tubs. A Spanish doctor practicing in Rome at the time, Blas Villafranca, wrote that this was the new way to cool wine and water, and that all the nobility and gentry of Rome used the method.[4]

In addition to slushy wine coolers, the new technique made possible all sorts of fanciful ice artistry. Cooks dipped fresh fruits in water, froze them until their icy exteriors sparkled, and then displayed them. They set marzipan boats afloat on seas of ice. They created tall pyramids of ice with fruits and flowers frozen within them. For a dinner in Rome celebrating the feast of the Assumption on August 15, 1623, Antonio Frugoli, a steward and author of *Practica e scalcaria*, made an ice pyramid with a fountain in its center. During dinner, fragrant orange-flower water splashed over the icy fountain for more than half an hour, according to Frugoli's account.[5] The coolness as well as the fragrance and beauty of the centerpiece must have charmed the guests.

Best of all, the new freezing technique made it possible for cooks and confectioners to begin experimenting with making ices and ice creams.

"The Stomach Grows Chilled"

Not everyone took to all this iciness immediately. Dietetic beliefs were still governed by the humoral doctrine in the early seventeenth century, and its adherents prized moderation above all. Based on the writings of Hippocrates, Aristotle, and Galen, the doctrine classified people according to four humors or temperaments: sanguine, phlegmatic, choleric, or melancholic. Each had its own characteristics and required particular foods or food preparation methods to achieve the ideal, which was defined as a slightly warm, slightly moist body.

Those whose dominant humor was sanguine were of a hot and moist character, so they required cooling, drying foods. Cholerics were hot and dry and needed cooling, moistening foods. Foods were classified as hot, cold, dry, or moist to varying degrees, a classification that had little to do with their physical properties. For example, strawberries were cold and dry in the first degree, and dates were hot in the second degree and moist in the first degree.[6]

Temperature was also important, since extremes of any kind were to be avoided. Very cold foods and drinks were considered especially dangerous. Hippocrates had written, "Cold things, such as snow and ice, are inimical to the chest, being provocative of coughs, of discharges of blood, and of catarrhs."[7] In the fifth century, Anthimus wrote, "The stomach grows chilled and loses its efficacy"[8] as a result of consuming cold drinks. Colic, convulsions, paralysis, blindness, madness, and sudden death were some of the problems attributed to putting ice in drinks. According to French food historian Jean-Louis Flandrin, the prejudice against iced drinks was based on the belief that wine turned into blood when drunk. To avoid serious injury it had to be drunk at body temperature.[9]

In addition, some believed that chilling drinks by immersing a decanter in ice and saltpeter was dangerous because particles of saltpeter could penetrate the decanter, get into the water or wine, and burn up the intestines.[10] Small wonder that, despite changing ideas about science and nutrition, many seventeenth-century doctors disapproved of cold drinks, not to mention ices.

Of course, people don't always follow their doctor's advice today, and many didn't then either. Their rationalizations—everyone else does it, I don't do it often, I don't use much—are familiar, too. The sixteenth-century French essayist Michel de Montaigne was visiting Florence when he wrote, "It is customary here to put snow into the wine glasses, I put only a little in not being too well in body."[11] The noted seventeenth-century English diarist John Evelyn blamed "an *Angina* & soare Throat" on drinking wine with "Snow & Ice as the manner here is" when he was staying in Padua.[12]

Long after humoral theory had been forgotten, some of its tenets remained in popular consciousness. At the turn of the twentieth century, famed cookbook writer and cooking school director Fannie Farmer wrote of ices, "Hygienically speaking, they cannot be recommended for the final course of a dinner, as cold mixtures reduce the temperature of the stomach, thus retarding digestion until the normal temperature is again reached."[13]

However, most physicians were leaving the humoral system behind by the latter part of the seventeenth century. Chefs and diners alike were only too happy to follow their lead. European eating habits were changing; heavily spiced and sweetened foods were off the table, herbs and salads were on. Wines sparkled. Sugar found its home in the dessert course.

A Sip of Sherbet

Once scientists had mastered freezing, and medicine had more or less given its approval, creating recipes for ices and ice creams was relatively simple. After all, cooks had for many years been making the drinks and creams that were the precursors of ices and ice creams.

In the Middle East, drinks known as sherbets—*sharâb* or *sharbât* (Arabic), *sharbate* (Persian), *serbet* (Turkish)—have been ubiquitous since medieval times. European travelers encountering them for the first time often wrote about them with great enthusiasm. Sir Thomas Herbert, who traveled in Persia from 1627 to 1629, wrote, "Their liquor is sometimes fair water, sugar, rose-water, and juice of lemons mixed, and sugar confected with citrons, violets or other sweet flowers; and for the more delicacy, sometimes a mixture of amber; this we call sherbet." He said sherbet was "a drink that quenches thirst and tastes deliciously." The Persians served their sherbets over ice or snow in large porcelain or gold bowls and sipped them from long-handled wooden spoons.[14]

A nineteenth-century English novelist, James Morier, described the flavor of Persian sherbets as "so mixed that the sour and the sweet were as equally balanced as the blessings and miseries of life."[15] Sour flavors were popular in Middle Eastern sherbets, and in fact, sour Cornelian cherries (*Cornus mas*) were so commonly used in Turkish sherbets that the cherries were also called, simply, sorbet. Pomegranate, citron, lemon, lime, and quince were also popular drink flavors in the Middle East. European drink flavors included lemon, strawberry, raspberry, cherry, apricot, peach, pistachio, and hazelnut. The drinks were made by blending fruit juices and other flavorings with sugar and water, or a sugar syrup, then chilling them with snow or ice. We make lemonade the same way today, although ice has replaced snow. To freeze the drinks into smooth ices requires added sugar, something cooks figured out after they had made a few very icy ices. Eighteenth-century drink recipes often directed the reader to double the sugar when turning a drink into an ice.

Iced sherbet drinks were also made from powders. That may sound like a modern-day shortcut, but the use of powders is centuries old. Jean Chardin, another seventeenth-century traveler in Persia, wrote, "In Turky they keep them in Powder like Sugar: That of Alexandria, which is the most esteem'd throughout this large Empire, and which they transport from thence every where, is almost all in Powder. . . . They keep it in Pots and Boxes; and when they would use it, they put a Spoonful of it into a large glass of Water. It mixes of itself with the Water, without being forc'd to stir it, as we do our Syrups, and makes a most admirable Liquor."[16]

Some nineteenth-century confectioners made what they called "essences" by combining the grated rind of a lemon or other fruit with sugar, pressing the mixture into a stone jar, covering it, and storing for a month before using it as a base to make ices.[17] The essences may have made something like the sherbet powder Chardin observed.[18]

The word *sharbat* appeared in Italian in the late sixteenth century as the name of a Turkish beverage. The frozen dessert became known as *sorbetto* in Italian, *sorbet* in French, *sorbete* in Spanish. The English language kept the *h* and called it sherbet. Middle Eastern sherbets are still drinks, but European and American sherbets are generally ices or ice milks.[19]

Iced Cream

Cooks had been making creams and custards, both simple and sophisticated, since the Middle Ages. In medieval England, "cream of almonde" was a popular dessert. Spanish cooks made a *crema Catalana,* which was golden with saffron. The Italian *crema della mia nonna* (my grandmother's cream) was sweetened with honey and flavored with citron. The English made a sage cream with red sage and rose water. They also made cabbage cream by building up skins of cream "round and high like a cabbage."[20] The cream did not contain cabbage. It was meant to look like the vegetable, not to taste like it.

A seventeenth-century Italian cook, Bartolomeo Stefani, made a custard he called *latte alla spagnuola,* or "Spanish-style cream." Made with milk, cream, sugar, and eggs, it is flavored with musk, the only ingredient that makes it seem dated. After it was cooked, Stefani heated a paddle in the fire and used it to brown the top, which he sprinkled with sugar. It's very like a crème brûlée.[21]

Another cream dessert, popular in France and Italy in the sixteenth and seventeenth centuries, was called *neige,* or "snow," in France; *latte miele,* or "whipped cream," in Italy; and snow in England. Cooks whipped cream, sugar, and sometimes a flavoring such as rose water or orange flower water, scooped off the frothy puffs of faux snow, and let them drain. As frugal as they were fanciful, the cooks put cream that drained off back into the original mixture and rewhipped it, so as not to waste any. After the snows had drained, they were either served immediately or set on ice to chill before serving. Occasionally they were stabilized with the addition of meringue. Later frozen desserts were also called snows.

Some creams were made with unusual (to us) ingredients such as laurel leaves, saffron, musk, tarragon, celery, violets, and rose petals. Others are as familiar to us as the flavors on an ice cream shop menu: caramel, lemon, ginger, almond, strawberries, raspberries, and even crumbled cookies. Some recipes were simple mixtures of cream, sugar, and flavorings or pureed fruit. Others were custards, made just as they are today with cream or milk or both, egg yolks, sugar, and a flavoring. In his 1685 work, *The Accomplisht Cook,* English chef Robert May made some of his creams with egg yolks, some with egg whites, some with whole eggs, and some, rather casually, "with eggs, or without."[22]

Often custards were baked in pies, and then as now, they were the stuff of farce. A clown jumping into a giant custard pie and splashing the filling on the guests was a high point of eighteenth-century English banquets. In the early part of the twentieth century, actors hurling custard pies at each other was the height of hilarity in American silent films.[23]

Most of the early creams and custards could have served as the basis for ice creams with very little change. In fact, in the early days of freezing, cooks gave detailed instructions on how to freeze ice cream but sketchy directions for making the mixture, perhaps because *everyone* knew how to make creams but not how to freeze them. Once they understood that, they turned their creams into "iced creams," as they were quite logically called at first.

Snow Wonders

Antonio Latini was one of the first to write in detail about making and serving ices. He was the author of *Lo scalco alla moderna,* or *The Modern Steward,* a two-volume work published in 1692 and 1694,[24] one of the most extensive European culinary texts published before the end of the century. Latini, whose title reveals that he considered himself a "modern steward," was at the forefront of many of the culinary changes of the day: using New World foods, promoting regional specialties, and taking advantage of the latest scientific discoveries. When he wrote the book, Latini was the *scalco* for the household of Don Stefano Carrillo Salcedo, first minister of the Spanish viceroy in Naples. It was a position of consequence in a noble household. As *scalco,* Latini was responsible for overseeing everything from food to finances. No detail was too large or too small for his attention, from planning menus and selecting wines to directing the fanciful folding of napkins. The *scalco* supervised the cooks, carvers, and other servants, selected the musicians and singers, and balanced the budget. He planned and managed everything from royal picnics to wedding banquets. Most important, he made sure all was carried out with panache.

Latini was an unlikely candidate for such a position. Born in a small town called Coll'Amato in the Marche region on the east coast of Italy in 1642, he was orphaned when he was five. He had to beg for food and a place to sleep until he found work as a servant. It was an inauspicious start to a remarkable life.

In seventeenth-century Europe, birth was generally destiny. Most people were poor and illiterate, and few ever traveled more than fifty miles from their birthplace. Latini was an exception. In one home where Latini worked, a priest who served as a cook taught him the rudiments of reading and writing. When he was sixteen, Latini went to Rome to try to better himself. There he worked as a cook, a waiter, and a wardrobe attendant in the household of Cardinal Antonio Barberini, nephew of Pope Urban VIII. Working for one of the most powerful families in one of the world's most sophisticated cities, Latini honed his skills. He became more literate; he learned the duties of a *cuoco* (cook), *trinciante* (carver), and *scalco*. Most important, he saw how a grand ecclesiastical household was managed. After working for officials in Rome and Faenza, Latini went to Naples and became the *scalco* for the Salcedo household in 1682.[25]

While working in Cardinal Barberini's household, Latini would have worn clerical garb since, at the time, the clothing of the staff reflected the style of those they served. When he moved to Naples and rose to the rank of steward, he wore elegant Spanish attire and was allowed to wear a wig. In his book's frontispiece portrait, Latini looks more like a king than a cook. He sports a lace jabot and flowing robes, and his wig's ringlets rival those of France's king, Louis XIV. Latini's intense deep-set eyes, imposing nose, and serious demeanor all convey the impression of a man of substance. To emphasize his intellect, he's depicted holding a book; Latin inscriptions and ornate curlicues decorate the oval frame around him. It's a portrait of a man of elegance and erudition.

In his book, Latini described the duties of a *cuoco*, *trinciante*, and *scalco* in detail. He devoted several pages to the many responsibilities of a *scalco* and stressed that he owed complete loyalty to his master. He wrote that a *cuoco* should be good and faithful and not overly fond of drink. He explained how a *trinciante* was supposed to carve all kinds of meats, fish, and fruit. In Latini's world, a carver not only had to be highly skilled, he had to be a showman as well. He was expected to be able to spear a roasted bird on a fork, hold it up in the air for the guests to see, and then, still holding it aloft, carve it precisely.

Latini listed food specialties from each region in the Kingdom of Naples, explained how to select fish, and noted where to find the best prosciutto, the finest rice, and the most abundant saffron. His recipes included soups, meats, fish dishes, pastas, sauces, drinks, and pastries. He offered multi-course menus for banquets, weddings, and other events, even one for a trip to watch Vesuvius erupting. Although he included a few medieval leftovers such as sugared pasta, *Lo scalco alla moderna* made it clear that Latini was embracing modern ways. In one chapter, he advocated cooking with fresh herbs such as parsley, thyme, and mint instead of sweet spices such as cinnamon and clove, citing the longevity of Capuchin monks as proof that the regimen was healthy.

So thoroughly have New World foods been integrated into the European diet that today people find it difficult to imagine Italy without tomatoes, France without haricots verts, and Ireland without potatoes. However, it took Europeans a long time to accept some of the new foods. Well into the eighteenth century, people looked on potatoes with fear and contempt, and some thought they caused leprosy.[26] Jean Le Rond d'Alembert and Denis Diderot's eighteenth-century *Encyclopédie, ou Dictionnaire raisonné des sciences, des arts et des métiers (1751–1780)* conceded that potatoes were nutritious, but suggested that they were more appropriate for peasants and laborers than for the upper classes. The now-ubiquitous tomato was not widely eaten in Europe until the eighteenth century, and it was not used as a sauce for pasta until later still. Most paintings of macaroni eaters show the pasta dressed only with cheese, and printed recipes for pasta with tomato sauce didn't show up until the nineteenth century.[27] So, even though he was writing two hundred years after Columbus landed in America, Latini's use of New World foods such as tomatoes, which he called variously *poma d'oro* and *pomadoro*, was modern and innovative. In fact, his recipes for tomato sauces are thought to be the first recorded in Italian. One, which he called "Sauce in the Spanish Style," was made with roasted and then peeled and minced tomatoes, along with minced onions, hot chili peppers, thyme, salt, oil, and vinegar. Latini wrote that it was a very tasty sauce for boiled dishes or anything else, but did not suggest using it with pasta.

Latini's *sorbetti* recipes were the first published in Italian, and to this day Italian ices and ice creams are prized. In his introduction to the section on ices, Latini said every Neapolitan was born knowing how to make them. He said great quantities were eaten in Naples, and they had the consistency of sugar and snow. Latini explained that he was not writing for the many Neapolitan experts, but was trying to help those who had yet to learn how to make ices. He promised he would not give away any professional secrets, and he did not. By today's standards, his recipes are not explicit enough to work from unless one is experienced. But they tell us what kinds of ices were eaten in Naples at the time and, roughly, how they were made. He also gave us nine recipes when others of the era offered no more than one or two. In his recipes, Latini used the feminine *sorbetta* (singular) and *sorbette* (plural) rather than today's masculine *sorbetto, sorbetti*.

Here is his recipe for lemon sorbet:

PER FARE VENTI GIARE DI SORBETTA DI LIMONE
Si richiedono trè libre di Zuccaro, Sale libre trè, e mezza, tredici libre di Neve, Limoni numero trè, quando sieno grossi, se saranno piccioli, ti regolerai a giudizio, particolarmente nella Stagione estiva.

TO MAKE TWENTY GOBLETS OF LEMON SORBET
You need three pounds of sugar, three and a half pounds of salt, thirteen pounds of snow, and three lemons, if they are fat. If they are small, you must adjust the amount according to your judgment, particularly in summer.

Latini was writing for professionals; they would have understood that the snow and salt were intended to go into the freezing pot, not into the sorbet itself. But if they weren't familiar with the method, they would not learn it from Latini. He didn't offer any instructions as to cooking, freezing, stirring, or timing. When he said ices had the consistency of sugar and snow, he implied that he was making what we would call scoopable ices rather than hard, icy ones.

The balance of sugar and liquid is critical in making ices. Use too much sugar, and you get a thick, sweet slush that never freezes completely. Use too little, and you get an ice so icy you can't get a spoon through it. Although it's difficult to judge exactly, since measurements and lemons have changed over the years, Latini's lemon sorbet would seem to have been tooth-achingly sweet, not very lemony, and unlikely to freeze very well. He was making enough to fill *venti giarre*, or twenty goblets. A *giarre* was just over six ounces, so twenty goblets would be nearly four quarts. But he used, roughly, eight cups of sugar.[28] For the same amount of sorbet, we'd use about four cups. He used just three lemons, but how big and how juicy were they? We'd use the juice of four or five lemons plus water to make one quart of lemon sorbet.

Among Latini's ices was one he called a milk sorbet. He never used the word *gelato*.

SORBETTA DI LATTE

Per fare altra Sorbetta di Latte, che prima sia stato cotto, ci vorrà di Dosa una Carrafa, e meza di Latte, meza d'acqua, trè libre di Zuccaro, oncie sei di Cedronata, ò Cocuzzata trita; nella Neve, e nel Sale, ti regolerai, come sopra.

MILK SORBET

To make another sorbet of milk, which first you must cook, you need a carafe and a half of milk, half of water, three pounds of sugar, six ounces of candied citron or pumpkin finely cut up; the snow and salt you'll measure as above.

Latini's *carrafa* was just over half a liter,[29] so a carafe and a half of milk plus a half carafe of water would be a little more than a liter of liquid, mixed with three pounds of sugar. A mixture that sweet seems unlikely to freeze well. And why use any water? How rich and creamy was his milk? We don't know. Interestingly, this was the only sorbet Latini cooked. Was this an early ice cream or, more likely, a harbinger of ice creams to come?

When Latini was writing, chocolate was a popular hot drink in Europe. Spanish conquistadors had first tasted it in the form of the bitter, cold drink of the Aztecs and rejected it. But after they sweetened it, added Old World spices like cinnamon and anise, and heated it, they adopted it as their own. Chocolate was introduced to Spain during the late sixteenth century, initially as a medicine. It traveled throughout Europe, in the words of Sophie and Michael Coe, authors of *The True History of Chocolate*, "from one court to another, from noble house to noble house, from monastery to monastery."[30] It was made in special chocolate pots, mixed not only with sugar and cinnamon but also with chili peppers, almonds, honey, milk, eggs, musk, bread crumbs, and ground maize. Finally, it was whisked into a froth with a grooved wooden beater called a *molinillo*. In the early seventeenth century, hot chocolate became a fashionable drink at the Spanish court. Royals and their guests sipped their chocolate from porcelain cups on saucers garnished with gold. They drank it first thing in the morning and in the afternoon, at court and at bullfights, and they dunked their biscuits into it.

Making ices with chocolate was an innovation, and Latini had two recipes. The first was frozen in tablets or bricks, which, he said, required more salt and snow to freeze. He called the second ice a chocolate mousse and said it should be stirred constantly during the freezing process to make it foam, then served as soon as it was frozen. This was his only comment about the necessity of stirring ices, something future cooks would emphasize.

Given the many ingredients people added to hot chocolate, it's interesting that Latini's chocolate ice recipes simply called for chocolate and sugar.

It's possible that he was using chocolate to which cinnamon or other spices had already been added. Or perhaps he preferred his chocolate plain and simple.

His cinnamon ice had the happy addition of pine nuts. Again, since he simply listed ingredients, we don't know exactly how he made the sorbet. He may have stirred in the pine nuts at the last minute to add crunch, as we would today. But it's more likely that he steeped them in the liquid to add flavor and then strained them out, as most recipes dictated throughout the next century. Smooth, not chunky, was the preference in ices for many years.

Latini was a little more explicit about some details. His recipe for strawberry sorbet specified that the strawberries be fresh, picked not more than a day before, and he instructed his readers to be sure to get every bit of the stones out of the cherries when making his sour cherry sorbet. He also had a recipe calling for dried cherries when fresh ones were out of season.

One of his more enigmatic recipes calls for *robba candita diversa*, which translates to "varied candied things," most probably lemon, citron, or pumpkin, as in the milk sorbet. However, although he included the recipe among the *sorbetti*, he says the mixture was intended to be frozen in the tall pyramid shapes so popular at the time; so it may have been destined to be a glistening icy centerpiece, one of the *trionfi*, literally "triumphs," that decorated royal banquet tables, rather than an edible dessert. In that case, the varied candied things could be almost anything.

Latini was as generous with his ices as he was with his recipes. At one of his banquets, the last course included an abundance of *sorbetti*, and he said that he had them served to guests and servants alike. When he made this highly unusual gesture, perhaps he was remembering his own days as a humble servant.

Sugar and Snow in France

Imagine Paris without coffee or cafés or sorbets. It is nearly impossible. Yet until the mid-seventeenth century, Parisians knew coffee only as an exotic

Middle Eastern beverage; the classic Parisian café did not yet exist; and ices were a dessert reserved for the privileged few. The three new arrivals would soon transform life in the City of Light.

Europeans began to hear about coffee from travelers' accounts of their experiences in Persia, Turkey, and other Middle Eastern countries where they first tasted the curious and bitter drink. Often they described it with less than enthusiasm. Sir Thomas Herbert, the early-seventeenth-century traveler, wrote of Persia:

> Here be coffee-houses, which also are much resorted to, especially in the evening. The coffee, or coho, is a black drink, or rather broth, seeing they sip it as hot as their mouth can well suffer out of small China cups; 'tis made of the flower of bunny or choavaberry, steeped and well-boiled in water; much drunk, though it please neither the eye nor taste, being black and somewhat bitter (or rather relished like burnt crusts), more wholesome than toothsome, yet (if it be true as they say) comforts raw stomachs, helps digestion, expels wind, and dispels drowsiness, but of the greater repute from a tradition they have that it was prepared by Gabriel as a cordial for Mussulmans.[31]

Coffee was introduced to the French royal court in the mid-seventeenth century, but some did not take to it initially. Madame de Sévigné, whose letters to her daughter so brilliantly described life among French nobility at the time, thought coffee drinking was nothing more than a passing fad at first. Then she discovered that, with enough milk and sugar, this "lait cafeté ou café laité" was "très jolie," and a great consolation during Lent.[32]

By the 1670s, coffee drinking was also becoming popular with the public. Coffee was sold by street vendors who often dressed up as turbaned Turks, regardless of their actual country of origin, to emphasize the exotic nature of the drink. One such vendor was a young Sicilian named Francesco Procopio dei Coltelli. He was employed by an Armenian man known as Pascal, who sold coffee in a stall at the popular Saint Germain

Fair in the heart of Paris. When Pascal decided to go to London to seek his fortune, Procope, as he became known, took over the stall. Later, he joined the guild of *distillateurs-limonadiers* and opened a small café on the Rue de Tournon. In 1686, he moved to the Rue des Fossés-Saint-Germain and opened the café called Le Procope. Although at the time Parisians could buy coffee at the fairs, from street vendors, and in a handful of dark and dank shops, there were few fashionable public places in which to enjoy the new drink. Procope's café boasted glittering crystal chandeliers, marble-topped tables, and shimmering mirrors and was, by all accounts, dazzling. It set the standard for all that followed.

Just a year after Le Procope opened, the Comédie Française moved in across the street. (The street name was later changed to the Rue de l'Ancienne-Comédie.) The café soon attracted writers, actors, and other artists, as well as audiences from the theater. Procope served coffee, chocolate, liqueurs, and ices. Although he did not introduce them to Paris, Procope made ices popular when he gave fashionable Parisians a setting in which to enjoy them.[33] Later, leading intellectuals of the Enlightenment, including Jean-Jacques Rousseau, Denis Diderot, and Voltaire, made Café Procope their headquarters. When he was in Paris, Benjamin Franklin was another of its habitués. Voltaire set one of his plays, *L'Écossaise*, in a café modeled on Café Procope.[34] Perhaps inspired by the ice cream he enjoyed there, he is credited with having said, "Ice cream is exquisite. What a pity it isn't illegal."

In 1692, the same year the first volume of *Lo scalco alla moderna* was published in Naples, *La maison réglée* was published in Paris. Written by Nicolas Audiger, it is a book about running what he called a household of quality. Audiger was writing toward the end of a long career as a confectioner, distiller, and maître d'hôtel, a position that corresponded to that of a *scalco*. When he had started working, more than thirty years earlier, France was becoming the culinary epicenter of Europe.

Over the years, Audiger served many of the members of the court of Louis XIV. He worked as a confectioner and *liqueuriste* for one of the Sun

King's favorites, the Comtesse de Soissons. He worked for the king's chief minister, Colbert, and for Colbert's son-in-law, the Comte de Saint-Aignan. Audiger helped prepare festivities at Versailles, Chantilly, and other royal settings. Eventually he opened a shop as a confectioner and *distillateur* at the Place de Palais Royal, and often provided refreshments, including *eaux glacées*, or ices, for royal feasts.

Audiger wrote that, early in his career, he went to Italy to learn how to make "en perfection" the ices, as well as liqueurs and other drinks that later became so fashionable in Paris.[35] He said that, although he was experienced in French confectionery and distillation and had traveled in Spain, Holland, and Germany, it was only in Italy that he could perfect his skills. He learned how to make chocolate, tea, and coffee there, and claimed that he helped introduce them to France. By the time he wrote his book, they were all very well known in Paris, but perhaps he was one of those who had helped to popularize them.

Audiger spent fourteen months in Italy, and after he returned to France, he tried—ceaselessly and unsuccessfully—to have the king give him the exclusive right to produce and sell the liqueurs of Italy in France. As he tells the story in his book, Audiger was on his way back to France in January 1660 when he happened upon some early peas growing in Genoa.[36] He says that he had them gathered up and packaged in a box along with some rosebuds, and took them back to France. He presented them to the king, who was impressed with their freshness and flavor and offered Audiger a monetary reward for the out-of-season treat. Audiger turned it down. He wanted, instead, the monopoly on producing the Italian drinks. The king and various court officials smiled on Audiger, but never granted him his request. He describes his quest in some detail in his book and seems never to have come to terms with his disappointment. He was furious when a guild of liqueur makers was established and people who, in Audiger's opinion, knew nothing of the craft were allowed to buy their masterships without undergoing a test of their skills. Procope may have been one of those who inspired Audiger's scorn.

La maison réglée, however, is a much greater legacy—if not so profitable at the time—than the liqueur monopoly would have been. In the book, Audiger described in detail how a noble household should be run. He discussed staffing, shopping, budgeting, menu planning, and table setting. He described the responsibilities of each member of the staff, including the maître d'hôtel and the redundantly titled *officier d'office,* both positions he himself had held. The development of haute cuisine brought about a division of kitchen labor in large noble households that would later be reflected in grand restaurants, and Audiger described the way it was organized. The large kitchen, or *cuisine,* was where most foods were prepared. This was the domain of the head cook, called the *écuyer* or *officier de cuisine;* the roastcook, or *rôtisseur;* and their assistants and aides. A smaller, cold kitchen was known as the *office* and was presided over by the *officier d'office.* He and his assistants made salads, pastries, liqueurs, jams, syrups, marzipan, and candy. They were responsible for the wine cellar, the silver, and the linens. When coffee, tea, and hot chocolate became chic, the *officiers* learned how to make and serve them. And when ice cream came along, it, too, was in their purview.[37]

In the section of his book devoted to making liqueurs and waters "à la mode d'Italie," Audiger gave instructions for distilling liquors and for making the nonalcoholic drinks called waters. His flavors included orange flower, lemon, strawberry, currant, raspberry, cherry, apricot, peach, pear, almond, pomegranate, *verjus* (literally "green juice," the sour juice of unripe grapes that is still used in place of lemon juice or vinegar), pine nut, pistachio, hazelnut, cinnamon, coriander, chervil, and fennel. The word *sorbet* was not yet in common use. Audiger used the phrase *sorbec de levant,* which would seem to refer to the Middle Eastern origin of sherbets. His book did not include any recipes specifically for ices. Instead, he wrote that, to freeze any of the waters into ices, one should double the sugar and increase the fruits, flowers, or seeds by half in order to make the taste stand up to the cold. Freezing does make flavors come through less strongly, and experienced cooks know mixtures should taste a little too strong when they're warm if they are to have enough flavor when frozen. Here is Audiger's lemonade:

POUR FAIRE DE BONNE LIMONADE

Sur une pinte d'eau metez trois jus de citron,[38] sept ou huit zestes, et si les citrons sont gros et bien à jus il n'en faut que deux, avec un quarteron de sucre ou tout au plus cinq onces. Lorsque le sucre est fondu et le tout bien incorporé, vous le passerez à la chausse, le ferez rafraicir et le donnerez à boire.

TO MAKE GOOD LEMONADE

Add the juice of three lemons to a pint of water, along with seven or eight zests, and if the lemons are fat and full of juice, you'll only need two, with a quarter pound of sugar, or at most five ounces. When the sugar has dissolved and is completely incorporated, strain it, chill it and offer it to drink.

To turn it into a lemon sorbet, Audiger would have us double the sugar to about ten ounces. Weighing sugar with a simple kitchen scale, that's about one and a third cups of sugar. So Audiger's sorbet was sweet but probably not as sweet as Latini's. He also added lemon zests, which Latini didn't mention, so Audiger's would have had more flavor.

Unlike Latini, Audiger gave us lengthy freezing instructions. He said that the waters should be put in containers, covered, and placed in a large tub at one finger's distance from each other. Then he filled the tub with ice that had been crushed well and mixed with salt. He explained that the containers had to be completely covered with ice and the tub had to be full. After letting the containers sit for half to three-quarters of an hour, he opened them and mixed the contents with a spoon. Then, being careful not to let any of the salted ice get into the containers, he recovered them and piled the ice back around and over them. Audiger instructed his readers to use a tub with a hole cut in the bottom and to supply it with a plug to let the melting water drain out from time to time.

Freezing ices was a chilly, laborious task; but neither Latini nor Audiger discussed that aspect of sorbet making. Having servants or apprentices to do the grunt work made it much lighter.

Audiger emphasized the importance of stirring the ices as they froze so their texture would be more like snow than ice. They would also taste better, he said, since otherwise the sugar would settle on the sides and bottom of the container, and the sorbet would be weak and watery. Except for his frozen chocolate mousse, Latini didn't mention stirring. Despite their very different recipes, both Latini and Audiger wanted sorbet to have the consistency of snow.

Audiger had just one recipe for ice cream:

POUR FAIRE DE LA CRÈME GLACÉE

Prenez une chopine de lait, un demi-setier de bonne crème douce, ou bien trois poissons, avec six ou sept onces de sucre et une demi-cueillerée d'eau de fleur d'orange, puis la mettrez dans un vaisseau de fer blanc, de terre ou autre pour la faire glacer.

TO MAKE ICE CREAM

Take a *chopine* of milk with a *demi-setier*, or three *poissons*, of good sweet cream, with six or seven ounces of sugar and a half spoonful of orange flower water, then put it in a container of lead, terra cotta, or other material to freeze.[39]

A *chopine* was sixteen ounces, and a *demi-setier* or three *poissons*, about eight ounces.[40] Audiger used more milk than cream (but how thick and rich were his milk and cream?), and a little more than a cup of sugar to make less than one quart of ice cream. Today, most recipes for a quart of ice cream call for from one-half to one cup of sugar. So Audiger's was on the sweet side but not achingly so. If he cooked the mixture, he didn't tell us.

Audiger made ice pyramids for centerpieces just as Latini did. But unlike Latini, he gave us explicit directions for making one. He said he filled a lead mold with fruits or flowers, which he selected carefully and arranged delicately so that the largest would be at the bottom and the tiniest at the top. He filled the mold with water and surrounded it with salted ice until it was frozen. Just before serving, he unmolded the pyramid by rubbing the outside of the mold with a cloth dipped in boiling water. Then he placed the pyramid on a platter and surrounded it with individual goblets of *eaux glacées*. This made a beautiful presentation on a table of consequence, Audiger noted. The spectacular ice pyramid would also have given the dessert ices arranged around it more prominence.

The great French chef François Pierre de La Varenne did not have any recipes for ices or ice creams in his 1651 masterwork, *Le vrai cuisinier françois*. But in *Le nouveau confiturier*, a supplement to a later edition attributed to him, he included two recipes for frozen *neiges*. The first, for *neige de fleurs d'orange*, "orange flower snow," is very like Audiger's *crème glacée*, except that it called for cream, not milk, and that he used fresh orange flowers when they were available, and a combination of candied orange flowers and orange flower water when they were not.[41] The other recipe, for *neige de coriante*, "coriander snow," is actually an ice. In both cases, measurements were less than precise. The first recipe called for sweet cream, no amount specified; two handfuls of sugar; a bed of ice; handfuls of salt. The second recipe called for two handfuls of coriander, some water, and a handful or two of sugar as well as the juice and peel of a lemon.

However, the freezing instructions were specific. The author said the containers should not touch; they should be a finger's width apart, just as Audiger instructed. Rather than stirring the mixture, he shook the ice cream container from time to time so that the ice cream wouldn't freeze into a solid lump of ice. Like Latini and Audiger, he was aiming for the consistency of snow—hence the name he gives his recipes—rather than that of ice. He also stated rather emphatically that the ice cream would be ready in two hours.[42] Limiting the freezing time may have also served as a way to keep it from freezing too hard.

English Creams

One ice cream recipe written in English predates those above. Called an "icy cream," it appeared in an unpublished manuscript cookbook by Lady Anne Fanshawe, the wife of Sir Richard Fanshawe, who was ambassador to Portugal and then to Spain during the Restoration. The manuscript is dated 1651–78, and the ice cream recipe is in the section that was written around 1665–66. Lady Fanshawe returned to England from Madrid in 1666, after the death of her husband. Perhaps she discovered the recipe in Spain.

TO MAKE ICY CREAM

Take three pints of the best cream, boyle it with a blade of Mace, or else perfume it with orang flowerwater or Ambergreece, sweeten the cream, with sugar let it stand till it is quite cold, then put it into Boxes, either of Silver or tinn then take, Ice chopped into small peeces and putt it into a tub and set the Boxes in the ice covering them all over, and let them stand in the Ice two hours, and the Cream Will come to be Ice in the Boxes, then turne them out into a salver with some of the same Seasoned Cream, so serve it up at the Table.[43]

There is just one problem with Fanshawe's recipe. Without salt, the ice would not freeze the ice cream. Did she forget to put the salt in the instructions, but remember it when she had her servants make the ice cream? Did she receive a faulty recipe from someone without realizing what was wrong? Did she ever have the ice cream made according to the recipe? We don't know.

There are similarities among these recipes. Fanshawe, like Latini, called for cooking the cream (or milk, in Latini's case). She, Audiger, and La Varenne all flavored their ice creams with orange flower water. It was the vanilla of its day. Used frequently in Middle Eastern cookery, orange flower water is still available, and a small amount adds a lovely flavor to ice cream.

The recipe considered the first published ice cream recipe in English appeared much later. It was in *Mrs. Mary Eales's Receipts,* a book on confectionery and pastry which was published in 1718. Mrs. Eales, who is identified as "Confectioner to her late Majesty Queen Anne" on the title page of the book, was specific about freezing techniques, but at first reading seems rather cavalier about her mixture.

TO ICE CREAM

Take Tin Ice-Pots, fill them with any Sort of Cream you like, either plain or sweeten'd, or Fruit in it; shut your Pots very close; to fix Pots you must allow eighteen or twenty Pound of Ice, breaking the Ice very small; there will be some great Pieces, which lay at the Bottom and Top: You must have a Pail, and lay some straw at the Bottom, then lay in your Ice, and put in amongst it a Pound of Bay-Salt; set in your Pots of Cream, and lay Ice and Salt between every Pot, that they may not touch; but the Ice must lie round them on every Side; lay a good deal of Ice on the Top, cover the Pail with Straw, set it in a Cellar where no Sun or Light comes, it will be froze in four Hours, but it may stand longer; than take it out just as you use it; hold it in your Hand and it will flip out. When you wou'd freeze any Sort of Fruit, either Cherries, Raspberries, Currants, or Strawberries, fill your Tin-Pots with the Fruit, but as hollow as you can; put to them Lemmonade, made with Spring-Water and Lemmon-Juice sweeten'd; put enough in the Pots to make the Fruit hang together, and put them in Ice as you do Cream.[44]

However, when Mrs. Eales said "any Sort of Cream you like," she may have been referring to her recipes for nonfrozen creams, which immediately precede the freezing instructions. They included creams flavored with mace and lemon, with chocolate, and with almonds. She also had a recipe for trout cream, but, happily, it was named for the basket it was shaped in, not for an ingredient. Her cream recipes did lack specific amounts. She simply said to sweeten the cream "as you like it." But someone who was skilled at making creams could turn hers into ice creams by following her freezing instructions.

Finally the stars were aligned. New World ingredients had made their debut. Science had discovered the secret of freezing. Medical opinion had come around. And cooks were embracing the chance to innovate. Latini's "sorbetta," Audiger's "crème glacée," La Varenne's "neiges," Lady Fanshawe's "Icy Cream," and Mrs. Eales's "Cream" were just the beginning. At the turn of the eighteenth century, people were poised to create and enjoy all sorts of splendid ices and ice creams.

TWO

Crème de la Cream

During the seventeenth and eighteenth centuries, France set the style in upper-class European dining and in the making of ices and ice creams. In fact, the first book completely dedicated to ice cream was written by a Frenchman, Monsieur (first name unknown) Emy, and published in Paris in 1768. French cookbooks were being translated and distributed in England, Holland, Denmark, Sweden, and Italy. Traveling chefs were disseminating the French culinary repertoire. Employing a French cook was the height of fashion, and well-to-do families in England, Russia, and Italy vied for them. In Sicily, they were called *monzu*, a word derived from *monsieur*. Although revolution and upheaval lay ahead on the political front, the empire of French haute cuisine was growing, and its influence was expanding.

François Massialot was one of the most influential French chefs of the time. Born in 1660, he cooked for many of France's nobles and was the author of *Le cuisinier roïal et bourgeois* and *Nouvelle instruction pour les confitures, les liqueurs, et les fruits*, both of which were updated and reissued several times. His combined works were translated into English and published as *The Court and Country Cook* in 1702, and *Le cuisinier roïal et bourgeois* was translated into Italian in 1741. Clearly, he was a man of some importance.

Yet, like everyone else, Massialot had to contend with the realities of ice cream making. It was still a difficult and laborious process. Nearly every ingredient that was needed presented a problem of one kind or another. The ice business was not yet widely established, so obtaining and storing ice was still expensive. Salt was costly. Sugar had to be purified before it was used. In an era without refrigeration, milk and cream often curdled and eggs were not always fresh. Cooks like Massialot stressed the importance of tasting ingredients such as cream to make sure they were still fresh before pouring them into a mixture and ruining it. Since the water supply was also of concern, Massialot noted that the water should come from a spring or a river and be very clear. In addition, the utensils used for making ices had not changed in any appreciable way since Latini's and Audiger's time.

Confectioners also had to be frugal. In explaining the process of freezing ices, Massialot wrote, "You'll find this expensive because of the salt." Until modern times, common salt was not so common. The *gabelle*, or salt tax, was one of the most hated and inequitable taxes in France.[1] The *gabelle*'s greatest burden fell to the peasants, but even an elite confectioner like Massialot could not afford to waste salt. He recommended that, after making ices, confectioners should collect the water from the melted ice and boil it to reclaim the dissolved salt. He said that the salt could be used several more times by repeating the process each time they made ice cream. Years later, the Italian government's monopolistic salt policy, too, turned this basic necessity into an expensive luxury. In 1891, in the first cookbook written in Italian for the home cook, the monumental *La scienza in cucina e l'arte di mangiar bene* (translated into English as *Science in the Kitchen and the Art of Eating Well*), author Pellegrino Artusi wrote in his introduction to making ice creams: "To save money you can re-use the salt by drying it out on the fire, thus evaporating the water that had resulted from the freezing process."[2]

The 1716 edition of Massialot's *Nouvelle instruction* began, as so many other books of confectionery would in years to come, with a chapter on sugar: how to select it, clarify it, and cook it to the different stages required for different types of confections. When Massialot was writing, sugar was becoming more available and affordable as a result of the use of slave labor on plantations in the French Caribbean colonies. However, it was sold in solid loaves that had to be crushed; and it contained impurities, so it had to be clarified before being used. Massialot recommended choosing the whitest and most beautiful sugar possible because it would be easier to work with than brown sugar. But, he pointed out, even the whitest and cleanest sugars still had to be clarified. The techniques he used to clarify sugar were typical. He suggested two different methods. In the first he crushed one or more eggs, shell and all, into a pot of water and whipped the liquid with birch branches before pouring it onto the sugar. The mixture was then put on the fire and heated to boiling. He stirred and skimmed the mixture continuously, adding water when needed to keep it from boiling over, until the foam at the top was no longer black and dirty, but white. The protein in the egg would attract impurities, so they could be skimmed off the surface of the mixture. Then he took the pot off the fire and strained the mixture through a wet white napkin. Again, being thrifty, he wrote that if one had clarified a large quantity, the residue of scum and sugar could be put back on the fire with some water and reclarified to recover a little more sugar.

His second method called for dissolving the sugar in water, adding beaten egg whites, and cooking the mixture. When it came to a boil, he added a little cold water to make it settle down, then repeated the process. After that, he took it off the fire and let it rest for about a quarter of an hour. He said a black crust would form on the top, which should be skimmed off carefully, and then the mixture should be strained. He said this technique resulted in sugar that was not as clear or as white as the first, but it was good for making jams. The same technique is still used to clarify stocks when making consommé or other clear soups.

Massialot then described *cuisson du sucre*, or sugar cooking, which he called the foundation of the art of candying. Although thermometers did exist at the time, it would be years before cooks and confectioners had them in their kitchens. Nevertheless, they cooked sugar to eight or more different syrup strengths, or stages, using a variety of methods to judge them. Massialot listed six stages plus a greater or lesser version of each. They included the *lissé*, or "thread"; *perlé*, "pearl"; *soufflé*, "blow"; *plume*, "feather"; *cassé*, "crack"; and *caramel*.[3] Other cooks listed even more, one of which was called the *queue de cochon*, or "pigtail," which came after *perlé*. Yet another was *manus Christi*, or "Christ's hand"; the name is thought to have come from the hand gesture used to test the syrup, which was considered similar to that used in the blessing of the Host and chalice during a Mass.[4]

To test for the *lissé* stage, Massialot dipped the tip of his second finger into the hot sugar syrup, then touched his finger to his thumb and drew the two digits apart. If the syrup was at the *petit lissé* stage, it would make a little thread and break. At the *grand lissé* stage, the thread would be thicker and stretch farther before breaking. It is no coincidence that, in addition to the first meaning, "cooking," the word *cuisson* also means a "burning sensation."

Despite Massialot's details on sugar cooking, he did not make a sugar syrup for his ices. He simply flavored water with fruit, flowers, or chocolate, then stirred in some sugar. In general, sorbets turn out better when they're made with a sugar syrup because all the sugar dissolves as it's cooked with water. When it's simply mixed into cold water or fruit juice, some of it may fail to dissolve, making the mixture less sweet, and often gritty and icy. Massialot also used more water than we would today. He did explain that the mixtures had to be stirred from time to time while they were freezing. But even when churned with a modern ice cream maker, his *eau de framboise glacé*, or "raspberry water ice," is thinner and icier than today's sorbets. Here is his recipe:

EAU DE FRAMBOISES

Prenez un livre de Framboises bien mûres, mettez-les dans une terrine; écrasez-les & y mettez une pinte d'eau fraîche avec une demi-livre de sucre, & vous les laisserez infuser une demi-heure; vous les passerez à la chausse, & la mettrez glacer comme les autres.[5]

RASPBERRY WATER

Take a pound of very ripe raspberries and put them in a terrine. Crush them and add a pint of fresh water, as well as a half pound of sugar. Let them infuse for half an hour, pass them through a strainer, and ice them like the others.

In his 1768 book, Emy said the earlier ices, which he called *fruits glacés*, had been made with a lot of water, a little fruit, and uncooked sugar; and they were icy. He stressed the importance of clarifying the sugar and cooking it to a syrup, generally to the *lissé* stage, and said the result would be lush, soft ices rather than icy ones.

Dites Fromage

The vocabulary of ices and ice creams evolved over time. Latini called all of his *sorbette*. Audiger called his ice cream *crème glacé;* his ices were *sorbec de levant*. Subsequently, the French used words such as *eaux glacés, fruits glacés,* or the simple *glace* for ices. The word *sorbet* was not used until the eighteenth century, when *sorbets* were more apt to be called *sorbets glacés*. The 1767 edition of the *Dictionnaire portatif de cuisine, d'office, et de distillation* used the word *glace*. Although the utensil used for making ices is often referred to as a *sorbetière,* the *Dictionnaire portatif* used two other spellings: *salbotiere* and *sarbotiere*. Emy called it a *sarbotiere*. The Italians generally used the word *sorbetto* for both ices and ice creams into the nineteenth century. Artusi, whose book was published in 1891, used *gelato* for both ices and ice creams. The most common French names for ice creams were *crèmes glacés, neiges, fromages glacés,* and *mousses*.

Massialot called his ice creams *fromages glacés,* or "frozen cheeses," although they were not cheeses. The first recipe was a combination of milk, cream, lemon zest, and sugar. It was cooked, cooled, and then frozen in a mold. The second, which he titled "Autre Fromage glacé," called for cream, a little curdled cheese, orange flower water, and sugar. This one was not cooked, although he said that in winter it should be. Massialot specified the amounts of the milk and cream but left the amount of sugar up to the cook. He simply suggested using a "reasonable" or "sufficient" amount. He said the flavors could be varied according to season and suggested using strawberry, raspberry, or fresh orange flowers in summer; and cinnamon, chocolate, lemon, or essence of bergamot during the winter months. The *fromages glacés* were preceded and followed in his book by recipes for fresh cheeses. Amid them all, there is the recipe "Fromage à l'Anglois." This seems to be the first printed ice cream recipe that calls for egg yolks. It is basically a *crème anglaise*, that is, a custard. Here is his recipe:

FROMAGE À L'ANGLOIS

Prenez une chopine de Crème douce, & chopine de lait, demi-livre du Sucre en poudre; y delayer trois jaunes d'oeufs, & faire boüillir jusqu'à ce que cela soit en petite boüillie; le descendre du feu, & le verser dans vôtre moule à glace, & le mettre à la glace l'espace de trois heures; & lorsqu'il sera ferme, vous retirerez le moule, & le chaufferez un peu, afin de tirer vôtre Fromage plus facilement; ou bien vous mettrez le moule un moment dans l'eau chaude; ensuite servez-le dans un Compotier.[6]

ENGLISH CHEESE

Take a pint of sweet cream, one of milk, and a half a pound of finely sifted sugar, mix in three egg yolks, and heat it until the mixture is barely at a boil. Take it off the fire and pour it into your ice cream mold. Put the mixture on ice for three hours, and when it becomes firm, take out the mold and warm it up a little in order to turn out your *Fromage* more easily, or put the mold in hot water for a few seconds. Serve in a compote dish.

The mixture itself would make an acceptable ice cream, apart from the fact that there is no added flavor, so it would be rather bland. But he did not call for churning it as it froze, so the texture would not have been as creamy as we would wish.

Why did he call these *fromages*, or "cheeses"? An early-nineteenth-century British traveler thought Parisians used the word indiscriminately. He wrote, "*Fromage* or cheese is a lax term at Paris for any substance compressed.

Thus a *fromage d'Italie* is a Bologna sausage, a *fromage glacé* is a kind of ice, &c."[7] Compression, or molding, seems to be the only thing the many ice creams called *fromages glacés* have in common. Despite frequent suggestions that the word *fromage* was used when the mixture contained more eggs than a *glace*, and *glace* was used when it contained fewer or none, the usage was contradictory. Massialot was typical. His *fromage à l'Anglois* was made with eggs, but his other *fromages glacés* were not.

Emy said the word *fromage* was used when the ice creams were molded into the shape of rounds or wedges of cheese. In fact, nearly all of his ice cream recipes close by explaining that one could mold the ice cream in different containers, including cheese molds, in which case it would be called *fromage glacé.* He called most of his ice creams *glace de crème* plus a flavor—for example, *glace de crème à la vanille* or *glace de crème aux fraises.* He said that, when an ice cream was put in a cheese mold, its name would be *fromage* plus the flavor. An ice cream made with pineapple and molded into a cheese shape would be called *fromage d'ananas.* But Massialot did not specify the shape of his molds, and other confectioners filled an assortment of molds with ice creams called *fromages.* The French *chef d'office* Joseph Gilliers, a contemporary of Emy and author of *Le Cannameliste français,* filled an asparagus mold with his *fromage à l'italienne,* for the white part of the stalks, and his *fromage de pistaches* for the green. He said the same mixtures, which he called *liqueurs,* could be used in an artichoke mold. Gilliers also made a *fromage glacé* with *fromage.* His *fromage de parmesan* was made with fresh cream, grated cheese, and sugar and flavored with coriander, cinnamon, and clove. It was cooked, churned, and frozen in a mold shaped like a wedge of Parmesan cheese. After turning it out of the mold, Gilliers used a little burnt sugar on top to simulate the browned rind of the cheese.

Another French cook, François Menon, also used the term *fromage glacé.* In the 1767 translation of *Les soupers de la cour,* called *The Art of Modern Cookery Displayed,* he included directions for making "*Fromage à la Crème glacé.* Iced Cream-cheese." Menon called for the mixture to be "moulded like a Cheese, which gives it the Name." He didn't specify what kind of mold he used for his *"Fromage à la Chantilly glacé. From the Name of the Place where made."* After turning it out of the mold, he topped it with flavored whipped cream "raised as high as possible," so perhaps Menon should be credited with creating the prototype for sundaes with whipped cream on top. His *"Fromage de Beurre glacé. As iced Butter"* was most unusual. It was made with cream and a dozen egg yolks and flavored with lemon peel and orange flower water. But it contained no sugar. It was frozen like the other ice creams; and then the reader was to "ice it in such a Manner, that you may take it with a Spoon, to serve like Pats of Butter stamped, and Bits of clean Ice between, to appear as Crystals."[8]

The Art of Ice Cream

The names were still evolving, but the techniques for making frozen desserts had reached new heights by the time Emy wrote his book. This is the book's title:

L'Art de Bien Faire les Glaces d'Office; ou Les Vrais Principes Pour congeler tous les Rafraichissemens. La manière de préparer toutes sortes de Compositions, la façon de les faire prendre, d'en former des Fruits, Cannelons, & toutes sortes de Fromages.
Le tout expliqué avec précision selon l'usage actuel.
Avec un traité sur les mousses. Ouvrage très-utile à ceux qui font des Glaces ou Fromages glacés.
Par M. Emy, Officier.

The title translates as:

The art of making ices for the *office;* or the real principles behind freezing all kinds of cold treats. The way to prepare all sorts of mixtures, how to mold them into the shape of fruits, *cannelons* and many cheeses. All explained precisely and according to present usage. Along with a treatise on mousses. This work is very useful for all those who make ices and ice creams. By M. Emy, *Officier.*[9]

Emy's book was published in 1768. In his introduction, he said that, although in earlier years ices and ice creams had graced the finest tables, they were not very good. Echoing Latini and Audiger, he believed the texture of ices should be like snow. Declaring that his own ices were "parfaites," Emy promised that, if the reader paid attention and read carefully, he too could, in very little time, achieve perfection.

Until this point, recipes for ices and ice creams were few and often seemed like works in process. Emy's book brims with confidence. He knew exactly what he was doing, having done it many times before, and he was ready to share his knowledge with others. According to the title page, Emy was an *officier*, and as such would have been in charge of the *office*. Gilliers and some others used the title *chef d'office* rather than the repetitive *officier d'office*. Since prerevolutionary France was essentially pre-restaurant France, it is likely that Emy worked for a large household, perhaps for a member of the aristocracy. He said he was writing for other *officiers* and for *limonadiers*, in other words, for professionals. No doubt he was responsible for teaching apprentices, since his writing was always instructive, and he often anticipated and answered questions as if he had been asked them many times before.

We do not know much about Emy. We do not know the date or place of his birth or even his first name. We don't know anything about his family, his education, or his marital status. We don't know whether he was tall or short, slender or stout. However, we do know he was a wonderfully talented and experienced confectioner and a man of strong opinions. Although he was a perfectionist about his craft, moderation and pragmatism were ingrained in him. He always counseled against excess and for discipline.

L'Art de bien faire les glaces d'office contained recipes for ices, ice creams, and frozen mousses in every flavor, from ambergris, the aromatic whale secretion that played a minor culinary role well into the nineteenth century, to *verjus*. But Emy's book was much more than a recipe book; it was a manual for ice cream makers. In it, Emy discussed the history of ices and ice creams, the techniques used to make them, and the utensils that were required. He stressed the importance of using the best ingredients and offered tips on judging their quality. He explained what to do when ices failed to freeze properly. He wrote about health issues and described New World foods and their usage. Emy believed there was a season for everything—even ices. He thought it imprudent to serve ices all year round, believing they should be reserved for the spring and summer months. They would be more precious for having desired them for six months, he wrote, just as fresh peas and strawberries tasted sweeter when they finally reappeared. The ice cream one made in season would taste better because of the fruit, and because of the anticipation.

Like all good cooks, Emy was serious about his ingredients, starting with the most basic ones—water and sugar. He called sugar "sel doux" (sweet salt) and said it had to be well clarified and then combined with water and cooked into a syrup to make the best ices, which he called "precieux rafraichissemens."[10] He believed that if sugar were simply stirred into the water or fruit juice when making ices, it might fail to dissolve and result in dry, sandy ices. Emy, like Massialot and others, explained how to test for the different stages of sugar syrups. But his directions were more precise than most of the others. He recommended cooling the syrup for two or three hours before using it with fruits such as oranges, limes, citrons, and lemons, because hot syrup would make the ices taste bitter. Similarly, he advised, to avoid bitterness one should not infuse the zests of the fruits in the syrup for more than five or six minutes.

Emy made ices and ice creams in more flavors than any of his contemporaries and, indeed, in many flavors seldom if ever tasted today. He used a master recipe followed by instructions on the variations for different flavors. Although his master ice cream recipe was quite simple, it covered three and a half pages because he included advice about technique and described the possible consequences of failing to follow his instructions properly. Here is his recipe:

MANIERE DE PRÉPARER LA CRÊME

Il faut quatre jaunes d'oeufs pour une pinte de crême, environ un quarteron de sucre, mettez quatre jaunes d'oeufs frais dans une poële ou poëlon, un peu de sucre en pain, battez le tout, mêlez ensuite la crême peu-à-peu pour délayer les jaunes d'oeufs: tout étant ensemble, mettez sur un feu doux pour faire épaissir cette crême sans qu'elle bouille, c'est-à-dire qu'elle ne fasse que fumer, ce qui fait évaporer la partie séreuse qui est considérée comme de l'eau. Lorsque la crême s'en trouve séparée, elle est bien plus grasse & délicate; faites attention de la bien tourner avec une cuiller de bois ou d'argent, tournez également & par-tout, parce que le jaune d'oeuf s'attache à la poële, & forme des petits grumeleaux qui empêchent la crême de bien épaissir; & lorsqu'on la fait prendre, elle graine; telles précautions que vous puissiez prendre après ne pourront y remédier, & la congelation ne sera pas heureuse, parce que l'oeuf qui s'est coagulé sur le feu, se durcit à la glace.

Tournez donc la crême, comme je le dis, jusqu'a ce qu'elle soit bien épaisse, comme une bouillie claire; ne la laissez pas bouillir, fassiez-vous une heure à la tourner, parce que c'est de cette première préparation que dépend tout le fini.

Si le feu poussoit trop vîte, mettez de la cendre dessus, & laissez épaissir; goûtez s'il y a assez de sucre: lorsque vous serez certain qu'elle est bien, ôtez-la du feu, elle épaisse encore en refroidissant; passez-la dans un tamis, & faites refroidir, remuez de tems à autre pour empêcher qu'il ne se forme une peau épaisse dessus, & dans le fond une espece de lait clair, ce qui désunit les parties.

Voilà en général la meilleure façon de préparer toutes sortes de crêmes cuites; il ne faut plus que vous dire comment donner les différens goûts. Je renverrai à cet Article pour éviter un nombre de répétitions qui seroient inutiles; faites seulement attention à cet Article, pour prévenir tous inconvéniens qui pourroient arriver à la crême: en suivant de point en point, on sera sûr de bien réussir.[11]

HOW TO MAKE ICE CREAM

You will need four egg yolks for a pint of cream and about a quarter pound of sugar. Put the four fresh egg yolks in a pot with a small loaf of sugar, and beat, then mix in the cream little by little to dilute the egg yolks; when it is all mixed together, put it on a low fire to thicken the cream without letting it boil, that is to say it should barely simmer, which makes the serous, or watery, part evaporate. When the cream has separated, it is far more fatty and delicate; pay attention and stir it well with a wooden or silver spoon, turn it evenly and all around, because the yolk sticks to the pot and makes little curds that prevent the cream from thickening well; and when it takes, it's grainy; the precautions that you might take afterward cannot remedy it & the freezing won't go happily, because the egg that has coagulated while cooking will harden while freezing.

Stir the cream, as I've said, until it is thick, like a clear stew, even if it takes you an hour, because it's on this first step that the end result depends.

If the fire heats too fast, sprinkle some cinders on it & let the cream thicken; taste to see if it has enough sugar; when you are certain that it is ready, take it off the fire, it will thicken more as it chills; pass through a sieve, & chill it, stir it from time to time to prevent its forming a thick skin on the top & a sort of clear milk on the bottom, which results in separate parts.

That is, generally, the best way to prepare all sorts of cooked creams; all that is left is to tell you how to make the different flavors. I will refer back to this Article to avoid a number of repetitions that would be useless; pay attention only to this Article, to prevent all the inconveniences that occur with cream: in following point by point, one will be sure to succeed.

The recipes for specific ice cream flavors explained how much of the flavoring or fruit to add, as well as when and how to add it. Emy often included his thoughts on the fruit or flavoring, and occasionally he also commented on the way other *officiers* made the creams, and whether he agreed with them. He told his readers to taste frequently while they cooked and pointed out that the flavors must be strong enough to stand up to the cold of ices. He also suggested that cooks wash their mouths out between tastes so that one flavor would not influence another.

Emy and other confectioners stored their ices and ice creams in a uten-sil called a *cave*, also known as an ice safe, freezer box, freezing box, or small icebox. Its design evolved and changed over time, but basically it was a simple oblong box made of metal and lined with sheet iron or zinc. The space between the two layers was filled with charcoal, sawdust, or fibers for insulation. Available in a variety of sizes, *caves* had movable tin shelves to allow for storage of either several small ice cream molds or a few tall ones, surrounded by ice and salt. They also had holes near the bottom to allow melted ice to drain out. Intended to keep items frozen for a couple of hours or even overnight, provided one did not open them frequently during that time, *caves* allowed confectioners to make ice creams ahead of time and keep them frozen until it was time to unmold and serve them. They could also unmold and decorate the ices and then place them back in the *cave* to firm up before serving. Some small *caves* had handles, and confectioners used them to transport ice cream to picnics and garden parties.

Not So Plain Vanilla

Vanilla was not as ubiquitous a flavor then as it is now. It came to Europe, originally from Mexico, in the sixteenth century but wasn't commonly used until the mid-nineteenth century, when a method of artificial polli-nation was developed and commercial cultivation was made possible.[12] So although Emy and his contemporaries did make vanilla ice cream—with vanilla beans rather than extract—it would be another century before it became the standby we know and love. Emy said vanilla had a very agree-able flavor and was a great help to confectioners. But, he said, you must se-lect vanilla beans that are big, fat, and healthy with a pleasant fragrance. Warning that unscrupulous dealers often tried to pass old, dry vanilla beans off as fresh by soaking them in oil, he said that to avoid being tricked, one had to smell the beans. Oil-soaked beans looked fresh, he pointed out, but were never as fragrant as fresh ones.

Emy made ice creams with cinnamon, cloves, anise, saffron, oranges from Malta, orange flowers, and raspberries. He made an ice cream with a spice mixture he called *houacaca* that was sold in Paris in powdered form and was the color of cinnamon or Spanish tobacco. He thought it came from Portugal, and said he had been told it was composed of cinnamon and ambergris, and it warmed the stomach. Emy was, apparently, the first to make *glace de crème aux truffes*. The truffles in the recipe are not chocolate truffles, nor are they the bittersweet chocolate ice cream Italians call *tartufo*. They are true truffles, the fungi that grow underground, are hunted by pigs or dogs, and are prized for their intense, earthy aroma and taste. Emy prefaced his recipe by saying truffles might be white, gray, or black, and that those from Piedmont tasted like garlic. His recipe called for a quarter pound of truffles along with his standard cream, sugar, and egg mixture; it was made in the usual manner. He did not comment on its flavor.

Another oddity of the era was Gilliers's *neige d'artichaux*, or artichoke ice cream. It was made with pistachios and candied orange, along with artichokes, and quite probably the finished product tasted less like artichokes than like pistachios and oranges. Almost from the beginning, confectioners have pushed the ice cream envelope. Vincenzo Corrado, author of *Il credenziere di buon gusto*, published in 1778, said there was no vegetable that a *credenziere* could not turn into an ice. Some confectioners seemed determined to prove him right.

Emy was meticulous about the fruits and flowers he used in his recipes. His favorite fruit was the pineapple. He called it the king of fruits both for its flavor, which, he said, surpassed that of any other fruit, and for its crown of leaves, a mark of royalty. He said it was unknown (to Europeans) until the seventeenth century. You could tell the fruit was ripe when it gave off a sweet, strong scent, he explained, and it had to be used at its peak of ripeness, because if it were kept more than three or four days, it would lose its flavor and fragrance. He made a pineapple ice by grating the fruit, straining it, and then mixing it with a sugar syrup and a little lemon juice. These three in the right proportions, he wrote, made a perfect ice.

If the pineapple was king to Emy, the strawberry was queen, for its delicious taste, agreeable aroma, and delicate flesh. Were it as rare as the pineapple and as difficult to grow, said Emy, it would be more sought after and costly, because it was not possible to eat a more perfect fruit. Although he advised adding a little lemon juice to many of his ices to heighten their flavor, he thought this was not a good idea with strawberries. When strawberries were not at their best, he said, one should add a little currant juice instead, because it blended more gracefully with the taste of strawberries. He topped his strawberry ice cream with more "belles fraises" (beautiful strawberries).[13]

Emy often named and described different varieties of a fruit and specified which variety he preferred. He thought muscats were the only grapes worth using for ices, but said they were difficult to find in Paris. He liked oranges from Malta better than those of Provence because the Maltese were sweeter. He said pomegranates from France were as tasteless as water; those from warmer countries were superior. Because he was so particular about flavors and freshness, he often began a recipe by telling his readers to choose the ripest nectarines, or to select some beautiful freshly picked violets, or to choose good ripe cherries. The better your fruit or flowers, he said, the better your ices. The fruit should not be too ripe or too green, neither spoiled nor flawed. It is clear that many of the ingredients available at the time were not pure and fresh. Emy warned of chocolate and nuts gone moldy, lemons that were black in the middle, sugar that tasted dirty or old. When explaining how to make *glaces de crème*, Emy said the most important thing to do was to taste the cream, especially in summer, because it was subject to souring. When in doubt, don't use it, he advised.

Emy made several different nut ice creams but always strained the nuts out of the mixture after letting them infuse long enough to give it flavor, as did most other confectioners of the time. His filbert ice cream called for pralined filberts, that is, nuts cooked in a sugar syrup, then chopped. He said cashew nuts were shaped like a hare's kidney and were very good for the stomach. He used both sweet and bitter almonds for his almond ice cream, and made another he called *glace de crème de Strasbourg* with peach stones in place of almonds. When he made cherry or apricot ices, he infused the ground pits of the fruits in sugar syrup, along with the fruits themselves, for the most intense flavor. Then he strained the mixture.

Crumbled cookies, macaroons, and even bread crumbs all found their way into ice creams as well, but the results were strained and turned into smooth ice creams, rather than the crunchy, chunky ones we enjoy today. Emy was the first to make an ice cream with rye bread crumbs, but again, after he steeped the crumbs in the mixture, he strained them out. Other confectioners, probably following his lead, made brown bread ice cream the same way, and it became especially popular in England. Emy did, however, suggest sprinkling dry biscuit or macaroon crumbs atop some ice creams just before serving, so he had a bit of crunchiness in his repertoire.

Chocolate, coffee, and tea were the three important new beverages in seventeenth-century Europe, and they were all used to make unfrozen creams. Menon made creams with all three: "Crème de Chocolat," "Crème de Caffé," and "Crème d'Herbages de ce que l'on veut," which was translated as "With Garden-Herbs of what kind you please."[14] The herbs he suggested were tea, aniseed, chervil, tarragon, celery, and parsley. But these were all creams, not ice creams. It took some time before all three of the new beverages were transformed into frozen creams and ices.

Emy made chocolate and coffee ice creams and mousses and chocolate ices, but he didn't use tea. He introduced his recipe "Glace de Crème au Cacao" by explaining that cacao was the nut with which one makes chocolate. He described four types, with different shapes and degrees of bitterness and fattiness, and said all could be used to make ice cream. He said it was necessary to understand how to distinguish among them, and that it was important to choose large heavy ones with no green or raw taste or mold. One bought cacao at a spice shop or from chocolate makers, either roasted or not, according to Emy. Naturally, he included detailed instructions for roasting it.

His recipe "Glace de Crème au Cacao" was more complex than his usual *crêmes glacés*. It was also unusual in its use of egg whites rather than yolks. He started by making a *glace royale,* which is an icing sugar made with stiffly beaten egg whites and sugar. It is still used in decorating cakes. Emy mixed cream into it and cooked it slowly, stirring it carefully until it thickened. Then he added two ounces of roasted cacao and cooked the mixture in a *bain marie,* or warm water bath, until the flavor of the chocolate permeated the cream. After an hour and a half to two hours, he strained the mixture, then chilled it and froze it. He suggested adding a little ambergris, cinnamon, or vanilla, and said he didn't think it was possible to make a better ice cream of its type.

Emy also made what he called a *glace de crème au chocolat blanc,* but it was not made with white chocolate. He said it was made the same way as his *glace de crème au cacao,* except that, before putting the cream on the fire, he added a half grain of ambergris, half a vanilla bean, and two grains of cinnamon. He said it would be *"delicieux"* (his italics).

His recipe for chocolate ice, "Glace de Chocolat a l'Eau," was less complicated. He simply melted some *bon chocolat de santé,* or "good chocolate of health," mixed it with sugar syrup cooked to the *petit lissé* stage, strained it, and froze it. He said that if one wished, one could use *chocolat à vanille* and add vanilla, clove, and lemon. He added that these made very tasty chocolate ices; and although vanilla, clove, and lemon were warm to the stomach, they were very good for those with cold temperaments. According to the *1767 Dictionnaire portatif de cuisine, chocolat de santé* was made with fewer of the warming ingredients or spices that could be harmful to people of a warm temperament. The dictionary also reported that people were making chocolate with an "infinity" of ingredients that its American inventors had never imagined.

Chocolate ices dated back to Latini's day, but coffee ices were late in arriving. Even though ice cream had been closely associated with cafés, apparently no one thought to use coffee as an ice cream flavoring until the eighteenth century. Emy had two recipes, one for *glace de crème au caffè blanc,* or "white coffee ice cream," and one for *glace de crème au caffè brun,* or "brown coffee ice cream." His white coffee ice cream was made with the *glace royale* like the chocolate ice creams. He steeped a quarter pound of coffee beans in the mixture, strained them out, and froze the ice cream. Steeping the beans and then straining them out gives ice cream an intense coffee flavor but only a whisper of coffee color. For his brown coffee ice cream, Emy reverted to his earlier preparation and simply flavored his mixture with a quarter pound of brewed and then clarified coffee. Gilliers also made coffee ice cream by adding strong, well-ground coffee to his basic ice cream mixture. He did not make a white coffee version.

The first to make a tea ice cream seems to have been Mr. Borella (first name unknown), identified on the title page of his 1772 book, *The Court and Country Confectioner,* as "head confectioner to the Spanish Ambassador in England." The recipe follows his general instructions for judging the proportion of eggs to cream in making cream ices:

TEA CREAM ICES

MAKE tea very strong in a tea-pot, have your cream ready mixt with the proper quantity of sugar and yolks of eggs, pass your cream through a sieve, pass likewise your tea over it, mix the whole well with a spoon, when that is done, put in it the *sabotiere* and make it congeal according to the usual method.[15]

The Art of Compromise

Emy was a professional, and he addressed the enduring problem of all professional cooks: how to remain true to one's own standards and still satisfy one's masters or, today, customers. Although he disapproved of some ingredients and techniques, he knew that *officiers* might be called upon to use them, so he explained how to do so most effectively.

Emy preferred making his ice creams with cooked cream because its water evaporated during the cooking process, and the result was an ice cream that was fat, soft, and delicate, like *un beurre glacé,* "frozen butter."

Nevertheless, he gave directions for making uncooked ice creams because many *officiers* served them. If the uncooked ice cream's color was not changed by its flavoring, he called it a *glace de crème vierge*, or "virgin ice cream." If its color was changed, he called it a *glace de crème naturelle*, or "natural ice cream." Both could be prepared with beaten egg whites added for a light, delicate texture, he said. The recipes repeated his earlier admonitions about the problems involved in using uncooked cream and advised that, if one were to make them, one had to use very fine sugar and make sure it was mixed in very well.

Emy and the other confectioners of the time made ices and ice creams according to the seasons. Coffee, chocolate, cinnamon, and other spices flavored wintertime ice creams; berries, fruits, and flowers were used in summer, when they were fresh and perfectly ripe. But when his superiors wanted strawberry or raspberry ice cream in the middle of winter, Emy used preserves. Many of his fruit ice and ice cream recipes were followed by another titled "En Hiver," or "In Winter," that explained how to use marmalade made from the same fruit to approximate the taste of the ice cream out of season. Of course, Emy would have used preserves he or his assistants had made themselves the previous summer. when the fruit was at its best. Surprisingly, one can make excellent ice creams with good marmalades and jams. The key is the quality of the preserves.

Just as he had to bow to his employers' wishes for out-of-season ice cream, Emy had to accommodate their desire for alcohol in their ices and ice creams. He said it was impossible to make good ices with wines and spirits. In fact, he wrote six pages of explanation, complete with experiments, to prove that they did not freeze properly and would result in diluted ices. Wines were bad and spirits were worse, according to Emy. Freezing diminished their taste, quality, and fragrance. The only possible exceptions were maraschino liqueur; *l'eau de créole*, or rum; a ratifia or cordial made with orange flowers; and muscat wine. He thought it was better to simply drink the wines and liqueurs at a normal temperature than to turn them into bad ices. But he said that, because he was afraid some people would insist on having them regardless of his explanations, he would provide instructions for doing it correctly. And he did. In another section of the book, after repeating that he did not recommend the practice, he offered several recipes using the wines and liqueurs he had previously named. He said he did so because he wanted his book to be useful, serving all people and all tastes. Emy knew that *officiers* had to please their masters, and he wanted to help them. At the same time, he made it very clear that his own standards were higher and flatly stated that he would "not answer for the quality of these concoctions."

Grand Delights and Deceptions

Eighteenth-century confectioners not only made ices and ice creams in all sorts of flavors but also molded them into a profusion of shapes. Surviving molds (now collectible antiques) and illustrations in early confectionery books reveal an imaginative assortment of shapes and sizes. There are peaches, pears, pomegranates, asparagus spears and bunches, cornichons, crawfish, boar heads, salmon heads, whole salmon, hams, and many more. To turn the ices out, one dipped the mold briefly in hot water. After the ice was turned out of the mold, confectioners often put it back in the *cave* to firm up, since the heat of the water softened the outer surface of the ice. Emy said returning it to the *cave* also gave the ice or ice cream a faint fuzziness, which he liked because it resembled the natural texture of a fruit such as a peach or apricot.

After ices were frozen and unmolded, they were often painted and decorated. Menon wrote, "When ready to serve, have the proper Colour of the Fruit ready, which you colour with a Pencil to imitate nature; the best method is to have a natural one, or one properly painted for a pattern."[16] Imitating nature was important. Another confectioner instructed his readers that, when preparing ice cream molded to resemble a fish, the belly had to be a paler shade than the back. Confectioners suggested having the colors ready in small pots with a light and dark version of each color at hand for nuance, along with paintbrushes and a container of water for rinsing them. (Some writers used the word *pencil;* others referred to paintbrushes; some called them camel's hair pencils.)

At the time, confectioners blended their own colors from a variety of vegetable and animal sources. To make red, they blended cochineal, extracted from insects, or carmine, a pigment made with cochineal and other ingredients, with water and a little sugar syrup. Emy explained that water alone would soak into the ices too much. Yellow was made from gomme-gutte, a product of the gamboge tree. Saffron was also a source of yellow coloring. Violet for plums was made from a mixture of carmine and indigo, a blue dye obtained from plants. Green was often made from spinach that had been blanched and put through a sieve. This was so common that recipes often simply called for "spinach green" without any further explanation. Sometimes, instead of being painted on, color was mixed into the ices when they were being made. Emy suggested tinting pistachio ice cream with spinach and reassured his readers that it wouldn't affect the taste. Burnt sugar and chocolate were both used for brown tints. Fresh cream or pounded, colored sugar brushed lightly over the surface of molded peach or apricot ice cream gave them the soft, fuzzy exterior of the natural fruits. Some confectioners painted powdered colors onto the inside of molds before filling them with ice cream to give the unmolded ice cream the proper color for serving.[17]

Emy was of two minds when it came to painting his ices and ice creams. On the one hand, he thought nothing offered more pleasure to the diner than to see the ices painted in the colors nature gave the fruits from which they were made. On the other hand, he said, some people thought the colors were poisonous; and since foods should inspire desire rather than fear, it was better not to paint them. But, again, he explained how to do so because an *officier* was bound to be asked to make them.

Presentation was of utmost importance to the confectioners. They tucked real fruit leaves and stems into the tops of molded fruit ices. They arranged orange tree branches alongside orange flower ice creams and topped pineapple ice with the fruit's crown. They filled scooped-out oranges with orange ice and called them *oranges en surprise*. Meringue eggs were cut in half, filled with ice cream, and put back together. Walnut ice cream was served in walnut shells; chestnut ice cream, in chestnut shells. Gilliers made ice cream eggs by freezing saffron-tinted ice in small round molds; then, when they were ready, he unmolded them and put them in the center of egg-shaped molds filled with white ice cream and froze them again. Sliced, they would look just like hard-cooked eggs. He colored pistachio ice cream with spinach to imitate sorrel, and arranged the ice cream eggs on it, either whole or cut in quarters. Confectioners also made almond paste containers in the shape of baskets, boxes, or fruits and sent them to the table filled with ice cream. Menon made small covered buckets out of sugar paste to be filled with ice cream, and he suggested the form of snuff boxes might be used as well. He wrote that "these small Dishes, although of no Consequence of themselves, shew the Ingenuity, and Delight the Workman takes in his Business, as those Things require a good deal of Time and Care."[18]

When ice creams were not molded or spooned into fanciful containers, they might be served in small glass dishes called *tasses à glaces*. Rather than being given the rounded scoop shape we are familiar with, the ice creams were formed into an elongated egg or oval shape with a spoon and drawn up as high as possible into a point. Emy said serving them that way took longer, implying they would start to melt, and it was more convenient to have them molded.

Some of the molded ices looked so realistic that diners could be deceived into thinking they were about to eat a fresh peach rather than peach ice cream, or a spear of asparagus, not ice cream shaped like asparagus. This dining trompe l'oeil was sometimes an intentional joke on the part of the confectioner and sometimes an inadvertent deception. Diners' reactions to the trickery revealed much about their character. One traveler in Sicily described such an event in a letter:

The desert [*sic*] consisted of a great variety of fruits, and still a greater of ices: these were so disguised in the shapes of peaches, figs, oranges, nuts,

&c. that a person unaccustomed to ices might very easily have been taken in, as an honest sea-officer was lately at the house of a certain minister of your acquaintance, not less distinguished for the elegance of his table, than the exact formality and subordination to be observed at it. After the second course was removed, and the ices, in the shape of various fruits and sweetmeats, advanced by way of rear-guard; one of the servants carried the figure of a fine large peach to the captain, who, unacquainted with deceit of any kind, never doubted that it was a real one; and cutting it through the middle, in a moment had one large half of it in his mouth; at first he long looked grave, and blew up his cheeks to give it more room; but the violence of the cold soon getting the better of his patience, he began to tumble it about from side to side in his mouth, his eyes rushing out of water, till at last, able to hold no longer, he spit it out upon his plate, exclaiming with a horrid oath, "A painted snowball, by G-d!" and wiping away his tears with his napkin, he turned in a rage to the Italian servant that had helped him, with a "D-n your macaroni eyes, you son of a b—, what did you mean by that?"—The fellow, who did not understand a word of it, could not forbear smiling, which still convinced the captain the more that it was a trick; and he was just going to throw the rest of the snowball in his face, but was prevented by one of the company; when recovering from his passion, and thinking the object unworthy of it, he only added in a softer tone, "Very well, neighbour, I only wish I had you on board ship for half an hour, you should have a dozen before you could say Jack Robinson, for all your painted cheeks."[19]

On another occasion, the trickery was intentional, the skill of the confectioners was appreciated, and the joke was enjoyed. Dr. John Moore, author of *A View of Society and Manners in Italy,* wrote that he, along with King Ferdinand IV of Naples, his wife, Queen Maria Carolina, and others paid a call on the sisters of the San Gregorio Armeno Convent in Naples one day. The royals and their entourage were surprised when they were ushered in and saw

a table covered, and every appearance of a most plentiful cold repast, consisting of several joints of meat, hams, fowl, fish and various other dishes. It seemed rather ill-judged to have prepared a feast of such a solid nature immediately after dinner; for those royal visits were made in the afternoon. The Lady Abbess, however, earnestly pressed their Majesties to sit down, with which they complied, and their example was followed by the Archduchess and some of the ladies; the nuns stood behind to serve their Royal guests. The Queen chose a slice of cold turkey, which, on being cut up, turned out a large piece of lemon ice, of the shape and appearance of a roasted turkey. All the other dishes were ices of various kinds, disguised under the forms of joints of meat, fish, and fowl, as above mentioned.[20]

Moore reported that the guests and the nuns alike all laughed heartily at the clever joke.

THREE

Ingenious Foreigners
and Others

Italians were celebrated for their ices, and, in turn, they celebrated ices. Italian poets and novelists wrote paeans to ices. Italian confectioners and even nuns delighted in fooling diners by sending ices to the table disguised as slices of turkey, bunches of asparagus, and lush, ripe peaches. Yet Italians did not give us the valuable printed guides to their art that French confectioners such as Emy and Gilliers did. Just two eighteenth-century Italian books dealt with ices, and they were written by a physician and a Benedictine monk rather than a cook or a confectioner.

The Neapolitan physician and author Filippo Baldini wrote a treatise on the health benefits of ices and ice creams called *De sorbetti*, which was first published in 1775. The book has no recipes; rather, it is one long argument in favor of eating ices and ice creams. Emy had discussed their health benefits and drawbacks in his own judicious way in *L'Art de bien faire les glaces d'office* just a few years earlier. He believed eating too much ice cream could be a problem, but thought that if one ate slowly and prudently it would do no harm. Emy said that overindulgence could stop perspiration and cause colics and other illnesses, but that ices and ice creams were good for those with a strong and nervous temperament. He often commented that a particular ice cream was good for someone with a cold stomach or that another might prove warm to the stomach but could be tolerated. In his strongest endorsement of the health value of ices, he reported that when a tax was imposed on ice and people ate fewer ices as a result, the incidence of common diseases went up. He attributed the increase in disease to the decrease in the consumption of ices.

Baldini was much more enthusiastic about their benefits. He saw ices and ice cream as cure-alls. The combination of sugar, salt, and cold was infinitely beneficial to our bodies, according to Baldini. He thought that if the salt from the melting ice and salt mixture used in freezing got into the ice cream, it was all to the good. As to sugar, he thought it was nearly perfect, and cited the example of a man who lived to be one hundred as a result of consuming large quantities of sugar every day.

Although he introduced one section of his book with the words "Sorbetti o Gelati," Baldini used *sorbetti* throughout, whether referring to items made with milk, cream, or even butter, or those made with fruit juices or flavored waters. He called ices made from lemons, citrons, strawberries, and pineapples *sorbetti subacidi,* since the fruits are acidic. *Sorbetto* made from lemons was good for those with fevers or weakness of the stomach, he wrote, and citron *sorbetto* conserved health and prolonged life. Baldini, like Emy, was enamored of the new pineapple fruit. The second edition of the book, published in 1784, concluded with a fifteen-page section extolling its merits. He said that pineapple *sorbetto* restored vigor and calmed fevers.

Ices made with chocolate, cinnamon, coffee, pistachios, or pine nuts were *sorbetti aromatici,* or "aromatic sorbets," according to Baldini. The cinnamon was one of the most valuable, he said. It relieved pain, was calming, increased perspiration, and improved circulation. It was an excellent cordial, and it had proved very successful in treating many maladies. Chocolate *sorbetto* was nearly as good. Baldini explained that the chocolate used to make it consisted of cocoa, cinnamon, sugar, and vanilla, all of which contained plenty of essential oils. As a result, ices made with chocolate were particularly nourishing. They were an effective remedy for atrophy, scurvy, and the pains of gout. In addition, he said he had personally witnessed the way chocolate *sorbetto* raised the spirits of hypochondriacs and melancholics. In recent years medical studies have discovered many health benefits in chocolate consumption. No doubt if he were alive today, Baldini would find an enthusiastic following.

Baldini titled the section on *sorbetti* made with milk "De Sorbetti Latti-ginosi," or "Of Milky Ices." He differentiated between ice creams made with milk from asses, cows, goats, and sheep and commented on the numerous health benefits of them all. Asses' milk *sorbetti* purified blood; goats' milk *sorbetti* were good for persistent diarrhea, hemorrhages, and many other atrocious ailments. Cows' milk *sorbetti* were excellent for a variety of ills from paralysis to scurvy. In his experience, he reported, they never failed to have a positive impact and to lessen violent symptoms. Finally, sheep's milk *sorbetti* provided good nourishment to emaciated bodies and were helpful against diarrhea, dysentery, hemorrhages, and scurvy.[1] Opinion had reversed. The diseases once thought to have been caused by ices—paralysis, dysentery, hemorrhages, scurvy—were now thought to be cured by them.

The only Italian book of the time that specifically described the duties of the *credenziere,* the equivalent of the French *officier,* was published in 1778. *Il credenziere di buon gusto,* or *The Confectioner of Good Taste,* was written by Vincenzo Corrado, a Benedictine monk who was born in Oria, a small town in Puglia, and educated by the Celestines of the Saint Peter Monastery at Maiella, in the Abruzzo region. After he took his vows, he traveled throughout Italy with the *padre generale,* Cherubino Brancone, studying and recording local culture and cuisine. He settled in Naples and wrote *Il cuoco galante* (The Gallant Cook), first published anonymously in 1773. His books attempted to document and elevate Italian cuisine and confectionery at a time when they were still heavily influenced by the French.[2]

Il credenziere di buon gusto included a chapter on ices and ice cream, both of which Corrado referred to as *sorbetti.* He did not use the word *gelato.* Like Baldini, Corrado used the terms *subacidi* and *sorbetti latticinosi* (their spellings differed). Corrado said that the *latticinosi,* or milk-based *sorbetti,* required less sugar than the acid fruit ones. He called ices noble frozen beverages, although it was clear that they were eaten rather than drunk, and he said making them took a lot of practice. Like Emy, Corrado stressed stirring the mixtures continuously so as to make a smooth ice or ice cream. His ice cream recipes usually specified cow's milk and sometimes called for a combination of milk and cream. A few recipes added butter as well, along with more eggs than Emy used. They would have been very rich ice creams. He used a sugar syrup to make ices, as did Emy and most other confectioners. Corrado's ices and ice creams also included some of the same flavors as Emy's—coffee, chocolate, strawberry, pistachio, and pineapple, which he called *sorbetto di ananas frutto Americano,* or "American pineapple fruit sorbet," using the French word for pineapple rather than the Italian, *ananasso.*

He also featured recipes for *sorbetti* that were considered typically Neapolitan.[3] Among them were a pomegranate ice, a jasmine ice, and *sorbetto di caroselle.* He explained that the word *caroselle* was a Neapolitan term for fresh fennel seeds. In addition to the crushed fennel seed, the ice was made with lemon juice and sugar syrup. He also made *sorbetto di torrone.* *Torrone* candies are Italian nougats made with egg whites, honey, and almonds. They are frequently a part of Christmas feasting, and Italian-American children often find small boxes of them in the toes of their Christmas stockings. Corrado replicated the flavor of *torrone* candies with cow's milk, eggs, sugar, almonds, coriander, and cinnamon water. This is Corrado's recipe for butter ice cream:

SORBETTO BUTIRATO

In tre libre di latte di vacca, cotto con sei gialli d'uova ci si metterà una libra di butirro; ed una e mezza di zucchero a maturatura; e condito il tutto con acqua di canella, si farà congelare, e mantecare.[4]

BUTTER ICE CREAM

Cook thirty-six ounces of cow's milk with six egg yolks, add twelve ounces of butter and eighteen ounces of refined sugar; flavor the mixture with cinnamon extract, freeze and whip.[5]

The ice cream that results, mixed in a present-day ice cream maker rather than whipped by hand, has a grainy, coarse texture as a result of tiny bits of butter that remain unincorporated into the ice cream. It leaves a greasy feel in the mouth. Made with cinnamon sticks rather than the now-uncommon cinnamon extract, it is quite flavorful.

Cinnamon in various forms was popular among the Italians. In addition to flavoring the butter and egg ice creams with it, Corrado used it as the main flavor of two different ices—a red cinnamon *sorbetto* and a white one. He made the red by steeping crushed cinnamon in boiling water, then straining it, adding sugar syrup, and freezing it. Just before serving it, he added some oil of cinnamon. He made the white with a mixture of sugar syrup, water, and cinnamon water along with several drops of cinnamon oil. He said it had to be worked well to become smooth and white.

His *sorbetto di candito d'uova*, or "sorbet of candied eggs," may sound more appealing if we give it the name a similar ice is known by today—*zabaglione* (or *zabaione*) *gelato*, or frozen *zabaglione*. The original unfrozen version of *zabaglione* is made by mixing egg yolks with sugar or sugar syrup, then adding marsala wine and whisking the mixture in a double boiler until it becomes light and foamy and increases in volume. Often served warm for dessert, it is sometimes prepared tableside with great fanfare in restaurants. Corrado's frozen version called for thirty egg yolks cooked with three pounds of sugar syrup until thickened. Then the mixture was strained, whipped until cold, and frozen. He suggested flavoring it with cinnamon extract or oil of cinnamon. In the nineteenth century, confectioners in London called a comparable preparation a *bomba*. Today, frozen *zabaglione* is usually made with marsala or rum, and whipped cream is often blended in to lighten the mixture.

Corrado made another whipped ice, which he called a *spuma*. The word means "foam," and the ingredients were whipped and the foam gathered up and placed on a strainer to drain off excess moisture. Then it was frozen. This is the same technique—minus the freezing—that had been used for many years to make light, frothy desserts called snows or snow creams. Corrado's *spume* recipes included a frozen chocolate *spuma*, a frozen milk *spuma*, and one he called *spume varie*, which he said could be made with a variety of flavors, such as cinnamon or coffee. *Spume* were probably a predecessor of the ice cream now called *spumone* or *spumoni*. Today the word is used to describe a molded ice cream dessert including two or three flavors of ice cream, at least one of which is made with whipped cream. The whipped cream makes for a lighter, frothier ice cream. Often cherries or nuts are mixed into one of the flavors.

Corrado did not describe molding or decorating ices in any great detail. He simply said that the *sorbetti* could be molded in *pezzi*, small fruit-shaped molds, or in *stracchini*, larger cheese-style molds. The latter required more sugar than the former, according to Corrado. He concluded his chapter with the comment that he had said enough about *sorbetti* and would leave further discussion to the professional confectioners, those who were so talented they could turn nearly any vegetable into a sorbet.

Ice Cream in England

Until the mid-seventeenth century, most cookbooks were written by men for professional cooks, who were almost exclusively male. Then some, like François Menon, began writing for women and their cooks and housekeepers.[6] But in the late seventeenth century, women began publishing cookbooks for women, both for ladies with servants and for home cooks. Hannah Glasse, who was the author of one of the most successful eighteenth-century English cookbooks, *The Art of Cookery Made Plain and Easy*, wrote for the home cook rather than for the elite or for professionals. In her introduction she revealed her great disdain for "French tricks," and said it was the folly of the age to prefer a "French booby" to a "good English cook."[7]

Perhaps ice cream did not come under her heading of good English cooking, because Glasse left that to the professional confectioners. In her 1762 book, *The Compleat Confectioner*, she wrote, "Ice cream is a thing used in all deserts [*sic*], as it is to be had both winter and summer, and what in London is always to be had at the confectioners."[8] *The Compleat*

Confectioner was less than complete when it came to ice cream recipes. The book had just one; it began: "Take two pewter basons [*sic*], one larger than the other; the inward one must have a close cover, into which you put your cream, and mix it with what you think proper, to give it a flavour and colour, as rasberries [*sic*], &c. then sweeten it to your palate, cover it close."⁹ She went on with directions for freezing. When the ice cream was ready to be served, she suggested, one could divide it into four parts and color one yellow, one red, and one green, and leave the fourth white, perhaps flavoring it with orange flower water. She suggested using saffron, cochineal, or any sort of fruit for the red and yellow shades. For the green, she wrote, "there are several sorts of juice; all must be well flavoured with different sorts of fruit." Few would be able to produce ice cream using Glasse's recipe, so it was fortunate that it could be had so readily from confectioners.

Another Englishwoman, Elizabeth Raffald, also limited herself to one ice cream recipe in her 1769 cookbook, *The Experienced English Housekeeper*. However, it was a more complete one. As the title of her book suggested, Raffald had been employed as a housekeeper. She had worked for an upper-class family in the English countryside; later, she moved to Manchester, where she ran a confectionery shop and an employment agency for servants, in addition to writing her book and raising a family. Seven editions of the book were published in her lifetime, and it remained in print until well into the nineteenth century.

One could make ice cream from her recipe because it is much more instructive than Glasse's. That may be why the editors of the 1796 edition of Glasse's *The Art of Cookery* (published after her death) decided to use Raffald's recipe under the heading "To make Ice Cream." Apart from a few word changes, the only difference was that Mrs. Raffald dipped her ice cream mold in warm water to release the ice cream, while *The Art of Cookery* directed the reader to dip the mold in "cold spring water." This was not the only time Raffald's recipe was used without attribution. Here is Mrs. Raffald's recipe:

TO MAKE ICE CREAM

Pare, stone, and scald twelve ripe apricots, beat them in a fine marble mortar. Put to them six ounces of double-refined sugar, a pint of scalding cream, work it through a hair sieve. Put it into a tin that has a close cover, set it in a tub of ice broken small and a large quantity of salt put amongst it. When you see your cream grow thick round the edges of your tin, stir it, and set it in again till it all grows quite thick. When your cream is all froze up, take it out of your tin and put it in the mould you intend it to be turned out of, then put on the lid. Have ready another tub with ice and salt in as before, put your mould in the middle and lay your ice under and over it, let it stand four or five hours. Dip your tin in warm water when you turn it out. If it be summer you must not turn it out till the moment you want it. You may use any sort of fruit if you have not apricots, only observe to work it fine.[10]

The first English confectionery book to include a whole chapter on ices and ice creams (including the recipe for tea ice cream in chapter 2) was *The Court and Country Confectioner or, the House-Keeper's Guide* by Borella, first published in 1770. Little is known about Borella, but in the first edition of his book he called himself an "ingenious foreigner," suggesting that he immigrated to London to find employment. The second edition, published in 1772, reported that he was "now head confectioner to the Spanish ambassador in England." Borella wrote that he had many years of experience working as a confectioner for noble families abroad and had lived several years in England, "in some of the most distinguished families as confectioner." He dedicated the book to "the Ladies of Great Britain" and wrote in "The Author's Address to the House-Keepers of Great-Britain" that "there are few or no receipts in confectionary and distilling but what may be easily and successfully practised by the English house-keeper."[11]

Borella offered housekeepers a dozen recipes for fruit and flower ices and fourteen recipes for what he called "cream ices," along with instructions for freezing and molding. His master ice cream recipe, "Pistachio Nuts Cream Ices," called for four egg yolks for each pint of cream, along with "some pounded loaf sugar." His subsequent cream ice recipes explained how to vary the pistachio recipe to make chocolate or apricot or other flavors. The master recipe included general directions and proportions to be applied to the other recipes, warnings about pitfalls, and instructions to ensure success. For example, he pointed out that the mixture should be cooked only until it "offers to boil." If it actually boiled, he warned, it could turn into whey. He also advised that the cream should be very fresh and sweet; otherwise as soon as it "would feel the warmth it would all turn into curds and whey."[12]

He said that both ices and ice creams could be made with preserved fruits instead of fresh ones. But unlike Emy, he did not comment on seasonality or say he considered preserves a second-rate option. His ice cream flavors included pistachio, chocolate, strawberry, brown bread, currant, and peach. He advised that the brown bread ice cream should be made with finely sifted crumbs because that would make it "infinitely more agreeable to the mouth." In addition to tea, he made both coffee and white coffee ice creams; the white coffee was made by putting roasted coffee beans in a "fine cloth, which you tye as a bag, and throw it quite hot in your cream."[13]

Borella's ice cream recipes were highly regarded, if imitation is any indication. In 1800, thirty years after Hannah Glasse's death, a new edition of her book, titled *The Complete Confectioner, or, Housekeeper's Guide*, was published under her name "with considerable additions and corrections by Maria Wilson." Wilson was not otherwise identified. Apparently recognizing the need to expand the ice cream section, Wilson appropriated Borella's recipes for both ices and cream ices. She copied the subtitle of his book, and she even used his explanatory remarks on freezing and molding. Borella had a unique and engaging writing style, one that was easily recognizable. For example, he introduced his comments on making ices with preserved fruit by writing, "There are none of the ices which we have directed you how to make with fresh gathered fruit, but may be made also with that same sort of fruit after it has been preserved."[14] Wilson used the same introduction.

At the time, cookbook authors frequently borrowed recipes from one another without attribution. Borella was considered unusual because he did credit Glasse and Raffald for cake recipes he used in his book. His brown bread ice cream recipe is thought to have been a variation on Emy's rye bread ice cream; however, he did not credit Emy. Frederick Nutt, author of a book that was also titled *The Complete Confectioner*, picked up Gilliers's recipe for Parmesan cheese ice cream.[15] A certain amount of plagiarism, or borrowing, was accepted at the time. Some considered recipes to be similar to folktales, public property to be shared with everyone rather than owned by an individual. However, many cookbook writers made strong claims of originality in the introductions to their works and stated emphatically that none of their recipes were copied. Clearly, they protested too much for people who accepted borrowing without a qualm. Even allowing for more relaxed standards than today's, Wilson's use of Borella's work was extreme.

Borella was not the only confectioner who went to England to practice his craft. Later, one of the ripple effects of the French Revolution was to spread the secrets of confectionery far and wide. Of course, cooks traveled before the Revolution, but they traveled in greater numbers afterward. When French and Italian confectioners working in France lost their positions with noble households, many of them went to England or America in search of employment. They found it in upper-class households, in cafés, restaurants, confectionery shops, and tea shops. Once established, they shared their knowledge with other cooks and confectioners. Some of them wrote cookbooks and spread their skills even farther. An Italian confectioner who had a long and illustrious career in London, Guglielmo (later changed to William) Jarrin, wrote, "The art of the Confectioner, in common with almost every other art, has been greatly improved by the aid of modern chemistry; the events of the French Revolution, also, which deprived many ingenious men of their situations in noble families, and compelled them to seek a subsistence by laying before the public the secrets of Confectionery, have done much towards the perfection of this agreeable art."[16]

Foreigners, ingenious or not, were frequently the ones who made the ice cream and eventually even owned the shops in London. They advertised goods in the "true Parisian style of excellence" or ices "in the best Italian manner."[17] In addition, some English confectioners traveled to France or Italy to perfect their skills and then returned to practice them in London. The famous Gunter's Tea Shop was a case in point. Founded by an Italian confectioner, Domenic Negri, in 1757, the shop was named after Negri's partner, James Gunter, who eventually took it over. The shop was located in Berkeley Square, later to become famous for the song "A Nightingale Sang in Berkeley Square." Gunter's elegant patrons liked to enjoy their ices outdoors under the shade of the plane trees in the square. The gentlemen lounged outside, chatting to each other, while the ladies sat waiting in their carriages for waiters to bring their ice cream to them.[18]

In 1815, Gunter sent his son Robert to Tortoni's Café in Paris to learn more about making ices. At the time, Tortoni's was the most stylish café in the city and was reputed to have the best ices. Some people thought Robert Gunter's visit to Paris indicated that the Gunters were not yet expert in the art of ices. Captain Rees Howell Gronow, an Englishman who spent years in Paris, wrote that Gunter had to study in Paris because "our London ices and creams were acknowledged, by the English as well as foreigners, to be detestable."[19] However, Gunter's was popular among people who had the means to be discriminating, and many other confectioners in London served ices and ice creams, so it is more likely that he went to Paris simply to learn about the newest trends and to acquire new recipes.

Two years later, Jarrin went to London and began working at Gunter's. Gunter's set the standard in London for many years thereafter, and the ices served there were considered to be excellent. Gunter's supplied ices and ice creams for the dining tables of London's upper class for decades. When the journalist George Sala described an evening party in his 1859 book, *Twice Round the Clock*, he did not have to explain who or what Gunter's was. He merely wrote, "How the horses champ! how the dresses rustle! how the jewels shine! and what fair women and brave men are here congregated! . . . Messrs. Gunter's men have brought the ices; there are flirtations in the conservatories, and squeezings of hands interchanged on the stairs."[20] The shop continued in operation until the 1930s, and Londoners remembered it fondly for many more years. In a 1974 novel titled *Tea at Gunter's*, the leading character looked back nostalgically on the era between the two world wars, when she and members of her family regularly met at Gunter's for tea and "jolly good" ices.[21] Gunter's symbolized the lost style and elegance of an earlier time.

Ices in Writing

Several of the confectioners who were employed by Negri or Gunter went on to write cookbooks with significant chapters on ice creams. They all proudly noted their association with the shop in their books, which include *The Complete Confectioner* by Frederick Nutt, first published in 1789; *The Italian Confectioner* by William Jarrin, first published in 1820; *Gunter's Confectioner's Oracle* by William Gunter, a son of James, published in 1830; and *The Modern Confectioner* by William Jeanes, published in 1861, then reprinted as *Gunter's Modern Confectioner* in 1871.

William Gunter, from whom one might have expected the best treatise on confectionery in general and ices and ice creams in particular, wrote the most frivolous and self-indulgent book. Filled with asides, gossip, dreams, and name-dropping, it was also humorous and entertaining, sometimes unwittingly so. In addition to recipes, the book included thoughts on exercise, digestion, and the stomach. One section of the book was supposed to be a dictionary of raw materials in use by confectioners. It started with A for apple, and skipped B because it "is to us an empty letter." C was a fourteen-page treatise on coffee, in French. Although the section was in quotation marks, Gunter did not name its source. The coffee entry described the plant and its origins, its introduction to Paris, and the story of Café Procope. The anonymous writer said medical opinion held that coffee excited the brain, and observed that great writers, such as Voltaire, drank a lot of it. The dictionary skipped D and E. The letter F was for flour.

Then Gunter wrote, "I now skip a number of useless letters until I arrive at P." Pears, spirits, sugar, and truffles completed the entire dictionary section.

The book's ice cream recipes were equally cavalier. The master recipe, which he titled "Creams for Icing," called for thirteen egg yolks, one and three-quarter pints of cream, flavor, and "some loaf-sugar." To turn that into a coffee ice cream, Gunter said, one could throw in some roasted coffee berries. To make chocolate ice cream, he called for adding chocolate, vanilla, cinnamon, almond, and liqueur. He did not specify amounts. Here is his recipe for fruit ice creams in its entirety:

> Fruit ice-creams,
>   Are made by adding a portion of the strained juice to the sugar in powder. Use a little lemon-juice to all.[22]

Emy, who was so specific in his choices that he preferred oranges from Malta to those from Provence and thought currant juice complemented strawberries better than lemon juice, would have been appalled at Gunter's lack of attention to detail.

Nutt, Jarrin, and Jeanes were serious about their work and confident about their own abilities. They all considered previous books on confectionery to be inferior to their own and said so in their introductions. Nutt, who had started as an apprentice at the shop in the early days, wrote in the lengthy subtitle to his book that it included "250 cheap and fashionable receipts. The result of many years experience with the celebrated Negri and Witten." (Witten was one of Negri's early partners.) Nutt was scornful of Mrs. Glasse, calling her work a "spurious production" in the 1789 edition of his book. In its fourth edition, dated 1807, he took the opportunity to remark, "only one work, except the present, was ever presented to the world, on the Art of Confectionary; that production has already met with the contempt which it justly deserved."[23]

Jarrin was born in Italy in 1784 in a small town near Parma and eventually made his way to Paris. After his time at Gunter's, he opened his own confectionery and catering business. His book, *The Italian Confectioner*, was reissued with numerous changes ten times over the years.[24] In the preface to the 1823 edition, citing his twenty years of experience, he wrote that his book would be "found to contain every important particular which relates to, or is connected with, confectionery; including a variety of articles, entirely new, and describing processes little, if at all, known in England."[25]

Like Nutt, Jarrin held existing confectionery books in low regard. But Jarrin did not disparage anyone personally; he simply said his book would make up for the defects of other works. He said the existing works were "very imperfect" and "totally silent on matters of the first importance." In fact, there was "not any treatise in the English language, which can be of essential use to the Confectioner."[26]

Jeanes was identified on the title page of the 1861 edition of *The Modern Confectioner* as "William Jeanes, Chief Confectioner at Messrs. Gunter's, Confectioners to Her Majesty, Berkeley Square." In his preface, he noted that confectionery, "like other processes of manufacture," had changed in recent years with advances in chemistry as well as new fashions and changing tastes. As a result, what was once popular and refined was now "obsolete and in bad taste." Jeanes praised the work of the famed French chef Marie Antoine Carême, saying that his "was almost the only treatise that offered any real assistance to the young or inexperienced practitioner." However, he reported, English tastes differed from those of the continent. Then he addressed Jarrin's work: "Jarrin (who was formerly employed at our establishment) wrote the *Italian Confectioner* in 1820. Some of the recipes given in his work were those formerly used by us, but they have since been remodeled or supplanted by fresh ones, to suit modern tastes. As given in his work, many of the recipes are entirely wrong, and several of the utensils he describes are old-fashioned articles that have long since been worn out or thrown aside to make way for superior articles."[27] Although Jarrin had died in 1848, another edition of his book was published in 1861, the same year Jeanes's book came out.

Perhaps Jeanes was responding to the threat of competition. Still his criticisms were harsh, particularly since his recipes were so nearly identical to those of Jarrin.

So Much in Common

It is not surprising that there were some similarities among the Gunter alumni's ice cream recipes, since they had all worked at the same shop and catered to the same fashionable clientele. But since their books span more than half a century, it is remarkable that there are so few differences. Despite the fact that ice cream makers with cranks were introduced in 1843, not even Jeanes seems to have used them. From the 1807 edition of Nutt's book to Jarrin's 1827 edition and, finally, the 1861 edition of Jeanes's book, the directions for freezing hardly changed. They still used freezing pots, or *sorbetières*. Both Jarrin and Jeanes specified using pewter ones rather than tin because pewter prevented the contents of the vessel from congealing too quickly. According to Jarrin, pewter allowed "time enough to mix them thoroughly; for on this circumstance, in a great measure, depends the excellence of the ice. Tin vessels occasion too rapid a congelation, and do not afford time to well mix the materials."[28] Jeanes said of the pots, "They should be *Pewter*, and not tin, as the former metal prevents the contents freezing quickly into lumps, and consequently allows time for mixing the ingredients well together."[29]

Nutt, Jarrin, and Jeanes still turned the freezing pot around in the ice using the handles at the top and then opened the pot at intervals to scrape the frozen mixture from the sides and then stirred the contents together. In their directions they differed slightly as to the intervals at which the pots should be opened and stirred. Nutt specified every ten minutes. Jarrin said every three. Jeanes recommended every five. However, they aimed for the same result. Nutt specified that it be mixed until "your cream is like butter, and as thick." Jeanes said to blend until "the whole is as smooth as butter." Jarrin simply said to mix "till your ice is completed."

Both Jarrin and Jeanes said it was untrue that freezing made mixtures taste less sweet. The problem, they said, was that the sugar wasn't mixed in well enough; it sank to the bottom and gave the ice cream a tart taste. Both recommended thorough mixing and stirring to prevent that, as well as to eliminate lumps. They said lumps had been a problem in the past. Jarrin and Jeanes shared a similar work ethic. Speaking of the tedious process of turning and stirring the mixture, Jarrin warned his reader, "Do not spare your labour, for on this part of the operation, as is said before, very much depends."[30] Jeanes said, "If you wish to produce satisfactory Ices, considerable labour and attention must be bestowed on them. *They must be thoroughly mixed and stirred, in order to prevent lumps.*"[31]

Jarrin, in his 1844 edition, and Jeanes, in his 1861 edition, recommended the use of the saccharometer, a new instrument that had been developed for the beer and wine industries. The device was used to measure the amount of sugar in a solution. It gave confectioners not only a more exact measurement than the manual tests but also one less painful to their fingertips.

As for the recipes, the greatest differences were between Nutt and the others, rather than between Jarrin and Jeanes. For example, Nutt made many of his ices and ice creams with jams, jellies, or preserved fruit. Other confectioners did the same, but generally said they were doing so only out of season or as an alternative. Nutt's first recipes under his ice cream heading—barberry, raspberry, strawberry, apricot, currant—were all made with preserves. Later he listed fresh versions, as if the preserved ones were his first choice and the fresh ones his second. Many of his water ices were made with preserves, jellies, or "essences." He used them in small amounts as flavorings for ices and other confections. Jarrin and Jeanes called for ripe fruits in their recipes, and substituted preserved fruits or marmalades only in winter. In his instructions on making "winter ices," Jeanes noted that unsweetened preserved fruit was better for water ices, but wrote that he preferred jam or marmalade for making cream ices in winter. In addition Nutt made his cream ices with a sugar syrup rather than loaf sugar.

Nutt departed from standard practice by putting a bit of crunch into some of his ice cream mixtures. Up until his day, the desired consistency of most ice creams was smooth and creamy. To make his burnt filbert and his burnt almond ice creams, he mixed roasted nuts with the cream mixture to get the maximum nut flavor, then he strained out the soggy nuts. Just before the ice cream was frozen, he added fresh nuts. This is still the best way to get both the flavor of nuts and their crunch into the mixture. Similarly, he added crumbs to his brown bread ice cream just before molding it. Emy strained out his rye bread crumbs.

Nutt's recipe for "royal" ice cream may have been inspired by Borella's recipe of the same name. The recipes have in common citrus peels and spices such as cinnamon and coriander. Borella strained his mixture before molding it. Nutt added citron, lemon, and orange peel as well as pistachio nuts prior to molding his.

ROYAL ICE CREAM

Take the yolks of ten eggs and two whole eggs; beat them up well with your spoon; then take the rind of one lemon, two gills of syrup, one pint of cream, a little spice, and a little orange flower water;[32] mix them all well and put them over the fire, stirring them all the time with your spoon; when you find it grows thick take it off, and pass it through a sieve; put it into a freezing pot, freeze it, and take a little citron, and lemon and orange peel with a few pistachio nuts blanched; cut them all and mince them with your ice before you put them in your moulds.[33]

Soon other confectioners began adding bits of cookies, bread crumbs, candied fruits, and chopped nuts to their ice creams and not straining them out. When iced puddings came into vogue, all manner of tasty additions found their way into ice cream.

Nutt, Jarrin, and Jeanes all had similar recipes for punch water ice, which was to become wildly popular in America by the end of the nineteenth century. Nutt's recipe called for oranges, lemons, sugar syrup, and rum. Jarrin flavored a lemon ice with white rum. Jeanes offered the options of either rum or a combination of brandy and rum. He also made a Roman punch ice by adding beaten egg whites and sugar to a lemon water ice, then mixing in "one wine-glass of Rum, one of Brandy, and one tumbler of Champagne."[34] Clearly, Emy's admonitions against adding liquors to ices had had little or no impact.

Despite Jeanes's claim of superiority, his recipes for ices and ice creams differed from Jarrin's only in minor details. For example, they both made a Champagne water ice with a bottle of Champagne, sugar, and the juice of lemons. Jarrin used six. Jeanes used seven. Jeanes preferred morello cherries for his cherry ice, while Jarrin liked Kentish ones. Jarrin added pounded apricot kernels to his apricot water ice. Jeanes did not. Jeanes added beaten egg white to his lemon ice, and Jarrin did not. They both molded ices in the shape of the fruits from which they were made, and both said that the natural stone of the fruit could be inserted in the mold after being "well cleaned."

To make the basic custard for ice creams, they each began with a pint of "good" cream and a slice of lemon peel. Jeanes added seven or eight egg yolks and "half a pound of pounded sugar (or what suits your taste)." Jarrin called for eight egg yolks and "half a pound of pounded sugar, more or less, according to taste." They both said it was possible to use half milk and half cream, along with two or three extra eggs, but that using all new cream and fewer eggs made better custard.

Sometimes Jeanes and Jarrin differed mainly in the titles they gave their recipes. For example, they both made ice cream with green tea. Jarrin called his "Tea Ice Cream" and specified "the finest and strongest green tea." Jeanes named his "Green Tea Ice Cream" and called for the "best Green Tea." Jarrin made "White Coffee Ice Cream" by steeping roasted coffee beans, which he called "berries," in hot cream, then straining them out and sweetening the mixture. He wrote, "You may likewise make it with a strong infusion of coffee, but then it will take the colour of coffee."[35] Jeanes made "Coffee Ice Cream" the same way and concluded his recipe by writing, "Some make it with ground coffee, well strained, but the Cream has then a disagreeable brown colour."[36]

Nutt, Jarrin, and Jeanes all had an unusual recipe that may have been borrowed or adapted from Borella's recipe for muscadine ice. Muscadine is a type of grape. However, Borella's muscadine ice was not made with grapes; it was made with elderflowers. He directed his reader to infuse elderflowers in hot water and then add the strained infusion to a mixture for lemon ice. Nutt, Jarrin, and Jeanes all called their recipes "Grape Water Ice," and each one was nearly the same as Borella's. They all infused the flowers the same way, then added the strained mixture to lemon juice and sugar syrup—in other words, to the ingredients that make a lemon ice. The ice tastes like a lemon sorbet with an added floral scent reminiscent of some teas. This is Jarrin's recipe:

GRAPE WATER ICE

Take a handful of dried elder flowers, put them into a freezing pot, and cover them with boiling water; let them stand for half an hour, strain them through a sieve, and add two lemons; sweeten it to your liking; when frozen, add a glass of white wine, but mix it only a little at a time, then put it in your moulds.[37]

In 1885, Agnes B. Marshall included a similar recipe in *The Book of Ices*. Marshall called hers "Grape Ice Water (*Eau de Grappes*)." She used elderflower water rather than the elderflowers themselves, mixed it with her lemon ice water, then added two glasses of sherry. Borella did not add liquor to his. Nor did Nutt, who, uniquely, molded his into the shape of a bunch of grapes. Jeanes added a glass of Madeira. Not one of the recipes called for grapes.

Elderflowers and elderberries have been used for teas, wines, jellies, syrups, and vinegars for many years. Some believe the flowers have a muscatel-like flavor,[38] so it is possible that the chefs named their ices "muscadine" and then "grape" because the flavor reminded them of the wine. Barbara K. Wheaton, in her book *Victorian Ices & Ice Cream*, suggested that the problem may have been that someone mistranslated the French name *grappes de sureau*, which means elderflowers, not, as might be assumed, grapes.[39] Or, possibly, Borella named his "muscadine" after the muscatel-like fragrance of the elderflowers, and everyone else translated *muscadine* into "grape." In addition to the muscadine ice, Borella's book included a grape ice recipe made with ripe grapes. Maria Wilson included both recipes in her edition of Glasse's book. Since Agnes Marshall's era, recipes for elderflower ice have been called just that, and most recipes for grape ices call for grapes.

Frozen Pudding

Frozen puddings became popular during the nineteenth century, and Jeanes was one of the first to offer recipes for them. His "Plombiere, or Ice Pudding" was made with cream and milk along with ten egg yolks and two whole eggs, mixed spices (a typical combination of the time consisted of allspice, cloves, cinnamon, nutmeg, ginger, and possibly coriander),[40] sugar, vanilla, a glass of maraschino liqueur, and one of brandy. His was a smooth ice cream, but soon candied fruit was added to *plombières* before molding. His "Nesselrode Pudding" was made the same way except for the addition of diced preserved fruit soaked in brandy. Neither followed what would become the classic recipes.

Larousse gastronomique and most other sources define *plombière* as an almond-flavored ice cream containing candied fruits that often have been steeped in kirsch. It is sometimes enriched with whipped cream. The name is thought to have come from the French word *plomb*, or "lead," for the lead molds in which the ice creams were shaped. Some sources cite the city of Plombières-les-Bains as the source of the name, and say the ice cream was created for Napoleon III when he was there meeting with the Italian diplomat Count Camillo Benso di Cavour regarding the expulsion of Austrian troops from the Italian peninsula. However since this event took place in 1858, years after Balzac mentioned *plombière* as a specialty of Tortoni's, the lead mold is likely the source of the name.

"Nesselrode" dishes are supposed to be made with chestnut purée or chestnuts, although recipes vary. They are named after a Russian count, Karl Vasilyevich Nesselrode, a prominent nineteenth-century diplomat. His chef, M. Mouy, is said to have created the original, nonfrozen Nesselrode custard, which was made with chestnut purée, candied fruits, currants, sultanas, and whipped cream. The custard has served as a pudding, a pie, and a dessert sauce, as well as being frozen. The British food historian Ivan Day believes frozen Nesselrode pudding may have originated as a sly joke intended to poke fun at the traditional English plum pudding, which it resembles when it is served turned out of a mold.[41]

Jeanes's *plombière* had no candied fruits or almond flavoring; his Nesselrode ice cream contained no chestnuts. But he was not alone in varying from the classic definitions. Other chefs have stirred figs, dates, peaches, pistachios, walnuts, macaroons, dry cakes, citron, maraschino liqueur, rum, and other ingredients into ice creams and called them variously *plombières*, Nesselrodes, and, perhaps most appropriately, frozen puddings.

Jarrin made a "*bomba* ice," which was very similar to Corrado's candied egg ice, or frozen zabaglione. He used the yolks of sixteen fresh eggs to a pint of water along with a glass of noyau or maraschino liqueur, and sugar syrup "to your liking." Noyau liqueur tastes of almond but is usually made from the kernels of apricots or peaches. Jarrin directed his reader to cook the mixture, whipping it with a whisk "as if you were whipping the whites of eggs." When it was ready to boil, he took it off the fire and continued whipping it until it became "a light froth." Today, instructions usually call for whipping until the mixture cools and doubles in volume.

Jeanes's recipe was similar but called for larger quantities: three half pints of water, twenty-five "new-laid eggs," two glasses of maraschino or noyau, along with a pint of syrup. They both suggested freezing the *bomba* in a mold and filling the center of the mold with a different ice cream. Initially, they did so by filling the mold, then scooping out the ice cream in the middle and replacing it with another kind. Jarrin wrote, "You can mask this ice by cutting out with a spoon the middle of the ice, and filling up the pot with cream ice of any other kind or colour."[42] Later, molds were designed to create a hollow center that could be filled with different ices or ice creams.

The word *bomb* was used for ices made in molds that did, in fact, resemble bombs. In the late nineteenth century, Victorians made joke ices in the shape of anarchists' bombs complete with flames erupting from the tops. The editors of *The Encyclopædia of Practical Cookery* wrote, "It is remarkable how much inclined some culinary practitioners are to introduce the arts of warfare into their peaceful and uneventful occupations. The Bomb-ice is just one of these remarkable productions, having no more than a very fanciful resemblance to the bomb-shell from which it is designed." Some of the bombs were intended for one serving; other, larger ones were sliced and served. The confectioners were skilled bomb-makers, according to the encyclopedia editors, who wrote, "The flame which should issue from the aperture of a live bomb-shell was imitated with spun barley sugar, and with excellent effect."[43] The practice was a clear indication that Italian confectioners were not the only ones who had fun playing with their ice creams.

Paris Fashion

When Gunter went to Tortoni's to learn more about ices, he went to one of the most famous and renowned cafés in Paris. Gronow called it "the center of pleasure, gallantry, and entertainment." He wrote, "Towards the end of the first Empire, and during the return of the Bourbons, and Louis Philippe's reign, this establishment was so much in vogue that it was difficult to get an ice there; after the opera and theatres were over, the Boulevards were literally choked up by the carriages of the great people of the court and the Faubourg St. Germain bringing guests to Tortoni's."[44]

Located at the corner of the boulevard des Italiens and the rue Taitbout, the café was named after its owner, a Neapolitan whose first name is not mentioned in contemporary accounts. He had been headwaiter at the café when it was owned by his fellow countryman M. Velloni (here, too, no first name is mentioned). After Tortoni took it over, in 1803 or 1804, the café became a raging success. In the morning, stockbrokers breakfasted there; late in the afternoon, artists sipped absinthe and showed off their latest works there; and at night, *tout le monde* went to Tortoni's for ices. In 1843, Jules Janin, author of *The American in Paris*, wrote, "At eleven o'clock in the evening, the Café Tortoni is no longer a place for eating, it is a saloon for sherbet and ices. . . . The most elegant beauties, and the most agreeable young men, hasten to this last rendezvous of the evening; for Tortoni's, they abandon the unfinished Opera; they leave the theatre before the last stab."[45]

Tortoni's was immortalized in paintings by Manet and Guérard, in stories and books by Balzac, de Maupassant, and Poe, and in an Offenbach operetta. A *Harper's* magazine article published in 1889 called it the "centre of fashion."[46] Its patrons included Manet, Baudelaire, Rossini, Flaubert, Talleyrand, and Balzac. Tortoni's even has a namesake: in 1858, Café Tortoni opened in Buenos Aires. Named in homage to the Parisian café, it is now the oldest café in the city and one of the most famous.

Although contemporary writers called Tortoni's ices the best in Paris, most did not reveal a great deal about the way they were made, what the most popular flavors were, or how they were served. However, in his novel *Splendeurs et misères des courtisanes*, first published in 1839, Balzac gave us a description of one of Tortoni's ice creams: "At the end of the meal, the ices called *plombières* were served. As everyone knows, this sort of ice contains delicate preserved fruits, placed on the surface without affecting the ice's pyramid form, and is served in a small glass." Balzac added that ices had been ordered from the famous establishment at the corner of the rue Taitbout and the boulevard: Tortoni's.[47] Perhaps Tortoni invented the *plombière*.

Today, one dessert bearing the Tortoni name still exists—biscuit Tortoni. Admittedly, no one has yet succeeded in tracing its origins directly to the Paris café. The frothy frozen mousse may have originated there and then crossed the ocean to become an American favorite. Or, since it seems to be better known in the United States than in France, it may have been an American creation named in honor of M. Tortoni.

Why was it called a "biscuit"? The term came to be used during the eighteenth century for frozen desserts that contained crushed biscuits, or cookies. Macaroons, nuts, or cakes that had been grated or finely chopped were also blended into some mixtures. Some were simply ice cream with cookie or cake crumbs folded into the mixture. Others were frozen mousses made with whipped cream or a stiffly beaten meringue or both, along with a flavoring. They were frozen, without being churned, in paper cups or molds. Their names included *biscuits glacés*, biscuit cream ices, biscuit ice creams, biscuits Americana, and even bisque ice creams or *bisques*. The last is odd, since the word is the name of a French soup typically made with shellfish. Perhaps it was a spelling error, or it may have been a misguided attempt to make a humble biscuit seem more sophisticated. The authors of a British confectionery book cited a menu listing of "bisque glaze" and called it "nomenclature gone mad with a vengeance."[48]

However biscuit Tortoni originated, it became nearly ubiquitous on the most fashionable American restaurant menus in the early twentieth century. Later it was a common dessert at more modest Italian-American restaurants in the Northeast. Since it was easy to prepare and did not require an ice cream maker, it became an extremely popular home dessert as well. Although it has faded from favor in recent years, recipes for biscuit Tortoni abound in cookbooks from the nineteenth century to the present, and everyone from Fannie Farmer to Julia Child has one. This is my version:

BISCUIT TORTONI

One-half cup crushed amaretti cookies
One cup heavy cream
One-quarter cup confectioner's sugar
Three tablespoons rum, amaretto, or Frangelico liqueur
Two egg whites
Crushed cookies or finely chopped almonds for garnish

Grind cookies to fine crumbs (but not a powder).

In a medium-size bowl, whip cream with sugar until cream forms soft peaks. Carefully fold in crushed cookies and rum. In another bowl, beat the egg whites until they form stiff peaks. Gently fold into cream mixture.

Spoon the mixture into paper-lined cupcake tins, swirling the mixture into peaks. Sprinkle with cookie crumbs or almonds. Cover with plastic wrap and freeze until firm.

Makes 12.

When the Paris café closed in 1893, the *Atlantic Monthly* magazine ran an article titled "The End of Tortoni's." Its author, Stoddard Dewey, attributed the demise of Tortoni's to the disappearance of the elites who had the leisure to while away their lives in cafés, to a general lowering of standards, and to the "melting sunlight of democracy." He blamed the growing influence of the British, and the English-style teashops that had become popular in Paris. Bemoaning the fact that brasseries and beer were replacing absinthe and ices, Dewey wrote, "Fashion, literature and art, and the green devil [absinthe] continue to exist; but they are not as they were, and the putting up of the shutters at Tortoni's is the sign of an age that has passed."[49]

FOUR

The Land of Ice Cream

England lagged behind the continent in ice cream making, and America lagged behind England. In America, until well after the Revolutionary War, ice cream was a rarity. Pastry chefs and confectioners were few and far between. Ice for freezing was not always available and was difficult to store, even for those who had icehouses. Sugar was expensive. Making ice cream was also, as we know, a physically taxing, time-consuming job. Even wealthy households with servants seldom served ice cream. It was not until the middle of the nineteenth century that ice cream was available to the average American, and even then it was a special treat.

In the mid-eighteenth century, simply eating ice cream was such an unusual pleasure that those who did have it often mentioned it in their journals and letters. When Maryland governor Thomas Bladen and his wife served ice cream at a dinner in 1744, one of the guests, William Black, wrote in his journal that the dinner was most elegant; it included a great variety of dishes, "after which came a Dessert no less Curious; Among the Rarities of which it was Compos'd, was some fine Ice Cream which, with the Strawberries and Milk, eat most Deliciously."[1] In Italy or France, a table covered with trompe l'oeil ices was worth mentioning. In America, a simple dish of ice cream was noteworthy.

America's founding families enjoyed ice cream. After the Revolutionary War ended, George Washington bought a "Cream Machine for Making Ice." Thomas Jefferson's papers include eight recipes written in his own hand, one of which is for vanilla ice cream. On the other side of the paper, he wrote out a recipe for biscuit de Savoy, a cookie he liked to eat with his ice cream. He probably wrote the recipes sometime after his diplomatic service in Paris in the late 1780s.

This is one of the first ice cream recipes written by an American.

ICE CREAM

2. bottles of good cream.
6. yolks of eggs.
½ lb. sugar

mix the yolks & sugar
put the cream on a fire in a casserole, first putting in a stick of Vanilla.
when near boiling take it off & pour it gently into the mixture of eggs & sugar.
stir it well.
put it on the fire again stirring it thoroughly with a spoon to prevent its sticking to the casserole.
when near boiling take it off and strain it thro' a towel.
put it in the Sabottiere [sic]
then set it in ice an hour before it is to be served. put into the ice a handful of salt.
put salt on the coverlid of the Sabotiere & cover the whole with ice.
leave it still half a quarter of an hour.
then turn the Sabotiere in the ice 10 minutes
open it to loosen with a spatula the ice from the inner sides of the Sabotiere.
shut it & replace it in the ice
open it from time to time to detach the ice from the sides
when well taken (prise) stir it well with the Spatula.
put it in moulds, justling it well down on the knee.
then put the mould into the same bucket of ice.
leave it there to the moment of serving it.
to withdraw it, immerse the mould in warm water, turning it well till it will come out & turn it into a plate.[2]

Jefferson could have found recipes for ice cream in English or European cookbooks of the day, but not in an American one. No American cookbooks were published until the end of the eighteenth century, and the first ones had no recipes for ice cream. The dearth of cookbooks is not remarkable, since only about one hundred books a year were published in America before 1842, when advances in printing technology revolutionized the industry. But many people brought cookbooks by authors such as Hannah Glasse and Elizabeth Raffald with them to America, and reprints of English books were published in America in the eighteenth century. An American edition of the *English Art of Cookery* by Richard Briggs, published in Philadelphia in 1792 with the title *The New Art of Cookery*, was one of the first to include a recipe for ice cream. However, it was Raffald's recipe, though he did not attribute the recipe to her any more than the editors of Glasse's work had. The first true American cookbook, *American Cookery* by Amelia Simmons, was published in 1796, twenty years after the American Revolution. It did not include any recipes for ice cream.

The Virginia House-Wife by Mary Randolph, published in 1824, was the first American cookbook with a significant section on ice cream. The book became the most influential American cookbook of the nineteenth century and was especially popular in the South. Randolph's Southern specialties included catfish soup, "Chicken Pudding—a favourite Virginia dish," and barbecued "shote," which she said was "the name given in the southern states to a fat young hog." Randolph also had recipes from other regions and other countries. She had a recipe for "Gaspacho—Spanish," and one for "Dough Nuts—A Yankee cake."[3]

She had many recipes for ices and ice creams. She made a fruit ice from lemonade and said the same recipe could be used to make ices with the juice of morello cherries or currants. Her ice cream recipes included almond, chocolate, citron, coconut, raspberry, strawberry, vanilla, and coffee. The coffee ice cream was a white coffee; she wrote, "If properly done, it will not be discoloured." She also said that, after the coffee was strained out of the ice cream mixture, it could be dried and used to make coffee, "allowing more for the quantity of water, than if it had not gone through this process." Oddly, among her ice cream recipes was one for frozen oyster cream. This was simply oyster soup, strained and frozen. She did not explain when or, more important, why it would be served. Here is one of her more appealing recipes.

PEACH CREAM

Get fine soft peaches perfectly ripe, peel them, take out the stones, and put them in a China bowl; sprinkle some sugar on, and chop them very small with a silver spoon—if the peaches be sufficiently ripe, they will become a smooth pulp; add as much cream or rich milk as you have peaches; put more sugar, and freeze it.[4]

In a section titled "Observations on ice creams," she explained how to freeze ice cream and specified that it was best made in a freezer twelve or fourteen inches deep and eight or ten wide. She said this size facilitated freezing "by giving a larger surface for the ice to form." However, the narrow cylindrical shape was still the norm for most ice cream makers, or *sorbetières*. Randolph's no-nonsense approach to cooking was evident in her statement "It is the practice with some indolent cooks, to set the freezer containing the cream, in a tub with ice and salt, and put it in the ice house; it will certainly freeze there; but not until the water particles have subsided, and by the separation destroyed the cream." She explained that instead it was necessary to turn and mix the ice cream well to make it smooth, before packing it in molds.[5]

Randolph was from a well-to-do family and was a distant cousin to the Jeffersons. After her marriage, she and her husband settled at his James River, Virginia, plantation, where she became a celebrated hostess. When the family met with reverses and had to sell their home, she ran a boardinghouse in Richmond and later wrote her very successful cookbook. Randolph and her family were exceptional. The average American family did not have an icehouse and did not make ice cream in the early nineteenth century. It was not until the end of the century that the increased availability of ice, advances in ice cream freezer design, and more afford-able ingredients made it feasible for ordinary Americans to make ice cream at home.

Public Pleasures

In the meantime Americans could enjoy ice cream at confectioners' shops, pleasure gardens (also known as ice cream gardens), and ice cream sa-loons in cities such as Philadelphia, Boston, and especially New York. French or Italian confectioners who had left political upheaval behind of-ten ran the shops, just as they had in London. One of the earliest ads fea-turing ice cream ran in the *New York Gazette* in 1777. In the ad, a confectioner named Philip Lenzi, who had come to America from London, promised that ice cream "may be had almost every day."

The French gastronome and author of *The Physiology of Taste*, Jean An-thelme Brillat-Savarin, visited America and wrote that a Captain Collet had earned a great deal of money in New York in 1794 and 1795 by mak-ing ices "for the inhabitants of that commercial town." Brillat-Savarin described the reaction of women to the ice cream: "It was the ladies, above all, who could not get enough of a pleasure so new to them as frozen food; nothing was more amusing than to watch the little gri-maces they made while savoring it. It was especially difficult for them to understand how anything could stay so cold in the summer heat of ninety degrees."[6]

Despite the patronizing tone of his remarks, they tell us that ice cream was still relatively novel in late-eighteenth-century America. In America, it would be a long time before ice cream was, in Hannah Glasse's words, "always to be had at the confectioners." In 1815, Francis Guerin, newly ar-rived from France, opened a café on Broadway and served ice cream only in summer.[7] In 1827, members of the Del-Monico family from Switzerland opened a confectionery shop on William Street in downtown New York City. Delmonico's, the name modified by a sign painter, would become the finest restaurant in America in years to come. But initially, the family ran a small café that became known for its cakes, coffee, chocolate, bonbons, and fancy ice creams.[8]

In 1818, Eleanor Parkinson opened a confectionery shop in Philadelphia, and her husband, George Parkinson, opened a tavern next door. The shop was so successful that her husband joined her, and together they ran one of the city's most prominent businesses. Their son would later found the country's first culinary trade magazine, the *Confectioners' Journal*. Parkinson's confectionery shop became renowned for the quality of its ice cream and helped make Philadelphia ice cream famous.[9] In the preface to her cookbook, *The Complete Confectioner, Pastry-Cook, and Baker*, first published in 1844, Mrs. Parkinson referred to the shop as "the oldest, most extensive and successful confectionery establishment in the country." In her introduction to the section on making ices and ice creams, she noted that "Philadelphia has for a long time enjoyed a pre-eminent reputation in the manufacture of these delicious compounds." But she warned her readers against using inferior ingredients or thickeners and said, "Use cream entirely, and on no account mingle the slightest quantity of milk, which detracts materially from the richness and smoothness of the ices." Philadelphia ice cream would come to be known as ice cream made, as Parkinson advised, entirely with cream.[10]

Her book included nearly fifty recipes for ices and ice cream, along with instructions for freezing and molding. However, as she acknowledged, most of the recipes were not original. She wrote, "We have consulted every authority, French or English, within our reach; but the basis of our little work is to be found in Read's *Confectioner*, a late London publication." Read was George Read, an English confectioner. One ice cream recipe that was original to Parkinson called for egg whites rather than egg yolks. Whites do appear in ice cream recipes from time to time. In fact, Emy used stiffly beaten egg whites in some of his ice creams and said that they made light, delicate creams. But the practice is not typical. This is Parkinson's own recipe.

BRAHMA ICE

One quart of cream, the whites of ten eggs, one and a half pounds of powdered sugar [today's finely granulated sugar] of the best quality; mix the whole in a tin saucepan; put it on the fire, stirring constantly, until it boils once, then add two wine-glasses of Curaçao, half a glass of orange-flower water; put it into the pot, and freeze.[11]

What is strange about the recipe is the inordinate amount of sugar Parkinson used. When weighed on an ordinary kitchen scale, a pound and a half of sugar amounts to about three cups. Similar recipes called for one-half pound, or one cup. When brahma ice is made with one cup of sugar, it is as sweet as anyone would wish. The combination of orange flower water and orange liqueur gives it a complex bittersweet, rather than fresh orange, flavor. The texture is light and silky smooth.

Pleasure, or ice cream, gardens began as adjuncts to taverns. They were small outdoor areas where patrons could enjoy their drinks and a light meal. By the beginning of the nineteenth century, they had become commercial spaces where for a small admission charge people could stroll, listen to music, and enjoy such popular refreshments as ice cream, pound cake, and lemonade. According to contemporary reports, vanilla and lemon ice creams were the most common flavors, along with strawberry "if in season."[12] Although most writers did not describe the ice creams served in pleasure gardens except to note the flavors, one, lamenting the closing of Contoit's New York Pleasure Garden, wrote that the ice cream was made from "soft-boiled egg sweetened with brown sugar!" And served with "iron spoons that nobody would carry off wrapped up by mistake in his handkerchief."[13]

New York's pleasure gardens were located in then-rural settings in what is now downtown Manhattan. When the Vauxhall Garden was opened in 1805 near Astor Place in New York, it was thought to be too far out of town to attract customers. However, town soon caught up to it, and it was successful for years. Although the gardens differed in their particulars, most featured shaded walkways, flowers, and trees, often with cages holding singing birds hanging from the branches. Initially, the gardens attracted the genteel and the fashionable. Ladies who would not have been seen in other public venues felt comfortable strolling in such elegant settings. Describing one New York garden, a writer recalled, "Small neatly fitted up boxes to represent mystic bowers were ranged along the fences, for the special accommodation of female visitors who desired refreshments, while benches and chairs were scattered under the trees for the use of male patrons who chose to sip their brandy and smoke their *principe* in the open air."[14]

Similar gardens had been popular in London for years, and American pleasure gardens were patterned and named after them. Vauxhall, one of London's most fashionable gardens, attracted thousands of visitors on summer evenings. It was famous for its balloon ascents, as well as for the quality of its music and refreshments. *Vauxhall* became a generic name for pleasure gardens in America. There was a Vauxhall Garden in Philadelphia, and Boston's Washington Garden was referred to as a "Boston Vauxhall." New York boasted several Vauxhall Gardens at different times and in different locations, although a British travel writer of the day called New York's pleasure gardens "poor imitations of those near London."[15]

Gradually, the gardens evolved into entertainment centers lit by colored lanterns with bandstands, theatrical presentations, displays of sculpture, illuminated fountains, panoramas, fireworks, sports, dancing, drinks, and refreshments. Thomas A. Janvier's *In Old New York* described one of the gardens as it was in the late nineteenth century: "Its dazzle of lamps in the arbors and shrubbery, and its fire-works and fire-balloons, and its music, and the performances of that killing comedian Twaits . . . to say nothing of the palate-tickling things to eat and to drink which there abounded—'twas as gay a place of recreation as was to be found at that period of an evening anywhere in the civilized world."[16]

Some pleasure gardens served liquor, and others professed not to, but, according to Abram C. Dayton's *Last Days of Knickerbocker Life in New York,* "a quarter slyly dropped into a sable palm would ensure a moderate supply of cognac to be poured over the lemon ice, which gentlemen almost always preferred to the more luscious vanilla, to the great surprise of their fair companions."[17]

New York's pleasure gardens did not welcome blacks, except as servers. In fact, according to a news report, "Among the number of ice cream gardens in this city, there was none in which the sable race could find admission and refreshment." So in 1821 William Alexander Brown, a free man of color and a former ship's steward, created a pleasure garden at 38 Thomas Street on the West Side. It was in a primarily white, affluent neighborhood. A contemporary news account referred to the garden as the "African Grove," a place where "the ebony lads and lasses could obtain ice cream, ice punch, and hear music from the big drum and the clarionet." Unfortunately, it did not last long. Less than a month after its opening, complaints from neighbors, thought to have been brought on by negative news coverage, forced its closure. Brown later became a pioneer in operating inclusive, integrated theaters. However, assaults by whites finally forced him out of that business as well. He was alleged to have responded by erecting a sign that read: "Whites Do Not Know How to Behave at Entertainments Designed for Ladies and Gentlemen of Colour."[18]

In Philadelphia, black cooks and caterers opened their own confectionery and catering businesses and pleasure gardens in response to discrimination. One of the first is thought to have been Monsieur (first name unknown) Collot, a French-Creole confectioner who came to the city from Haiti after a slave rebellion.[19]

By the middle of the nineteenth century, working-class whites were visiting pleasure gardens, usually at night or on Sunday, their only day off. In Manhattan, the working class patronized gardens located in the Bowery area, while gardens located in the Broadway area attracted a more well-to-do crowd. In 1852, the Southern writer William Bobo called one garden "a sort of ice-creamery, and general rendezvous for the Bowery fashionables, who assemble, mostly at night—not having time during the day like the Broadway dandies."[20] By then, the upper classes had started to desert the gardens rather than hobnob with the working classes. According to the *New York Herald*, by 1856, when Vauxhall Garden closed, "the fashionables had deserted it and the democracy of society took it altogether to themselves."[21]

As pleasure gardens changed, newspaper accounts of drinking, unruly crowds, and a riot at one garden altered the public's perception of them. They were no longer seen as resorts for genteel ladies and gentlemen, but rather as playgrounds for boisterous crowds. When designs for Central Park were being evaluated in the 1850s, the pleasure garden model was considered and rejected. Although the working classes enjoyed the lively diversions it offered, and Irish American and German American newspapers argued for it, the prevailing view was that it was too commercial, perhaps too democratic. In an 1857 *New York Times* editorial, a writer opined, "Better the Park would never be made at all if it is to become the resort of rapscallions."[22] The "claptrap and gewgaw" of pleasure gardens, as another contemporary account described their attractions,[23] no longer appealed to the upper echelons of society, who, following the lead of European trendsetters, preferred picturesque natural landscapes. The chosen Greensward Plan, designed by Frederick Law Olmstead and Calvert Vaux, was a model of the rustic and picturesque.

London's pleasure gardens had begun their downward spiral earlier, and the city's famed Vauxhall Garden was shut down permanently in 1858. During the same year, the last pleasure garden to be built in New York, the Palace Garden, opened on Fourteenth Street near Sixth Avenue. According to its advertising, it was designed to appeal to the "refined, fashionable and the intellectual."[24] Instead, it attracted housemaids and their young charges and other members of the working classes. When the elite stayed away, the owners of the garden added children's attractions, built a new amphitheater, and welcomed circuses to serve their new customers. But the Palace Garden lasted just four years. One factor in its demise may have been that it did not sell liquor, which made profitability much less likely. But it was also simply the end of the era. Pleasure gardens were fast disappearing and being replaced by such entertainments as vaudeville and amusement parks.

Saloons for Ice Cream

In addition to being served in the pleasure gardens, ice cream was sold in ice cream saloons and ice creameries. Like the pleasure gardens, different shops catered to different customers, from the most fashionable to the least. George Foster, a flamboyant writer for the *New York Tribune* in the mid-nineteenth century, wrote about their differences in his columns on life in the city, which were later reprinted in the books *New York in Slices* and *New York by Gas-Light*. Describing an elegant Broadway shop, he reported that its entrance was dominated by long counters laden with cakes, fruits, and confectionery. The dining area was located up a few steps at the back of the shop, and ladies occupied most of the tables. Although it was daytime, the room was dimly lit, he wrote, adding, "Ladies love such subdued atmospheres, unless they are very young and handsome."[25]

The ladies were unlikely to go hungry in such a shop because, in addition to ice cream, they could enjoy tea, coffee, chocolate, sandwiches, oysters, porterhouse steaks, and sherry cobblers. The cobblers were then-fashionable drinks made with sherry, sugar, lemon, and ice and served decorated with fruit. Sherry cobblers were generally sipped through a straw, a practice some proper Victorian ladies thought altogether shocking.

"Quite a different set of customers," Foster reported, frequented the "Patent Steam Ice-Cream Saloon," so-called because the ice cream was made in a steam-driven freezer. Foster joked that the ice cream must be warm, then described the customers as the wives and daughters of "the substantial tradesmen, mechanics and artisans of the city, the great middle class." He wrote, "They are altogether a pleasant sight, this glorious autumn afternoon, sitting at these handsome tables, every matron attended by a 'little horde' of hungry expectants, clinging full of hope and confidence to mama's knee—hope that they will get now and then a spoonful of the delicious Patent Steam Ice-Cream, (which after all, dear reader, is *not* warm,)—and confidence that their reasonable expectations will not be disappointed."[26] At night, the class distinctions at the various ice cream saloons were even more evident. Foster reported:

> The Broadway establishments are generally fitted up in a style of exaggerated finery, which has a grand effect from the street, but is a little too glaring and crushing when you are within. At night, when the gaudy curtains, silver paper, and gilded mirrors are highly illuminated by gaslight, the scene rises to splendor itself or at any rate to that which most people are willing to accept for it, and never know the difference. In the sultry summer evenings, every one of these fashionable Ice-Cream Saloons is crowded with throngs of well-dressed men and women, belonging for the most part to the great middle classes; while the establishments in the Bowery are crammed to the very threshold with the b'hoys and their buxom and rosy sweethearts, their veins leaping with the fire of health and youth, and their round cheeks glowing with happiness.[27]

Finally, he wrote, there was "no lack of ice-cream shops of a lower grade than those of which we have been speaking—where, although the company is not 'picked,' the pockets of the unwary visitor generally are."[28]

The Ice Harvest

During the first half of the nineteenth century, several events, inventions, and innovations brought about enormous changes in the production and consumption of ice cream. The invention of ice cream freezers with built-in churns, the expansion of the sugar industry, and especially the development of the ice business all helped make ice cream a household word and a family treat. Ice, the winter crop of frozen ponds, lakes, and rivers, gave America its favorite summer dessert.

For years, ice had been harvested and used to chill drinks, preserve food, and freeze ice cream. But it had been limited to those few who could afford it and had the means to store it. Jefferson had an icehouse at Monticello that, like most built in the late eighteenth and early nineteenth centuries, was more like an ice cellar. It was dug into the ground on the coldest side of the house, under the north terrace. It could hold sixty-two wagonloads of ice, which was taken from the Rivanna River in winter and used throughout much of the year. In 1815, the supply lasted until October 15.[29]

The British confectioner William Jeanes included advice on building icehouses in his 1861 book, *The Modern Confectioner: A Practical Guide.* He wrote, "In America, almost every small farmer enjoys the luxury of an Ice-house. In this country they are unknown, except in large establishments." Jeanes discussed materials, sites, and insulation in some detail and suggested walls measuring from fourteen to eighteen inches thick. "If you have a cool dairy, let your Ice-house be built at the side of this, entering from the dairy," he advised. "This arrangement serves a double purpose: the Ice cools the dairy in the warm months, and the low temperature of the place does not thaw so quickly the frozen mass within." Warning that the icehouse must be as nearly airtight as possible, he said, *"The great thing to guard against being the admission of warm air"* (italics in the original).[30]

Actually, Jeanes was wrong. In addition to having good drainage to keep meltwater away from solid ice, the great thing was to have good ventilation so that warm air could be released. Icehouse construction continued to evolve in the nineteenth century, and as people better understood freezing, they built aboveground icehouses with good ventilation and drainage, often painting them white to reflect the sun's rays. Sawdust or straw was used to insulate the ice. Prosperous farmers or homeowners with ponds or lakes on their properties often had small icehouses. In some communities, neighbors joined together to cut ice, and they stored it in communal icehouses.[31] The owner of a lakefront hotel might build an icehouse so he could cut ice in winter to supply his business. Some harvested ice and sold it to local businesses, restaurants, confectionery shops, or hotels. But it was not a big business until the middle of the nineteenth century, decades after Frederick Tudor first shipped ice from Boston to Martinique in 1806.

Tudor was a member of a prominent Boston family and was expected to attend Harvard University, as his father and older brother had done. But he had other ideas. He left school and drifted for a few years. He served a brief apprenticeship, traveled a bit, notably to Havana, and spent time at the family farm in Saugus, outside Boston. There the family had an icehouse where they stored ice from their pond and, in summer, made their own ice cream.

Tudor saw his future in the clear ice from the pond. Remembering the intense summer heat of Havana, he decided that supplying the West Indies with ice would be a successful business. Few agreed with him. No one wanted to invest in the enterprise. Nevertheless, in 1806 he managed to get the exclusive right to sell ice in Martinique, harvested enough to fill a ship, insulated the ice with hay, and set sail from Boston on February 13. The ship arrived on March 5 with much of the ice intact. However, according to Gavin Weightman, author of *The Frozen-Water Trade*, when Tudor landed in Saint-Pierre, then the island's capital city, he discovered that his brothers, who had gone ahead to make arrangements, had not managed to secure an icehouse. There was nowhere to store the ice. People were not eager to buy it, since they did not know how to store it or what to do with it. Tudor, probably recalling the ice cream his family made every summer, persuaded the owner of a restaurant called the Tivoli Garden to use the ice to make ice cream and sell it. Tudor provided the ice, the restaurateur provided the cream mixture, and together they made ice cream. Afterward, Tudor wrote in a letter to his brother-in-law, "The Tivoli man rec'd for these creams the first night $300; after this he was humble as a mushroom."[32]

The Saint-Pierre newspaper reported on the momentous occasion: "It will be a remarkable epoch in the history of luxury and enterprise that on the 6th March ice creams have been eaten in Martinique probably for the first time since the settlement of the country. And this too in a volcanic land lying 14 degrees north of the equator."[33]

Although Tudor's initial foray into the business lost money, it proved ice could be shipped successfully. It took years, but eventually the business became profitable and Tudor became known as the "Ice King." One secret of his success was that he was not content to simply wait for ice to form and then harvest it. He and his associate, Nathaniel Wyeth, developed innovative techniques and equipment that made the process efficient and lucrative. They improved on the design and effectiveness of icehouses and ice-harvesting tools. They were the first to use horse-drawn ice plows to cut regularly sized blocks of ice, which stored better than irregular ones. They pioneered the technique called "sinking the pond," in which holes were drilled into the ice to allow the water below to wash over the ice. The fresh water froze quickly and the ice became that much thicker. They discovered that sawdust was an excellent insulator, and found a reliable source at Maine lumber mills, where, previously, it had been considered worthless. The ice trade opened up a new market for lumber companies.

In 1833, Tudor shipped ice from Boston to Calcutta, to the amazement and delight of all concerned, especially the British, who suffered in India's heat. The *Tuscany* sailed from Boston on May 12 and docked in Calcutta on September 13 with enough ice to supply the city for up to sixty days, according to an ad in the local newspaper.[34] When regular shipments were established, ships carried American ice to India and returned with holds full of goods, including Indian jute, which New England mills turned into rope, fabrics, and sacks. Closer to home, ships brought ice to Southern states and returned loaded with cotton for Northern textile mills. Previously, the ships had sailed south with rocks in their hold for ballast. Although the North's blockade of Southern ports during the Civil War interrupted the Southern ice trade, it increased the Indian trade in both ice and cotton. Providing ice to the Union Army also became a profitable business.

Naturally, Tudor's success generated competition. Others entered the business, and soon large wooden icehouses lined the shores of New York's and New England's lakes, ponds, and rivers. One of Tudor's rivals began harvesting ice from Wenham Lake, north of Boston, in 1845 and selling it in London. When he displayed a large block of the ice in the window of his office in the heart of London, passersby were amazed at its clarity and its apparent longevity. It seemed the ice never melted. Unbeknownst to them, a fresh block of ice was substituted for a melting one whenever necessary. The ice was so clear many Londoners believed it was glass and had to touch it to be convinced otherwise. Wenham Lake ice became so renowned that it became a generic name for ice, much as Vauxhall had for pleasure gardens. Later, a lake in Norway was renamed Wenham Lake so that its ice would sell well in London.

When he was seventy-five, in 1859, Frederick Tudor created a public pleasure garden he called Maolis on land he had bought in the town of Nahant, north of Boston, then a fashionable seaside resort. The pleasure garden's many attractions included picnic areas, a teahouse, a dance hall, a "Witch House" where children could delight in being frightened, a bowling alley, a bear den, and an ice cream pavilion. It was not a big financial success, but it gave him much enjoyment in his last years. He died at the age of eighty, five years after opening it.

For years, the natural ice industry continued to thrive in America. In 1879, it was estimated that eight million tons of ice was harvested annually. The industry employed thousands of workers, some year round, many more during the winter ice harvest season. Ice was harvested from ponds, lakes, and rivers from Maine to California, and was transported to other parts of the world on ships, barges, trains, and horse-drawn wagons. Ice created and transformed businesses. Toolmakers devised a vast array of implements for harvesting and delivering ice. Ice boxes became must-have appliances both for businesses and homes. (Confusingly, they were often called refrigerators.) Meat could be slaughtered and shipped from Chicago across the country in railroad cars loaded with ice rather than being delivered on the hoof. Milwaukee's beer could be brewed year round rather than only in the winter, thanks to the natural ice supply. California's fruits and vegetables reached Chicago's markets in ice-cooled railroad cars. Butter was sent by rail from the Midwest to New York, then by ship to Europe.[35] Ice was used in medical practices, especially for treating feverish patients. In cities, ice depots held large stores of ice throughout the year. The iceman filled his wagon there and delivered the dripping blocks to homes and businesses daily or even more frequently. By the last quarter of the century, ice was available nearly everywhere, and, as a result, so was ice cream. The May 13, 1887, edition of the *Clinton Public* newspaper, of Clinton, Illinois, reported that the new West Side Bakery and Confectionery had ice cream for sale "every day."

The same year, nearly two million tons of ice was harvested in Maine.[36] Jennie Everson, who was born in Dresden, Maine, in 1890, wrote that, as a young girl, she had been able to see eleven commercial icehouses from the front lawn of her riverside home. They varied in size, but the capacity of a commercial icehouse ranged from 15,000 to 50,000 tons of ice.[37] In addition to the commercial houses, many families in the area had their own small icehouses, which were frequently filled with leftover ice from the commercial operations.

Despite the plethora of natural ice and the scope of the business, a number of inventors were experimenting with making ice artificially. Some machines used compressed air; others used ether or ammonia. However, the early machines were flawed. Occasionally one would explode, a fact that the natural ice industry exploited. The machines used corrosive chemicals, and oil sometimes got into the ice and ruined it. Artificially made ice was not cost-effective compared to natural ice. Most important, the public had plenty of natural ice and believed that artificially made ice was not quite real and not really necessary. When a machine that made ice artificially was demonstrated at the 1862 International Exhibition in London, some visitors thought the ice was produced through a sort of magic trick. They did not take it seriously. However, the Indian government did, and ordered one for the use of Her Majesty's troops, thus foreshadowing an end to the natural ice trade to India.[38]

During the American Civil War, the artificial ice business gained from the blockade that ended shipments from the North to the South. When Southerners could not get natural ice, they turned to artificially made ice to supply their needs. A Frenchman, Ferdinand Carré, had designed and patented a steam-driven ice-making plant that used vaporized ammonia. His machines helped the South get the ice it required during the war and proved that the business had possibilities.

The new machines did not capture a significant portion of the ice business quickly, yet they were harbingers of changes to come. In the late nineteenth century, the natural ice industry began to face many new challenges. During mild winters, there was not enough ice even in the far reaches of Maine to supply the ever-growing demand. Waters near growing cities were becoming polluted and could no longer be used for ice. At the same time, mechanical refrigeration continued to improve and became more cost-effective. The tide was turning, although not everyone recognized it. In 1895, the president of New York's Knickerbocker Ice Company, Robert Maclay, said of the machine-made ice business, "The cost of manufacturing such ice, even without the additional cost of making a chemically pure article, precludes the prospect of ever bringing it profitably into competition with ice formed by nature's own hand."[39]

Others predicted the future more accurately. In August 1894, an early issue of the *New England Kitchen,* a magazine published by the Boston Cooking School, summed up the situation concisely in an article titled "Ice and Ices." After explaining that the problem of oil in artificially produced ice had been overcome, the article stated:

> Thus to-day in most large cities we are offered a choice between natural and artificial ice, at about the same cost. . . .
>
> The probability is that every year manufactured ice will gain a stronger hold, for there is a constant increase in the demand for ice, because of the larger population of the country, and the same cause interferes with the natural ice supply.[40]

In 1920, according to the U.S. Census Bureau, forty million tons of ice was produced artificially and only fifteen million tons of natural ice was harvested.[41] The change would have taken place even sooner had it not been delayed by the U.S. government's need for ammonia for ammunition during World War I. After the war, the industry swiftly gained ground, and the once-thriving natural ice business failed.

The Price of Sugar

Another impediment to widespread ice cream making prior to the nineteenth century was the high cost of sugar. However, happily for ice cream makers, at the same time that ice became more available and affordable, sugar prices began to fall and sugar changed from a luxury item to a staple.

In the eighteenth century, sugar was expensive, and its quality varied depending on the level of clarification, from the coarsest brown sugar to refined white sugar. It was sold in hard loaves or cones that had to be broken up, pounded, and sifted before being used. Some used a mortar and pestle; others recommended rolling the sugar loaf with a bottle, then sifting it, because they thought this method wasted less sugar than pounding it in a mortar. The origin of the sugar was also a factor. For example, Elizabeth E. Lea, in *Domestic Cookery, Useful Receipts, and Hints to Young Housekeepers,* warned, "You should always clarify white Havana sugar."[42] Since even most refined sugar still contained many impurities, both confectioners' books and cookbooks written for home cooks included detailed instructions on how to clarify it, just as confectioners' books had. In her instructions for making jellies, author Eliza Leslie told her readers that sugar "will be improved in clearness by passing it through a flannel bag. Skim off the brown scum, all the time it is boiling."[43]

To save money, some homemakers bought different grades of sugar and put them to different uses. Catharine Beecher, sister of Harriet Beecher Stowe and author of *Miss Beecher's Domestic Receipt Book,* published in 1850, recommended keeping four qualities of sugar on hand: "Refined loaf for tea, crushed sugar for the nicest preserves and to use with fruit, nice brown sugar for coffee, and common brown for cooking and more common use." Storing sugar was also a challenge. Miss Beecher warned that sugars should not be bought by the barrel, because "the brown is apt to turn to molasses, and run out on the floor." She said that loaf sugar could be stored in its paper on a shelf, but that the others should be kept in "close covered kegs, or covered wooden articles made for the purpose."[44] Making a virtue of necessity, many cooks sweetened cakes and cookies with molasses rather than sugar.

As the cultivation of sugar spread throughout the Caribbean, originally by means of slave labor, the price began to drop and use began to increase. In 1700, according to Sidney Mintz, author of *Sweetness and Power,* per capita sugar consumption in England was four pounds per year. By 1800, it had gone up to eighteen pounds.[45] Between 1840 and 1850, the price dropped by 30 percent, and it fell another 25 percent in the next two decades.[46] By the latter half of the nineteenth century, even poor English families could afford sugar for their tea. American sugar consumption lagged behind England's, but according to Wendy Woloson, author of *Refined Tastes,* by the early 1870s Americans were consuming almost forty-one pounds of sugar per person, per year.[47] The British were up to a remarkable ninety pounds per person in the 1890s.[48]

Another factor behind the plummeting price of cane sugar was the development of beet sugar. Although the process of producing sugar from beets had been known for some time, it had not been used to any great degree. In 1812, when the Napoleonic wars cut off France's sugar supplies, Napoleon ordered the cultivation of sugar beets and the production of beet sugar. For the first time, beet sugar became a factor in the market and, by vastly increasing the sugar supply, helped drive down the price. Beets, unlike sugarcane, can be grown in temperate climates, and in the late nineteenth century they became a significant crop for the United States. In addition, Hawaiian cane sugar plantations were by then adding substantially to the sugar supply. By 1906, the United States and its territories were producing more than three hundred thousand tons of sugar annually. The United States would soon become a key world producer.[49]

Sugar-refining methods were also improving. During the latter half of the nineteenth century, industrialization was changing the way many products were made and distributed. In the sugar industry, steam-powered machines, centrifuges, evaporators, and other improvements in refining equipment and methods were making the process more efficient and less expensive. They also resulted in sugar that was ready to use without further clarification, thus saving time and effort. By the turn of the twentieth century, sugar was an easy-to-use, affordable, ordinary household product. In fact, it was so affordable that an article in the *American Kitchen Magazine* suggested that Marie Antoinette's directive was an idea whose time had come. According to the writer, who was not named, "sugar is so cheap in this world that you can make cake which shall contain more *calories*,—more of that which sustains life,—which will be cheaper than the bread which you can make from the same weight of good wheat flour." The article went on to say, "So, had she lived a hundred and twenty years longer, poor Marie Antoinette would be justified in her ejaculation."[50]

Stirring the Pot

Toward the middle of the nineteenth century, when the natural ice industry was still gaining strength, another big improvement in ice cream making occurred. The *sorbetière* had been in use for nearly two centuries, even though it was difficult to operate. Then several people invented new and improved ice cream freezers, at roughly the same time. Their biggest advantage was that they were all designed to stir the ice cream mixture without opening the pot. Each had a crank on the outside of the container, which was attached to a dasher, or churn, on the inside. The person making the ice cream turned the crank, and inside the pot the ice cream was mixed to the smooth, snowy consistency that everyone from Emy to Jarrin had recommended.

An American woman from Philadelphia, Nancy Johnson, invented the first such ice cream freezer in 1843. Intended for home use, it looked like a *sorbetière* but had an outer crank and an inner dasher. Little is known about Johnson, and many reports have stated that she never patented her invention. She did. Her "Artificial Freezer" received patent number 3,254 on September 9, 1843. Her application began: "Be it known that I, Nancy

M. Johnson, of the city of Philadelphia and State of Pennsylvania, have invented a new and useful Improvement in the Art of Producing Artificial Ices, and that the following is a full and exact description of the machinery for carrying into effect the said improvement." She went on to describe the way the freezer was constructed and how its internal "wings," or dasher, worked. She also explained that her device used less salt and ice because its outer tub had a diameter only three or four inches larger than the freezer. The application concluded:

> What I claim as new in this my invention and for which I desire to obtain Letters Patent is—The above described revolving curved beater with its vertical axis, in combination with a freezing apparatus as above described and adapted to the purpose herein set forth. Nancy M. Johnson.
> In the presence of—John Thompson, Samuel Day.

Five years later, Eber C. Seaman, a New Jersey Quaker, invented a crank-turned ice cream machine. His made large batches and was intended to allow professional confectioners to turn out more ice cream faster. It, too, helped lower the price of ice cream production. He later developed a smaller version for home use.[51]

Thomas Masters was an English confectioner to the Royal Zoological Gardens and to the Royal Polytechnic Institution, as well as something of an inventor. He also devised an ice cream maker, but his produced its own ice in addition to churning the ice cream. Masters, who was skilled at attracting publicity, demonstrated it at London's Crystal Palace, as well as before the Queen. He described his ice cream maker in his 1844 book, titled *The Ice Book: Being a Compendious & Concise History of Everything Connected with Ice from its First Introduction into Europe as an Article of Luxury to the Present Time: With an Account of the Artificial Manner of Producing Pure & Solid Ice, and A Valuable Collection of the Most Approved Recipes for Making Superior Water Ices and Ice Creams at a Few Minutes' Notice*. The book explained how to make ice with his machine and his chemical mixtures, as well as how to make ice cream. It had descriptions and diagrams of his ice- and ice-cream-making equipment, wine chillers, and knife-polishing machines. It included a chapter with recipes for more than four dozen ice creams and ices, some flavored with "nectar (a delicious beverage, prepared only by the author)." Masters claimed his machine could make ice cream in four or five minutes, and that "no mansion can be henceforward complete without it."[52] He said the machine could also be used to chill wine and churn butter. He wrote, "Any lady or gentleman having the same apparatus in their breakfast-room in the morning, may have butter for their own breakfast, with only a little beneficial exercise being required for its production."[53]

Masters believed that producing ice with his machine would have an enormous impact on the ice business. In fact, he wrote, "we anticipate nothing less from it than the speedy and entire abandonment of the present traffic in natural ice."[54] Despite his undeniable confidence and marketing skill, his timing was not perfect. Wenham Lake ice was poised to capture the British public's fancy at the time. Artificially made ice was not yet popular or even trusted. In addition, critics claimed that his devices used corrosive materials and required constant attention. But he was one of the first to make ice cream with artificially made ice.

It was years before the new freezers completely replaced the old *sorbetières*, including those in professional kitchens. When Charles Ranhofer, chef at Delmonico's, wrote *The Epicurean*, a cookbook for professionals, in 1893, his instructions for ice cream making showed four different types and sizes of freezers. Two of the four were old-style *sorbetières*, one with a two- to three-quart capacity, and the other with an unspecified but smaller, probably one-quart, capacity. The other two were machines with exterior cranks and interior dashers. One turned out thirty quarts of ice cream at a time; the other, twelve to eighteen quarts. Both could be operated by hand or by steam. The implication was that all four were in use in professional kitchens at the same time.

During the latter half of the nineteenth century, most of the new ice cream machines still used natural ice and salt for freezing, and initially even the larger professional machines were hand cranked. Before long, as designs evolved and improved, some were run by pedal, then by horse, then by steam power. Advertisements in trade publications such as the *Confectioners' Journal* showed a steady progression of modifications and changes in the machines over the next several years. The ad copy promised that the new machines could freeze a forty-quart can in thirty minutes, a twenty-four-quart can in twenty-five minutes, and an eighteen-quart can in twenty minutes. An 1875 ad for Thomas Mills and Brother featured a forty-quart machine for ninety dollars and a boiler, engine, and patent ice cream freezer complete for six hundred dollars. A smaller ad for a horizontal ice cream freezer promised that it would "save Ice enough in one season to pay for the Machine." Most of the machines were intended for use in ice cream saloons, hotels, and confectioners' shops. There were also ads for freezers for the home that made one or two quarts at a time.

In the early 1920s, the writers of a British cookbook for confectioners called *All about Ices, Jellies, and Creams,* wrote that the "old-fashioned" type of freezer was "the most generally used, and is in many respects the most useful, especially for small quantities." The illustration accompanying the text was of a *sorbetière*-style freezer. The authors also preferred natural ice to artificial. They said that there were many types of freezers on the market, "all of them claiming to be the best. If one is to believe all that is said of them, they all use the minimum amount of ice, with comparatively little labour, and give the best possible results."[55]

Wholesale Operations

Until the middle of the nineteenth century, ice cream making was a local business. Confectioners and cooks made small amounts of ice cream and sold them directly to their customers or occasionally to a local hotel or caterer. But ice cream, like so many other products, was about to become a large-scale commercial enterprise. Many factors were responsible for the change. The improvements in freezers, the plentiful supply of ice, and the low cost of sugar were all responsible for expanding production. Now, with the advent of the railroad, distribution was about to be transformed.

The first ice cream wholesaler in America was Jacob Fussell, a Quaker from Maryland. Fussell was a Baltimore milk dealer, a businessman rather than a dairyman. He bought milk, butter, and cream from Pennsylvania Dutch farmers in York County; had them shipped, packed in ice, in Northern Central Railroad cars to Baltimore; and sold them to city dwellers. They were glad to have fresh-from-the-countryside milk rather than problematic city milk, and business was good. However, during the summer of 1851, Fussell found himself with an oversupply of cream. Rather than let it go sour, he made some ice cream and sold it. It proved to be popular, no doubt partly because he sold it for twenty-five cents a quart rather than the sixty cents a quart the city's confectioners charged.

Quick to see the possibilities in the ice cream business, Fussell opened a factory in Seven Valleys, Pennsylvania, near the source of his cream. His listing in the 1853–1854 Baltimore City Directory read: "Fussell Jacob, Jr. country produce dealer (ice cream at 25 cts. per quart, delivered in moulds or otherwise, day or night)."[56] In 1854, he moved his operation to Baltimore, having decided that it was better to be close to the customers than to the supply. Over the next few years, he added factories in Washington, D.C., Boston, and, in 1863, New York. He was the first significant wholesale dealer in New York. When he arrived in the city, a committee from the Associated Confectioners of New York welcomed him by warning that, if he did not agree to abide by their price-fixing scheme, they would put him out of business. Fussell refused, and although he suffered retaliation from some suppliers, he prevailed. Fussell believed in open, transparent pricing rather than secret backroom deals. He priced his ice cream at one dollar a gallon for those who bought more than five gallons, one dollar and twenty cents for those who bought less. He sold to hotels, festivals, and churches for one dollar a gallon. He summed up his pricing philosophy in this statement: "While there must be no discounts, no donations or no subterfuge used to gain customers, we may be allowed discretionary liberty with churches and benevolent objects, but not to intimate this liberality beforehand with a view of gaining an order."[57]

Clearly a man of principle in addition to being an astute businessman, Fussell was an ardent abolitionist whose fiery speeches sometimes enraged audiences and put him at risk. Nevertheless, he worked with the Underground Railroad to help slaves escape, and, after the Civil War, he financed a housing development for newly freed slaves. As his business developed and prospered, Fussell took on partners and protégés, one of whom, James Horton, took over the business in 1874. The J. M. Horton Ice Cream Company became the first company to ship ice cream to foreign ports. On Christmas Day, 1891, the steamer *Hamburg American Packet* left New York for a voyage around the world with a thousand bricks of Horton ice cream in its hold.[58] Thereafter ice cream was always on the dessert menu on transatlantic steamships. Horton's company was bought out by a division of the Borden Company in 1928.

The wholesale ice cream business began in England at about the same time that it did in the United States, but under different circumstances. Carlo Gatti was born into a prosperous family in the Italian-speaking Swiss canton of Ticino in 1817. As a young man, he made his way to Paris, where, in winter, he sold chestnuts and *gaufres*, a wafflelike pastry and the precursor to the ice cream cone. In 1847, he went to London and began selling *gaufres* in the Italian quarter. He soon opened a café in the hall of Hungerford Market. With its plate-glass windows, marble tables, plush red velvet seats, and, most important, ice cream at prices the general public could afford, the café soon attracted a large following.

However, Gatti did not limit himself to running a café. He soon became the first mass manufacturer of ice cream in England and, by 1858, claimed to sell up to ten thousand penny ices a day. He formed a company to import ice from Norway and, by the 1870s, owned more than sixty ice wagons. Over time he, often in partnership with family members and compatriots, opened other cafés, restaurants, music halls, a chocolate company, and a pastry shop. He also aided and encouraged other Swiss and Italian immigrants and helped them set up businesses of their own. Gatti was only sixty-one when he died in 1878, but some of the family business interests survived until 1981.[59]

However, the wholesale ice cream business was most successful in the United States. After the Civil War, as food production became increasingly commercialized, America assumed ice cream leadership. European confectioners began to look across the Atlantic for ideas. They bought American ice cream makers, copied American ice cream products, and referred to America as the "land of ice cream."[60] After years of living in the shadow of Europe, America now set the standard. In 1875, according to the *Confectioners' Journal*, thirty Philadelphia confectioners were large enough to be considered wholesalers. In 1892, Pennsylvania State University became the first university to offer a course in commercial ice cream making. Ads for American ice cream freezers ran in French and Italian publications. Author Pellegrino Artusi recommended the new American ice cream makers in his classic Italian book *La scienza in cucina e l'arte di mangiar bene*, first published in 1891. In its English-language edition, the passage reads: "And today, thanks to the American ice cream makers, which have triple action and need no spatula, making ice cream has become so much easier and faster that it would be a shame not to enjoy much more frequently the sensual pleasure of this delicious food."[61]

Giuseppe Ciocca, in his 1907 book, *Il pasticciere e confettiere moderno*, pointed out that American ice cream makers did not need to be opened to stir the mixture, and that they made a very light, soft gelato. The noted Italian food historians Alberto Capatti and Massimo Montanari, writing in *Italian Cuisine: A Cultural History*, explained the decline of Italian ice cream making and the rise of American by pointing out that professional Italian ice cream makers lacked the capital to invest in new equipment at the turn of the century, and that few had artificial refrigeration until well into the 1920s. They quoted a famous Italian cook and writer, Amadeo Pettini, who consoled himself on Italy's loss of ice cream hegemony with the statement "Whatever the technical procedure might be in the future, the historical fact is that we were the first to introduce ice cream to civilization, and Italians were for centuries the foremost ice-cream makers in the world."[62]

The achievements of the American ice cream business did not please everyone. In particular, confectioners saw the wholesalers' success as a threat to their own and took advantage of every opportunity to cast aspersions on wholesalers' products. The editor of an 1883 issue of the *Confectioners' Journal* counseled a man who was interested in entering the ice cream business:

> Your whole aim and effort, as a beginner, should be to make an honest article, pure and unadulterated, as to ingredients; and a quart for a quart, not a sham-puffed-up article with no soul or body in it. People don't want to pay for atmospheric air instead of ice cream. My advice is for you to let the slop-shop, Cheap-John-Factorymen's processes severely alone; do not try to make the fraudulent and depraved wares of the factories, pinch-back creams, church fair and charity creams, boarding-house and almshouse creams, which are no creams but only frothy, watery slop and slush and still viler "flavorings," whose make up is only known to the devil's chemical emissaries.[63]

But the traditionalists were fighting a losing battle. Wholesalers, ice cream saloons, drugstore soda fountains, and street vendors were all making ice cream a democratic product rather than an exclusive one. The era of the elite confectioner was nearing an end.

FIVE

Screaming for Ice Cream

When ice cream peddlers began appearing on city streets in the early nineteenth century, children were no doubt delighted. Adults had a more ambiguous reaction; initially welcoming, their response quickly turned sour. Before long, they questioned the quality of the ice cream, the cleanliness of the vendor, and the health problems associated with ice cream made in less-than-pristine environments. When vendors cried their products in the streets, the noise offended some ears. Fashionable confectioners and ice cream shopkeepers disdained the peddlers. Social reformers didn't approve of them, because they believed the poor should not waste what little money they had on such frivolities. The fact that by the latter part of the century many, if not most, of the peddlers were immigrants also raised issues of prejudice and cultural misapprehensions. For ice cream peddlers, life was anything but sweet.

Peddlers had begun selling ice cream on American city streets in the early part of the nineteenth century, with some coming to the city from the surrounding countryside to hawk their products. At first, their ice cream was praised, albeit faintly. In 1850, a writer in the Philadelphia area, identified only as "an Observer," published a book called *City Cries* about the city's various street vendors. Under "Ice Cream!" he wrote, "The countryman . . . sells an excellent article. It is really country ice cream, fresh from the farm, and although cried and sold in the streets, the market, and the public squares, it will please the most fastidious palate." The "loudest criers of ice cream," according to the author, were blacks who carried tin cans of lemon and vanilla ice creams on their shoulders.

He had not tasted their ice cream, he admitted, but said he had been told that, although "the African article will not bear a comparison with Parkinson's [the highly regarded Philadelphia confectionery shop], it is by no means unpalatable."[1]

In London, where everything from apples to eels was hawked on the streets, ice cream was still not well known in 1851, when Henry Mayhew, the renowned chronicler of street life in Victorian England, asked a peddler about it. The peddler replied in astonishment, "Ices in the streets! Aye, and there'll be jellies next, and then mock turtle, and then the real ticket, sir. . . . Penny glasses of champagne, I shouldn't wonder."[2]

When, despite the peddler's skepticism, ice cream was sold in the streets, those who tasted it for the first time sometimes found the experience distressing. Mayhew wrote about a street seller at the Smithfield Market in London who had a handsome pie-cart drawn by a pony, from which he sold pies, milk, and ice cream, crying, "Raspberry cream! Iced raspberry-cream, ha'penny a glass!" Mayhew wrote:

> This street-seller had a capital trade. Street-ices, or rather ice-creams, were somewhat of a failure last year, more especially in Greenwich-park, but this year they seem likely to succeed. The Smithfield man sold them in very small glasses, which he merely dipped into a vessel at his feet, and so filled them with cream. The consumers had to use their fingers instead of a spoon, and no few seemed puzzled how to eat their ice, and were grievously troubled by its getting among their teeth. I heard one drover mutter that he felt "as if it had snowed in his belly!"[3]

In the second half of the century, the street vending of ice cream expanded rapidly as a result of an influx of immigrants from Italy. Destitute Italians were flooding into American and English cities, fleeing the political upheaval and poverty of their home. Rural Italy, in particular, had suffered as a result of revolution and changes in the feudal system. Even after the establishment of the new Italian state in 1861, peasants and laborers faced many hardships, and many sought a better life in other countries, particularly England and the United States. When they arrived, they faced all the problems of finding their way in a foreign land, along with widespread prejudice against immigrants. Prominent politicians and writers used language such as "good-for-nothing mongrels," "small, swarthy, black-haired, long-skulled people," and "human flotsam"[4] to describe them. A widely published turn-of-the-century poem titled "Unguarded Gates" railed against the "wild, motley throng" that was arriving in America with its "tiger passions, . . . strange tongues," and "accents of menace."[5] In 1891, when a local mob in New Orleans shot and killed a group of Sicilians who had just been acquitted of a murder, the *New York Times* described the Sicilians as "sneaking and cowardly" in its coverage of the event.[6] The anti-immigration fervor culminated in the Immigration Act of 1924, which effectively slowed the immigration of newcomers from southern and eastern Europe to a trickle.[7]

The Italians who had arrived in America between the 1860s and the 1920s were most often poor, illiterate young men and boys from rural southern Italy. Ill-prepared for life in the new country, they were met with not only the xenophobia of Americans but also mistreatment at the hands of their fellow countrymen. Most of the Italian immigrants were controlled by men called *padroni*, or bosses, Italians who had immigrated earlier, who spoke English, and who used their experience to dominate and profit from the newcomers. Acting as middlemen, the *padroni* helped the newcomers find work and housing. However, the housing was usually in a crowded tenement with a dozen or more sharing a room, and the work was no better. In return for their services, the *padroni* either extracted a portion of the immigrants' pay or took the entire amount and gave them back an allowance. In addition, the *padroni* received commissions from employers and tenement owners. Although there were exceptions, many *padroni* abused their power, took advantage of the fact that the immigrants did not speak English, and overcharged them for the services they provided. Dr. Egisto Rossi, of the Italian Immigration Bureau in New York, quoted in a 1901 immigration report, said, "The *padrone* system, or bossism, can be defined as the forced tribute which the newly arrived pays to those who are already acquainted with the ways and language of the country."[8]

Since most of the immigrants did not have a trade, they went to work as laborers or peddlers of small plaster statues. Some became organ grinders, a job that required no musical ability. The organ grinders simply cranked a wheel on the organ to make music, and, in theory, passersby paid them for the pleasure of listening. In practice, so many took up the trade that they became a nuisance, and some people began giving them money not to play or to play elsewhere. The police, too, were quick to tell them to move on. As a result, the bosses had newcomers take up ice cream vending instead of organ grinding. Making and selling ice cream was a practical alternative because supplies had become cheaper and more readily available. It was relatively easy to mix the ice cream, freeze it in a simple ice cream maker with ice and salt, pack it into containers surrounded by more ice and salt, load it onto a cart, and push it around the city. Generally, the *padroni* supplied the ice cream and the carts. The workers went out with carts full of ice cream and were expected to come back with empty carts and all the money they had earned.

Italians who emigrated to England in the latter half of the nineteenth century fared no better than their counterparts in America. Mostly men and boys, they walked from Italy to France and crossed the English Channel by ferry. Most were from rural areas and became street vendors in British urban centers. As in America, they started out as organ grinders or statue sellers, but by the 1880s they were selling food. Since many of the *padroni* had come from chestnut-growing regions in Italy, they imported chestnuts, fitted barrows with small braziers, and sent men and boys off to sell hot roasted chestnuts in winter. In summer, again like their compatriots in America, they made ice cream at night in the cellars of the Italian quarter, froze it in the morning, and loaded the ice-packed buckets onto the pushcarts and barrows to be cried in the streets. If the ice cream vendors returned at the end of the day with less money than expected, they had to answer for it. Sometimes, street toughs would pretend they wanted to buy a dish of ice cream and then, when the vendor opened the pail, they would toss dirt or stones into it, ruining his supply and subjecting him to punishment at the hands of his master.

Though Italian vendors in England were controlled by *padroni*, the system differed from that in America, according to Terri Colpi, author of *The Italian Factor*. Rather than acting as middlemen, the *padroni* were the employers in England. They recruited the immigrants, housed them, and put them under two- to three-year contracts. Generally, the contracts stated that a *padrone* would feed, clothe, and house the immigrant; in return, the latter would turn over all his earnings to the *padrone*. At the end of the contract's term, the *padrone* was supposed to give the immigrant a lump sum of from eight to ten pounds. The workers were housed in squalid, overcrowded apartments, according to contemporary news reports. In 1875, a British newspaper reported on their living conditions: "The accommodation is wretched in the extreme, all sanitary laws being set at defiance. Some of the sleeping rooms contain as many as sixteen beds, upon each of which three or four boys lie huddled together, dreaming of the sunny skies of their native country."[9]

The *padroni* held the workers' passports, so men could not return to Italy before their contracts were up. Although some bosses treated workers fairly, many did not. Some never paid them their promised wages. Tragically, many of these immigrants were young children, sent to England by parents who couldn't afford to feed them and who hoped they would be well cared for by a fatherly *padrone*. Instead, as Colpi put it, "at its worst, this process could become virtual slavery."[10]

The system largely died out at the end of the nineteenth century, both in the United States and in England, in part because by then most of the men had fulfilled their contracts, become acclimated, and learned to speak English. Many had either sent for their wives or gone back to Italy, married, and returned. Newly arrived immigrants were able to find the help and support they needed within the Italian community, often in neighborhoods made up of people from their home region if not their village. Ultimately, family connections replaced the *padroni* system. In addition, authorities in England, the United States, and Italy passed laws regulating child migration and labor after the abuses were publicized.

Recipes for Disaster

Toward the end of the nineteenth century, a flurry of news reports and books revealed that many of the foods whose safety Americans took for granted actually were contaminated or adulterated or both. The public learned that its meats were tainted, its dairy products were unclean, and foods such as tea, jams, spices, mustard, coffee, and candies contained such dangerous ingredients as lead, copper, and mercury. Indeed, it was said that, whereas once a young woman might have wanted her beau to prove his love by buying her candy, now she might think he was plotting her death if he gave her such a gift.[11]

The milk supply was especially vulnerable. As cities became more populated, cows were housed in crowded pens and fed refuse from city distilleries. Their milk became known as "swill milk." Legislation controlling the feeding and housing of cows began to be passed in many cities by the 1860s. But the American milk supply was not pasteurized until the 1890s, and until then bacteria in the milk frequently caused outbreaks of scarlet fever, diphtheria, and bovine tuberculosis. Ice cream containing such milk would be contaminated whether it was made in a fashionable shop or a teeming tenement. But the latter was more vulnerable. Hygiene was generally lacking. No one inspected the premises for cleanliness or made sure the cooks' hands and equipment were washed. If there was not enough ice and salt for proper refrigeration, the ice cream mixture would become rancid. "Sour milk, sweetened, for ice cream," was a typical description of the vendors' ice cream.[12]

The manner in which their ice cream was eaten was also an invitation to contamination. The vendors carried small glasses called penny-licks that they filled and handed to customers. The customers would either lick the ice cream out of the glass or push it out with their fingers. When they returned the empty glass, the vendor would give it a swish through a bucket of water and a wipe on a rag he carried, and fill it up for the next customer.

By the end of the century, several forces converged and led to the regulation, inspection, and labeling of many foods and transformed the way some products were made and sold, both in the United States and in England. The pure food movement, a grassroots interest group that began in the 1870s in reaction to publicity about food adulteration, supported the passage of legislation regulating food production. A Pure Food and Drug Act was passed in 1906. The new awareness of bacteria and the importance of cleanliness, coupled with publicity about the immigrants' terrible living conditions, also had an enormous impact on ice cream vending both in the United States and in England.

After chemists in England found dangerous levels of bacteria in ice cream and in the water used for washing licking glasses, the London County Council prohibited the manufacture of any ices and ice creams in any "shed, room or place used as a living room."[13] The chemists' reports were widely publicized, and the news hurt all ice cream makers. P. Michael, a British confectioner and author of *Ices and Soda Fountain Drinks*, wrote that the news caused "a great drop in the sale of ice cream, even in the best-kept shops." Michael, who was more sympathetic to the plight of the Italian peddlers than some of his colleagues were, wrote, "Perhaps the finest thing brought about by this scandal was the breaking up of the 'boss system' in the various Italian quarters throughout the kingdom, where poor agricultural and very ignorant and illiterate lads, fresh from Italy, lived under cruel bosses and under nauseating conditions at a very miserable wage, which was often replaced by kicks and bullying, especially if the day's takings had been very low, in spite of the weather being bad."[14]

In Philadelphia in 1908, Mary Engle Pennington, a bacteriological chemist who had earned a doctorate in chemistry from the University of Pennsylvania, was put in charge of ensuring the safety of the city's milk and dairy products. She convinced ice cream peddlers of the need for improved cleanliness by showing them slides of bacteria growing in their buckets. They agreed to begin boiling their pots and ladles. She also worked with dairy farmers to improve their standards. Her work was one of the reasons that Philadelphia ice cream and other dairy products had such a positive reputation.[15]

In New York in 1906, the National Consumer's League issued a report, "Manufacturing of Foods in the Tenements," describing the making of ice cream, candy, and macaroni in New York's crowded apartments. It told of a man making macaroni in an apartment where his child lay sick with diphtheria. He would hold the child and then, without washing his hands, pull the macaroni from the machine, drape it over racks to dry, and later sell it up and down the streets. Other foods were made under similar conditions. In addition to its concerns about health issues, the league was worried about the well-being of the children who lived, and often worked, in the tenements. The report stated, "It is not only that home-work in any food trade is dangerous to the health of the community when there is no supervision or restriction by law, but like all home-work it is poorly paid and there are no limits to hours of work or to the number of children that may be engaged in it."[16]

Shortly thereafter, New York passed laws regulating work in homes and specifically prohibited the making of ice cream in tenements. Additionally, the city began to regulate and license peddlers and their carts. Ice cream vendors had to buy their ice cream from wholesalers and sell it either in shops or from a licensed cart. To operate a cart, vendors had to pay a license fee of a minimum of ten dollars, depending on the location. Two kinds of licenses were issued: traveling and stationary. The traveling licenses were issued to peddlers in less crowded districts; the stationary, in congested neighborhoods. According to Ralph Selitzer, a historian for the dairy industry and author of *The Dairy Industry in America*, the vendor made about $5.00 a day; but after paying a rental fee of $1.50 for his cart and $2.50 for his ice cream, he would wind up with only $1.00. Some wholesalers let the vendors use the pushcarts for nothing as long as they used only that wholesaler's ice cream.[17]

Doing the Hokeypokey

Clearly there was a bias against the Italian vendors, and not all the concern expressed about the quality and safety of their ice cream was altruistic. The scorn that shop owners, wholesale ice cream makers, and others heaped on street vendors often had more to do with prejudice and fear of competition than concern over the spread of germs. An article in the May 26, 1901, edition of the *New York Herald* described poor, ragged children crowding around an ice cream pushcart: "From morning until night the children stuff themselves. . . . Where does the money come from? . . . Thriftless, but affectionate, is the lower class parent. Shoes the child must do without, for the father has not quite enough money to purchase them. But here is five cents to buy hokey-pokey. That much he can afford."[18]

Hokeypokey was a derogatory term used to describe a type of ice cream the peddlers sold, as well as the vendors themselves. It may have originated with the Italian-speaking vendors' cry of "Ecco un poco," or "Here's a little," as it was heard and repeated by their English-speaking customers. Or it may have come from the phrase used by magicians and jugglers in blasphemous imitation of a Latin phrase used in the Catholic Mass. *Hocus-pocus* was a corruption of "Hoc est corpus meum," or "This is my body," which was recited during the holiest moment of the Mass. At the time, street vendors and street performers were regarded as tricksters and charlatans. They were accused, sometimes justly, of cheating or, as the expression of the time went, hocusing—watering their milk or selling meat pies made from cats or dogs. Ice cream vendors were no more highly regarded, and it would have been natural for them to have been given the same derogatory nickname.

Confectioners were always contemptuous of the street peddlers. As early as May 1878, in an issue of the *Confectioners' Journal*, editor James Parkinson, a confectioner himself, wrote from Paris, "In Europe, as in America, I find also that ice creams are hawked about the streets. The low-priced stuff which is sold in all countries to the poor, I regret to say, is apt to be adulterated with ingredients which sacrifice health to cheapness. . . . There is entire safety only in purchasing from first-class manufacturers."[19]

In a book titled *Ices: Plain and Decorated,* published at the turn of the twentieth century, Frederick T. Vine, a British confectioner, wrote of the making of ice cream:

> Without a doubt there is no more profitable branch of the confectionery art than this, and there is no reason why confectioners should not practice and excel in it, and put into their pockets what too often goes into that of the swarthy sons of Italy, who annually visit us with their gaudily-painted barrows and questionable ices. That these cheap ices are appreciated by the populace cannot be gainsaid, or we should not be so regularly invaded by these foreigners in such increasing numbers; and there can be no question of the trade proving a profitable one, or, one may depend upon it, they would not keep coming.[20]

Vine was writing for fellow confectioners, not for the general public, but his description of the men was a common one. The more privileged members of society looked down on the ice cream vendors, which may be why they became known as "hokeypokey men."

Over time, *hokeypokey* lost its pejorative associations and became part of a popular children's rhyme with many different variations:

> Hokeypokey, penny a lump.
> Freeze your belly and make you jump!
> Hokeypokey, sweet and cold.
> For a penny, new or old.

It also became a popular song and dance:

> *The Hokeypokey*
> You put your right foot in,
> You put your right foot out;

You put your right foot in,
And you shake it all about.

You do the hokeypokey,
And you turn yourself around.
That's what it's all about!
You put your left foot in . . .

Earlier, the British author Andrew Tuer had drawn a distinction between penny-lick ices and hokeypokeys in his 1885 book, *Old London Street Cries*. Oddly enough, Tuer, unlike other writers, did not attribute hokeypokeys to Italian vendors. However, he explained the differences between the two novelties, and his observations about their advantages and ingredients are noteworthy.

The buyers of the so-called penny ices sold in the London streets during the summer months are charged only a halfpenny; and the numerous vendors, usually Italians, need no cry; for the street *gamins* and errand boys buzz around their barrows like flies about a sugar barrel. For obvious reasons, spoons are not lent. The soft and half-frozen delicacy is consumed by the combined aid of tongue and fingers. Parti-coloured Neapolitan ices, vended by unmistakable natives of Whitechapel or the New Cut, whose curious cry of "Okey Pokey" originated no one knows how, have lately appeared in the streets. Hokey-pokey is of a firmer make and probably stiffer material than the penny ice of the Italians, which it rivals in public favour; and it is built up of variously flavoured layers. Sold in halfpenny and also penny paper-covered squares, kept until wanted in a circular metal refrigerating pot surrounded by broken ice, Hokey-pokey has the advantage over its rival eaten from glasses, inasmuch as it can be carried away by the purchaser and consumed at leisure. Besides being variously flavoured, Hokey-pokey is dreadfully sweet, dreadfully cold, and hard as a brick. It is whispered that the not unwholesome Swede turnip [rutabaga], crushed into pulp, has been known to form its base, in lieu of more expensive supplies from the cow, whose complex elaboration of cream from turnips is thus unceremoniously abridged.[21]

Hokeypokeys were slices cut from bricks of ice cream. Michael described them as "cheap Neapolitan ices, which, in their turn, are small slices, generally 2 in. by 2 in. by ½ in. thick, cut from the large brick, packed in white paper, and then in the container."[22] The bricks were generally about eighteen inches long, twelve inches wide, and two and a half to three inches deep. The flavors were arranged lengthwise in a mold with tin dividers, which were removed once the ice cream was packed into the mold. They were usually layered with three different flavors of ice cream, and each crosswise slice would reveal all three. Michael said they cost one or two pennies, and that children could buy half a slice for half the price. After it was cut, the children would wonder how the colors "got in like that."[23] The wrapped slices were sold to ice cream vendors. Whole bricks were sold to ice cream shops to be sliced and served, and also to householders, who had to rush home to serve them to their families before the ice cream melted.

Although rutabaga seems far-fetched, it is impossible to know exactly what went into either penny-licks or hokeypokeys in the earliest days. But when the vendors were required to buy their ice cream from wholesalers, recipes began to be published in trade papers and books. An American book titled *Dispenser's Formulary* included four different recipes for hokeypokey. Three of the four called for cornstarch or gelatin or both; the other ingredients were simply milk, sugar, and a flavor extract. One recipe called for eggs. The fourth recipe, and the most complete one, follows:

HOKEY POKEY

Into a bright and perfectly clean basin put 1 pound of fine sugar and 1 dozen eggs; mix these well together; then add and stir in 2 quarts of fresh cream or milk, 1 spoonful of salt and 1 tablespoon of extract of vanilla; set the mixture on the fire and stir constantly till it thickens, but not curdles; strain into an earthen pan, cool, and stir into it 1 ounce of gelatin, dissolved in milk or water; now pour it into the freezer and work slowly during the whole process till it becomes well frozen; then remove the dasher and pack the cream firmly in brick molds and bury them in ice and salt until the cream is thoroughly frozen and hard; then turn them from the molds in the usual way and keep them in the ice cave or in a can imbedded in ice, or it may be cut with a knife, dipped in warm water, into suitable squares, wrapped in waxed paper and put in boxes and kept in the ice cave ready for sale.[24]

The American *Ice Cream Trade Journal* offered a brick recipe with the following ingredients for the peddlers' trade:

FIVE CENT BRICKS

3 gallons of milk
1½ gallons of cream
1 gallon of condensed milk
8 pounds of sugar
12 ounces of gelatine [*sic*]
4 ounces (or more) of vanilla extract[25]

In none of the recipes do the ingredients sacrifice "health to cheapness." They are perfectly adequate, though not first quality, assuming the recipe was followed as written. The gelatin and cornstarch were intended to help thicken a mixture that generally contained more milk than cream. Michael's opinion that the best gelatin was "free from arsenic and other undesirable chemicals" is not particularly reassuring.[26] Nonetheless, gelatin became a common ingredient in commercial and even homemade ice creams, as did cornstarch and condensed milk. Confectioners and wholesalers alike soon learned how to make less expensive versions of ice cream treats for different markets. In fact, Michael advised ice cream makers to "decide what prices your customers are likely to pay for the bricks, so that you will know whether to make a cream, milk, or sherbet one."[27]

In a book titled *Thirty-six Years an Ice Cream Maker*, published in Iowa in 1907, author Val Miller offered advice to proprietors of both wholesale and retail ice cream establishments. Along with recipes, Miller offered guidance on managing, serving, and pricing based on his extensive experience in the business. On the subject of hokeypokeys, Miller recommended using a "medium cheap, or cheap ice cream with a little more gelatine than for ordinary use." He provided a recipe and said it should be made up into one-quart bricks, each of which would be cut into eight slices or hokeypokeys. To cut the slices evenly, he suggested making a cutter by "nailing or bolting blades (cut out of heavy tin or galvanized iron) between strips of wood of the proper width." He said such a cutter was "good for quick work." Miller said that his recipe would produce 320 slices. Priced at five cents each, they should bring in between $8.00 and $9.60, depending on the amount charged to the retailer. Buyers of larger quantities paid slightly less per brick than those who bought smaller ones. Miller said the margin for profit and labor should never be less than five dollars a batch. He also advised his readers that they should "never recommend mixed colors in 5-cent bricks, and never agree to take back unsold bricks; it is always unprofitable."[28]

In both the United States and England, some of the hokeypokey men managed to open ice cream shops, often in partnerships in which one provided the capital needed and the other provided the labor. Some of the *padroni* even helped such men establish their own businesses. Many prospered and continued in the café and restaurant business. Michael, who was writing in the early 1920s, said, "These old Italians now possess fine ice cream shops, barrows are a mere relic here and there, and the trade is well boomed up. Still, there is a bias. This, however, will disappear more and more in the face of better shops."[29]

Not all ice cream bricks were made of medium-cheap or cheap ice cream. Although they disparaged street vendors, confectioners were not too proud to adapt peddlers' products to their own use. Confectioners began making bricks themselves and even turned them into decorative desserts for their customers. Flags were a favorite motif: flavors and colors were chosen to mimic the flags of different countries, and a tricolored slice of the ice cream was served with a piece of wafer cake representing the flag's staff. In an 1878 issue, the *Confectioners' Journal* suggested using chocolate, strawberry, and bright orange ice to stand for the black, red, and gold of a German flag. For an Italian flag, the *Journal* called for green, made with pistachio; red, made with red fruit or rose ice cream; and yellow, made with orange ice. It was an odd selection of colors since the Italian flag is red, green, and white, not yellow.

The Ice Cream Sandwich

The street vendors' hokeypokeys were covered with paper, which made them easy to store, convenient to carry, and sanitary. It was a practical arrangement. Then someone was inspired to replace the paper wrapping with cookies or crackers and thus created an enduring innovation—the ice cream sandwich. Whether the ice cream sandwich creator was a wholesaler who sold the idea to ice cream peddlers, or an entrepreneurial ice cream peddler who improvised the sandwich himself, will probably never be known. In most accounts, New York peddlers were given credit for the idea. A column in the March 1901 issue of *American Kitchen Magazine*, reprinted from the *New York Mail and Express*, was headlined "A New Sandwich" and began: "There are ham sandwiches and salmon sandwiches and cheese sandwiches—a down-town restaurant advertises 30 varieties—but the latest is the ice-cream sandwich. As a new fad the ice-cream sandwich might have made thousands of dollars for its inventor had the novelty been launched by a well known caterer, but strangely enough the ice-cream sandwich made its advent in an humble Bowery push-cart, and is sold for a penny." The columnist, who was not identified, went on to say that the ice cream sandwich was a good idea for children who wanted their ice cream warmed, explaining that "the thin wafers which go to make up the sandwich help to modify the coolness of the ice-cream, so that it can be eaten more readily." The article described the making of the sandwich:

A thin milk biscuit is placed in a tin mold just large enough to receive it. Then the mold is filled with ice cream from a freezer, and another wafer is placed on top. There is an arrangement for forcing the sandwich out of the mold when complete, and the whole process takes only a few seconds. The ice-cream sandwich man is the envy of all the other push-cart restauranteurs [sic] on the Bowery, as he has all the patrons he can attend to, and the cart is always surrounded by curious customers.[30]

Actually the new sandwich had been around for at least a couple of years before *American Kitchen Magazine* discovered it. An article in a 1902 edition of the *New York Tribune*, describing the way it was made as well as commenting on its price, dated the ice cream sandwich to 1899.

He places the thin, oblong wafers in a little tin mould made for the purpose, spreads it with loose cream, and claps another wafer on top. There is a blanket price of one cent for the ice cream sandwich. This was challenged by the boys of New York. The sandwich was introduced three years ago and sold at two or three cents. It was longer and contained more cream but the boys would have none of it. . . . they desired a penny sandwich . . . and last year the ice cream sandwich came down to one cent.[31]

Ice cream sandwiches were so popular that news accounts describe crowds of customers, from bankers to bootblacks, lining up to buy them. One account reported that on Wall Street "the brokers themselves got to buying ice cream sandwiches and eating them in a democratic fashion side by side on the sidewalk with the messengers and the office boys."[32] Some mentioned the mold into which the biscuit was placed before being topped with ice cream and then another biscuit. Others reported that a wafer was simply topped with ice cream and another wafer clapped atop. The wafers were variously described as milk biscuits, thin wafers, water wafers, and ice wafers. One account reported that sandwiches were made from "two graham wafers and a slab of ice cream between."[33]

Sylvester Graham, creator of the graham wafer or cracker, disapproved of meat, sugar, white flour, hot and spicy foods, coffee, tea, and alcohol.

Although Graham, who had died in 1851, did not specifically condemn ice cream, it's doubtful that he would have approved of his healthy whole wheat crackers being used for anything as sensuous as an ice cream sandwich.[34]

Fashionable confectioners also made ice cream sandwiches, and cookie manufacturers took full advantage of the new trend. A book published in 1900 titled *Ices, and How to Make Them,* written by Charles Herman Senn, who was identified as the "Inspecting and Consulting Chef, National Training School of Cookery, London," included this recipe.

DENISES GLACÉS (ICE CREAM SANDWICHES)

This is a most convenient and dainty way of serving almost any kind of ice. The ice wafers manufactured by Messrs. Peek, Frean & Co. are best adapted for this dish. These wafers being quite plain and of delicate light make, the true flavour of the ice is in no way impaired. When the ice cream or water ice is sufficiently frozen to allow it being spread, cover a number of ice wafers with a layer of the ice; place a wafer on the top of each like a sandwich. Pack them in a charged ice pail or cave, place a paper between each layer, and keep thus till required for table. Messrs. Peek, Frean & Co. supply a most useful Ice Cream Sandwich suitable for this purpose.

Conveniently, Messrs. Peek and Frean ran an ad for the very wafers in the back of the book. It invited "special attention" to their "Ice wafers, two of which may be used to form an *ice cream sandwich,* as per instructions on page 69" (emphasis in the original).[35]

Several years later, *Dispenser's Formulary* called for "two nabisco [*sic*] wafers, chocolate, vanilla or strawberry, whichever the customer may prefer, and place a slice of ice cream between them." The sandwich was served on a small plate with an ice cream fork. The author said that it was necessary to use an ice cream sandwich mold to "make a neat service."[36]

Ice Cream in Ink

By the time the ice cream sandwich made its appearance, the ice cream trade was, in Michael's words, "well boomed up." Trade publications were proliferating. Books and magazines offered business advice to confectioners, wholesalers, ice cream parlor operators, and increasingly, soda fountain operators. The first and one of the most important publications was the *Confectioners' Journal,* founded by Edward Heinz and James Parkinson, the son of famed Philadelphia confectioners Eleanor and George Parkinson. It began publication in 1874 and reported that there were already four hundred confectioners in Philadelphia. The magazine soon had subscribers from all over the country and claimed a circulation of five thousand. By volume 3, it had subscribers in England, Australia, France, Germany, Spain, Italy, and South America.

The magazine was an odd mixture of valuable information and peculiar gaffes. The first column, in volume 1, number 1, was headlined "Preface." However, it was not a statement about the mission of the new publication or its editorial philosophy. It was largely a reprint of the preface to the 1861 edition of *The Modern Confectioner* by William Jeanes, and it included his comments on Jarrin being out of date. It was not attributed. If anyone reading it wondered why a new American confectionery trade publication introduced itself by running a column taken from an English confectioner's thirteen-year-old book, it went unmentioned in subsequent issues.

Since his mother had been completely forthcoming about George Read being the source of most of the recipes in her book, it was odd that years later James Parkinson would exaggerate his parents' role in the development of ice cream as egregiously as he did. In one issue he said that his father, George Parkinson, was the first person to make ice cream. In another, a columnist for the magazine gave George Parkinson credit for inventing pistachio ice cream. James Parkinson actually wrote that Europeans did not make ice cream; they made only custards—baked, boiled, or frozen. They were a "nice dessert," he wrote, but they were not ice cream.[37]

Despite these lapses in editorial judgment, the *Confectioners' Journal* was an important and prophetic publication for many years. Through its columns and its advertisements, it demonstrated how the confectionery business grew and changed over the course of the nineteenth and twentieth centuries. Professional confectioners wrote columns that shared trade secrets with those just starting out in the business. They explained the nuances of sugar boiling, taught readers how to carve ice stands on which to display and serve ice creams (or oysters), explained how to mold ices in the shape of fruits and vegetables, and explored the history of sugar production. They answered queries about the business, reported industry news, and shared many recipes. The magazine ran advertising for all sorts of confectioners' supplies, from candy furnaces to pastry display cases, from popcorn balls to foreign fruit such as dates, bananas, and pineapples. The numerous ads for ice cream freezers for hotels, saloons, and ice cream parlors showed how commercial the business was becoming, and how competitive.

The *Confectioners' Journal* and other publications also documented the development of the soda fountain business and its transition from a dispenser of therapeutic drinks and medicines to a social center for ice cream lovers. When the first soda fountains made their debut at the beginning of the nineteenth century, ice cream was not on the menu. The fountains came from the world of medicine, the spa, and the apothecary. They served carbonated waters for medicinal purposes. The tradition of taking waters dated back to the baths ancient Romans soaked in and the mineral waters Europeans drank for the sake of their livers. When chemists learned how to reproduce the waters artificially in the eighteenth century, they became even more popular and widespread. Taking the waters, whether by bathing in them or drinking them, was and is considered by many to have health-giving properties. Soda, or "carbonic acid water," was listed in the *Pharmacopoeia of the United States* through the fifth revision of 1870.[38] The 1898 edition of *King's American Dispensatory* noted that it was a "refreshing, refrigerant beverage" that could be used in "fevers, inflammatory diseases, chronic inflammation of the stomach, vomiting of pregnant females, etc."[39]

The first establishments to sell soda waters in the United States did so in the style and spirit of European spas and pump rooms. A "soda water concern" opened in New Haven in 1807.[40] The Tontine Coffee House on Wall Street in New York, a popular gathering place for the city's merchants at the turn of the nineteenth century, featured fountains that dispensed a variety of waters. The apparatus that produced the waters was in the cellar. The waters themselves were carried up to the bar in tin tubes concealed by mahogany pillars crowned with gilt urns.[41] An advertisement in the 1809 edition of *Longworth's American Almanac* created a spa-like image for another New York establishment:

> Those who desire to frequent the Fountains in the morning for the benefit of their health will find here the important advantage of the Park for taking the necessary exercise in the intervals of drinking the waters. Papers, pamphlets and novels for Mr. Longworth's store will always lie on the tables in the pump room, so as to combine amusement with utility in this novel and salutary establishment, and render it not only conducive to the health of the city, but an elegant and fashionable lounge for ladies and gentlemen throughout the day.[42]

Although the apparatus required to produce the waters was cumbersome, druggists began installing it in the early 1800s and soon took over the business of selling medicinal soda drinks. Elias Durand, who emigrated from France to the United States and opened a pharmacy in Philadelphia in 1825, was one of the first to add elegance to the drugstore soda fountain. Durand's shop was considered "quite the handsomest drug store in the Quaker City." It featured French glassware, porcelain jars, mahogany drawers, and marble counters, along with "an apparatus for making and vending carbonic acid water."[43]

The early waters were most commonly called soda waters, since some were produced using bicarbonate of soda. But many chemists and druggists thought *soda water* was a misnomer and suggested other terms, including *carbonade, mephitic julep, mephitic gas, seltzer, spa, gaseous alkaline,* oxygenated waters, marble water, spirit of chalk, gaz oxide de carbone, and gaseous acid.[44] Seltzer was the only name, besides soda water, that had any longevity.

By the middle of the nineteenth century, most druggists had a counter set aside for serving medicinal waters. As time went on, soda fountains became more and more elaborate and whimsical. In 1858, Gustavus D. Dows of Lowell, Massachusetts, created a white marble soda fountain in the shape of a cottage. Before long, soda fountains became architectural wonders decorated with nymphs, sphinxes, cherubs, clocks, domes, Greek columns, and every other embellishment known to Victorian design. The cost of fountains ranged from a few hundred dollars to many thousands.[45] The pinnacle of soda fountain excess was reached during the 1876 Centennial Exposition in Philadelphia, when soda fountain manufacturers James W. Tufts of Massachusetts and Charles Lippincott of Pennsylvania joined forces and paid fifty thousand dollars for the exclusive privilege of serving soda water within the exhibition grounds.[46] In addition to operating thirteen or fourteen soda water fountains within the grounds, Tufts spent thousands more to erect a soda water saloon outside the exhibition. James Dabney McCabe, author of The Illustrated History of the Centennial Exhibition, described it: "The exterior of the edifice is neat and tasteful, and the interior is fitted up very handsomely and adorned with elaborate frescoes. In the centre stands a splendid fountain of variegated marble, with silver trimmings. It is forty feet in height, and was erected at a cost of between twenty-five and thirty thousand dollars. It is the largest fountain in the world, and is by far the handsomest."[47]

By then flavorings were being blended into the soda waters, and fountains featured a dozen or more spigots to dispense them. Flavored waters were not common until the 1830s, but the idea of adding them originated much earlier. In 1781, Thomas Henry, an Englishman, had suggested that a glass of lemonade should accompany what he called "Mephitic Julep" for additional medicinal benefits.[48] The 1809 American edition of Conversations on Chemistry proposed adding sugar and wine, explaining, "The Soda

Water is also very refreshing, and to most persons a very grateful drink, especially after heat and fatigue, and may be made a complete substitute for the beverages of which ardent spirits form a part. With wine and sugar it is very grateful."[49]

In the 1830s, many soda fountain operators began adding fruit syrups to sodas. The first edition of the *Dispensatory of the United States of America*, published in Philadelphia in 1833, had a recipe for mulberry syrup and suggested that similar syrups could be made from strawberries, raspberries, and pineapples. Syrups, the authors wrote, "are employed to flavor drinks and are much used as grateful additions to carbonic acid water."[50] When the 1868 edition of *The Manufacture of Liquors, Wines, and Cordials; also the Manufacture of Effervescing Beverages and Syrups* was published, the list of flavors had grown to include sarsaparilla, lemon, orange, vanilla, peach, grape, almond, spirit of aromatics (ginger, cloves, sassafras, lemon, bergamot), spirit of roses, blackberry, mulberry, neroli (orange and orrisroot), and more.[51]

Soda fountains' offerings depended on their locations and their clientele. Soda fountains at drugstores in business districts attracted and catered to men. They specialized in medicinal waters and beverages intended to aid digestion, calm nerves, check diarrhea, and offer relief when "we had too much fun the night before." The beverages they offered might alleviate headaches with Bromo Caffeine, treat hangovers with aromatic spirits ammonia, check nausea with soda mint water, and cure headache and exhaustion with something called Coca-Cola. E. F. White, the author of *The Spatula Soda Water Guide*, cautioned his readers that they had to be careful about treating customers. "Inexperienced dispensers should ask advice of the druggist before serving medicine," he wrote. "Medicinal drinks should never be recommended. Tell a customer what you have but let him decide."[52]

By the middle of the nineteenth century, some druggists were setting aside separate areas where ladies could sip their soda waters in a more refined atmosphere, away from men. Soda fountains located in department stores or in drugstores near shopping areas catered to female customers and offered drinks that were less medicinal and more flavorful. The proprietors also began to blend flavors and create fancifully named drinks for the ladies. A "Queen's Favorite" was made with orange syrup, grape juice, ice, lemon juice, Jamaica ginger, and soda.[53] "Ambrosia" was a mixture of raspberry, vanilla, and hock wine. A "Siberian Flip" was made of orange, pineapple, and angostura bitters. Many soda fountains reserved a spigot for a "Don't Care" soda. This was the mixture given to customers who, when asked what flavor they wanted, replied, "I don't care." A typical one was a blend of pineapple, strawberry, vanilla, and port wine.[54]

The next addition to soda drinks was not ice cream but cream. Beginning in about 1860, fountains began selling a mixture of soda water, fruit syrup, shaved ice, and cream that was called variously an "iced cream soda," a "frigid cream soda," or an "ice cream soda," despite the fact that it did not contain any ice cream. It was not until about 1874 that ice cream became an ingredient in the ice cream soda. The stories as to how it evolved are varied, but most involve a fountain operator substituting ice cream when he ran out of cream to make a soda. In the most widespread version, Robert M. Green of Philadelphia was operating a soda fountain at the 1874 semicentennial exhibition of the Franklin Institute when he ran out of cream. He went out and bought some ice cream, planning to let it melt before he substituted it for the cream. But his customers were so eager to enjoy their sodas that he did not wait for the ice cream to melt. He simply spooned it into the sodas. *Voilà!* The creation was born. The question raised by this scenario is that, if he ran out of cream, why didn't he simply go out and buy cream rather than ice cream?

A more likely explanation, reported by Anne Cooper Funderburg in *Sundae Best*, is that prior to the exhibit, Green was trying to think of a way to stand out, because his fountain was not as lavish as others. While at a confectioner's shop having a dish of ice cream, accompanied as always by a glass of water, he hit on the idea of combining the two. After much experimentation, he settled on vanilla ice cream with different flavored sodas, including lemon, vanilla, pineapple, strawberry, raspberry, ginger, orange, coffee, chocolate, and coconut. To introduce the drink, he printed and distributed flyers proclaiming, "Something New! Green's Ice Cream Soda," along with a list of all the flavors. He also gave away sodas to young people at the exhibit who agreed to tell their friends about the new drink.[55]

Despite its popularity with everyone who tried it, the ice cream soda did not become widespread immediately. An ice cream soda recipe in an 1877 edition of the *Confectioners' Journal* called for chilled cream, flavored syrup, and soda water but made no mention of ice cream. The 1877 and 1878 editions of a quarterly trade magazine called *Carbonated Drinks* did not include ice cream sodas. Some soda fountain proprietors were reluctant to begin offering the new drink because it meant they would have to either buy or make ice cream, which they had never done previously. Even if they simply bought ice cream, they still had to store it, which meant more ice and salt and more mess and bother. They feared the new sodas would not be profitable, because making them took more time and customers spent too much time lingering over them. Soda fountain publications began encouraging fountain operators to offer ice cream sodas by printing ice cream recipes and detailed directions for making the sodas. In his guide, White noted that if an ice cream soda was not made correctly, the customer's first taste would be nothing more than soda water; the last taste, merely sweet syrup. He recommended following these directions to make a good ice cream soda:

> We now draw one ounce of syrup, or if it be a fruit flavor one-half the amount will be sufficient, into the glass. Then with the coarse stream we draw the glass about one-fourth full of soda, and with the fine stream mix the soda thoroughly. Your glass is then about one-half full. Now add your ice cream, and where fruits are used add them at the same time, then fill the glass nearly full with soda and syrup as well as possible, taking care not to cut the ice cream any more than is necessary.[56]

Eventually the proprietors' objections were overcome and the ice cream soda triumphed. In an 1891 edition of *Harper's Weekly*, Mary Gay Humphreys wrote, "On a bright exhilarating day, to achieve a cup of ice-cream soda, a place should be engaged some time in advance. Beauty and fashion surge about the counter. One of the sights of the town is the rows of bright faces, two and three deep, bent over their cups, and fishing within with long-handled spoons."[57]

Six Ways to Sundae

The ice cream sundae too was a product of the soda fountain. Again, stories about its origins are many and facts are few. Most stories revolve around the idea that blue laws regulating activities on Sundays forbade eating ice cream sodas. To outwit the law, a clever soda fountain operator left out the soda and topped ice cream with syrup. One story has it that when the predominantly Methodist town of Evanston, Illinois (also known as Heavenston), legislated against the "Sunday Soda Menace," a soda fountain employee circumvented the law by creating the sundae. Another, set in Two Rivers, Wisconsin, gives credit to a customer. George Hallauer was having an ice cream at Ed Berner's soda fountain when he noticed the chocolate syrup used in sodas and, on a whim, asked to have it poured on his ice cream.[58]

The city of Ithaca, New York, may be the strongest claimant for *first* prize. This story has a minister instigating, rather than opposing, the Sunday treat. It seems that the Reverend John M. Scott visited a local drugstore after services at the Unitarian Church one Sunday. When he ordered a dish of vanilla ice cream, Chester Platt, who operated the fountain, topped it off with a candied cherry and some cherry syrup. It was such a wonderful combination that Platt kept it on the menu and later created strawberry, pineapple, and chocolate Sundays. This story has some documentation. An ad for a "Cherry Sunday" ran in the *Ithaca Daily Journal* on April 6, 1892. The ad copy read: "A new 10 cent Ice Cream Specialty, Served only at Platt & Colt's Famous day and night Soda Fountain."[59]

Regardless of who invented them, the early sundaes were spelled *Sunday* and were simple confections. According to the *Spatula Soda Water Guide*, "They are nothing more or less than a portion of ice cream over which a small quantity of syrup or crushed fruit has been poured."[60] In some college towns, they were called "college ices" or "college sodas" and were said to be especially popular with female students. They were also called "throwovers" because the toppings were thrown over the ice cream. Before long, simplicity was out and the sundae was being topped with syrups, fruits, whipped cream, marshmallow, nuts, cherries, and more. A popular early variation was a "Chop Suey Sundae," ice cream topped with a mixture of dates and figs that had been cooked to a jammy consistency and mixed with chopped walnuts.[61]

Ice cream sodas, sundaes, and other treats were transforming the soda fountain and making it ubiquitous. In 1906, the *New York Herald Tribune* reported that the soda fountain had surpassed the saloon in popularity. In New York City, there was a saloon for every 590 persons, according to the article, but there were seven thousand soda fountains, or one for every 535 persons.[62] The Chicago, Burlington and Quincy Railroad converted one of its cars to an ice cream parlor and served sodas and sundaes to riders day and night.[63] The temperance movement and, later, Prohibition gave added impetus to the business. Soon, save for an occasional early morning Alka-Seltzer, the carbonic acid waters of the early fountains would be forgotten.

SIX

Women's Work

In 1850, *Godey's Lady's Book* called ice cream "one of the necessary luxuries of life" and proclaimed that "a party, or a social entertainment, could hardly be thought of without this indispensable requisition." The writer was trying to persuade readers to buy "a recent valuable invention, in the shape of an 'ice cream freezer and beater.'" According to the article, Masser's Self-Acting Patent Ice-Cream Freezer and Beater would make ice cream more easily and much faster than the old method, which it called difficult, laborious, and uncertain. It said, "And if there is any one article, above all others, that the lady of the house would desire to have well made, it is her ice cream, as there is no article on the refreshment table that is more certain to undergo the ordeal of criticism. How important therefore is it to have it as it should be and can be, smooth, light, and well made."[1]

Making ice cream at home was not yet as widespread as *Godey's Lady's Book* implied. In fact, it would take most of the rest of the century before ice cream became as indispensable as the magazine suggested. At midcentury, well-off householders in eastern cities could have their servants prepare ice cream for them, or they could send out to the confectioners for ice creams molded into fanciful shapes for their elegant parties. The not-so-well-to-do might make ice cream at home themselves, assuming they had the necessary ingredients and implements. However, many were not so fortunate. Women living in rural communities or on the frontier often did not have iceboxes, much less ice cream makers.[2] Nor were there confectioners or, as yet, drugstore soda fountains where they could buy ice cream. For them, ice cream was a rare luxury, not a necessary one. Even for those with the wherewithal, but without household help, making ice cream was an occasional extravagance, a summer ritual, a weekend treat. Maine's Jennie Everson called it "Sunday ice cream" and described it wistfully. "One of the most popular and tasty uses for ice was for the making of ice cream. Here is another reason why farmers had a cow or two but not enough milk or cream to sell. Those were the days when ice cream was made of heavy cream, sugar, several fresh eggs, and some vanilla extract. Or perhaps, around the Fourth of July when the strawberry patch was at its best, some fresh, crushed strawberries were stirred in."[3]

But cookbooks and magazines were beginning to offer homemakers advice on acquiring ice cream makers and the other implements that went along with making ices and ice creams. Recipes for everything from lush frozen puddings rich with cream and brandied fruits to wan dishes of cornstarch-thickened ice milk began to appear in print. Writers offered recipes and serving suggestions for both prosperous households and modest ones. If not everyone served ice cream at special occasions, it was not for a lack of information.

By Women, for Women

During the nineteenth century, many cookbooks and household magazines were written by women for other women. The authors were professionals—not chefs, but writers, lecturers, and teachers. Although some of them were inexperienced in running a household or cooking for a family, they took on the task of teaching others how to do so by applying the skills and techniques of business and science to housekeeping and cooking. They were working women, and many of them were very successful; nevertheless, they glorified the role of the homemaker. They believed that, with instruction, women could improve the family's, and by extension the country's, morality, health, and education. Sarah Tyson Rorer, one of the leaders of the movement, was the author of nearly two dozen books, the director of the Philadelphia Cooking School, domestic arts editor of the *Ladies' Home Journal*, and a contributor to *Good*

Housekeeping magazine. Her career had begun when she took a cooking class at Philadelphia's New Century Club. Looking back years later, she explained, "Before I had taken the second lesson I saw the great possibilities of right living and a well-organized school of domestic science. In fact, I saw, a hundred years ahead, the influence that this knowledge would have over the health and homes of the people."[4]

The women became known as "domestic scientists," and ultimately they created the field of home economics.[5] They wrote from a woman's point of view, and thousands of women found this reassuring. It was a time when many women, and men as well, needed reassurance. After the Civil War, the rapid pace of industrialization created economic dislocation as well as opportunity. Families settling the frontier faced loneliness and poverty in addition to adventure. Immigrants were discovering a world of problems along with possibilities. Even the well-to-do sometimes found themselves in straitened circumstances, and women who had never expected to work had to support families. Several of the women who wrote cookbooks at the time had experienced just such difficulties in their own lives and had to take on chores they had never expected to perform. As a result, along with their recipes they offered their readers advice on everything from how to render lard to how to make mattresses. Their experiences also explain why the titles of their books so frequently include adjectives such as *frugal, economical, practical,* and *useful.*

Women, for the most part, were also responsible for another source of recipes and advice: community cookbooks. These books originated during the Civil War to raise funds to help care for soldiers and their families. After the war ended, the books continued to be produced to support local churches, schools, and other worthy causes. Indeed, they are still being published today. Since homemakers submitted their own recipes to make up the cookbooks, in general they reflected a reality where ingredients were sometimes scarce, time was limited, and indulgences were few. Nevertheless, many community cookbooks included ice cream recipes.

Ice Cream Utensils

In 1850, author Catharine Beecher called an ice cream maker *"almost indispensable"* (italics in the original), but she, unlike *Godey's*, did not expect her readers to simply buy one. Rather, she explained how to substitute a tin pail and a tub for an ice cream maker. She also suggested that anyone who did not own an apparatus might have one made. She wrote:

> If you wish to have a freezer made, send the following directions to a tinner.
>
> Make a tin cylinder box, eighteen inches high and eight inches in diameter at the bottom, and a trifle larger at the top, so that the frozen cream will slip out easier. Have a cover made with a rim to lap over three inches and fitted tight. Let there be a round handle fastened to the lid, an inch in diameter, and reaching nearly across, to take hold of to stir the cream. This will cost from fifty to seventy-five cents.[6]

At the time, kitchen utensils were few and often handmade—if not at home, then by a local handyman. But this was changing. During the latter half of the century, machine-made cooking implements were flooding into the marketplace and replacing the homemade, improvised, or custom-made utensils that had been the norm. The practice of going to a local tinsmith to have a cooking implement made to one's own specifications was giving way to shopping in stores or the new mail-order catalogs for mass-produced, uniform products. The new products coming out of factories not only increased the number of utensils in the kitchen, they also changed the way women cooked. They made cooking more scientific, less intuitive. Standardized products allowed for standard measurements. The domestic scientists embraced the new implements because they had the potential to save women time and effort. They also welcomed the precision these new tools offered. Recipes calling for a teacupful of this, a sufficiency of that, or "as much ground cinnamon as will cover a threepenny piece"[7] were being replaced by those calling for one teaspoonful or one-half a measuring cup. Tables of weights and measures began to appear in cookbooks. Authors began listing ingredients at the head of a recipe, rather than simply including them in the text, although sometimes they called for additional ingredients in the text. Change took time.

In 1882, *Miss Parloa's New Cookbook: A Guide to Marketing and Cooking* included almost twenty pages of illustrations and descriptions of "utensils with which a kitchen should be furnished." Among them were an egg-beater, a confectioner's ornamenting tube for decorating cakes, an apple parer, a lemon squeezer, a colander, a whip churn for whipping cream, and a quart measure. Maria Parloa, a well-known teacher, lecturer, and author, wrote, "A kitchen should be furnished with two measures, one for dry material and the other for liquids."[8] Sarah Tyson Rorer's *Philadelphia Cook Book* listed more than two hundred utensils needed for a "well-furnished kitchen," including a quart measure and a graduated glass measure. Her list also included three ice cream molds.[9]

The change in kitchen equipment did not happen overnight. More than thirty years after Beecher's book was published, many women did not own an ice cream maker, and some of those who did preferred the old-fashioned style to the newer ones. According to Marion Fontaine Cabell Tyree, the author of *Housekeeping in Old Virginia*, published in 1878, "After trying many new and patent freezers, some of the best housekeepers have come to the conclusion that the old-fashioned freezer is best[,] . . . especially as servants are so apt to get a patent freezer out of order." (The newer ice cream freezers with the built-in cranks were commonly referred to as "patent" freezers in contrast to the old-fashioned *sorbetière*-style freezers.) In 1884, Mary Lincoln, one of the most influential writers of the day, described how to make ice cream with either "a patent or home-made freezer" in *Mrs. Lincoln's Boston Cook Book*. Demonstrating the belief in frugality and emphasis on nutrition, rather than flavor and style, so characteristic of the domestic science movement, she also explained how to improvise an ice cream maker: "A good ice-cream freezer should be in every kitchen; for with it a great variety of wholesome and attractive dishes may be prepared with very little expenditure of time and strength. Fruit, cream, and eggs, when frozen are more palatable in hot weather than when served in other ways. A deep can, four inches in diameter, with a tight cover fitting outside the can, and packed in a firkin with ice and salt, makes a good substitute for a freezer."[10]

Lincoln was the first principal of the Boston Cooking School, author of—in addition to *Mrs. Lincoln's Boston Cook Book*—*The Peerless Cook-Book* and *Frozen Dainties*, as well as cofounder of the *New England Kitchen Magazine*. She had begun her career as a domestic because of her husband's ill health, and went on to become one of the country's most famous and successful women.[11] An early issue of her *New England Kitchen Magazine*, published in 1894, offered a brief overview of the evolution of the ice cream freezer and then recommended the more up-to-date ones over old-fashioned methods: "Many a country housekeeper today who does not possess a freezer and cannot order ice-cream from a caterer packs a tin pail of custard in a wooden one of ice and salt, and prepares her dessert in the same fashion. The modern freezers accomplish better work with less expense of time and strength, and thus will soon pay for themselves."[12]

Other writers also encouraged their readers to buy freezers. Parloa wrote, "If there be much fancy cooking, there must be an ice cream freezer." She called it a "great luxury" and said that it was best to buy the gallon size. One could make a small quantity in it for the family, she pointed out, but in addition, "when you have friends in, there is no occasion to send to the confectioner's for what can be prepared as well at home."[13] Under the heading "Ice-Creams, Etc.," *"Aunt Babette's" Cook Book*, published in 1889, stated, "To begin with, you must procure the best triple-motion patent freezer, plenty of ice and rock salt (common salt will not do so well)."[14] In 1898, more than fifty years after Nancy Johnson's invention, Rorer said, "Good ice cream cannot be made without a good freezer—one working easily with a side crank and a double revolving dasher."[15]

Making the Ice Cream

Even the most up-to-date ice cream makers still required ice, which was sold in large, awkward pieces that had to be cut or broken for use. In describing the process of preparing ice for freezing ice cream, many writers simply offered such instructions as: "Take a bucket of ice and pound it fine." Others were more specific and detailed. The 1877 edition of *Buckeye Cookery*, originally published to raise money to build a parsonage in Marysville, Ohio, offered these directions: "Put the ice in a coarse coffee-sack, pound with an ax or mallet until the lumps are no larger than a small hickory-nut."[16] (The book also included directions for building your own "cheap" icehouse.)[17] Aunt Babette suggested pounding the ice to the size of a walnut. She said, "To do this easily lay the ice in the folds of an old piece of carpet or blanket and pound it with a hammer or mallet. In this way you will not waste any ice or soil the floor."[18] Professional confectioners, hotel keepers, and restaurateurs could buy mechanical icebreakers, chippers, and shavers to make the chore easier. Eventually these were produced for home use as well. Churning ice cream, whether by opening the container and stirring it from time to time or by turning the outer crank, was still a tedious job, and no one described the process with more wit and candor than Marion Harland. Harland, whose real name was Mary Virginia Hawes Terhune, was born in Virginia in 1830 to a family who believed in educating its daughters. As an adult, she wrote popular novels, married a minister, traveled, had six children, and in 1871 published *Common Sense in the Household: A Manual of Practical Housewifery*. She said she wrote the book to teach others the lessons she wished she had learned when she was young; it seems she had not been educated in cooking or running a household. Readers responded to Harland's personal tone and humor. The book was a best-seller, remained in print for fifty years, and was translated into several languages.

Although she had household help, Harland empathized with homemakers who did not. She introduced her section on making ice cream by first describing how difficult it was. She wrote, "My earliest recollections of ice-cream are of the discordant grinding of the well-worn freezer among the blocks of ice packed about it—a monotone of misery, that, had it been un-relieved by agreeable associations of the good to which it was 'leading up,' would not have been tolerated out of Bedlam. For one, two, three, some-times four hours, it went on without other variety than the harsher sounds of the fresh ice and the rattling 'swash' as the freezer plunged amid the icy brine when these were nearly melted." She went on about the difficulties of freezing for several more sentences. Her basic ice cream recipe followed, along with an explanation of how to break the ice into pieces no larger than "pigeon eggs," layer it with salt, and finally, fill the container with the ice cream mixture. Then she shared the method she called "Self-Freezing Ice Cream":

> With a long wooden ladle or flat stick (I had one made on purpose), beat the custard as you would batter for five minutes, without stay or stint. Replace the lid, pack the ice and salt upon it, patting it down hard on top; cover all with several folds of blanket or carpet, and leave it for one hour. Then remove the cover of the freezer when you have wiped it carefully outside. You will find within a thick coating of frozen custard upon the bottom and sides. Dislodge this with your ladle, which should be thin at the lower end, or with a long carving-knife, working every particle of it clear. Beat again hard and long until the custard is a smooth, half-congealed paste. The smoothness of the ice-cream depends upon your action at this juncture.

Harland then covered the ice cream again, buried it in ice, and waited for two more hours, at which point, she wrote, it would be ready to turn out as "a solid column of cream, firm, close-grained, and smooth as velvet to the tongue." She claimed the whole process took no more than fifteen minutes of actual work. She suggested making the ice cream mixture the night be-fore it was to be served and putting it in the cellar. In the morning, she said, "by choosing the times for your stolen visits to the lower regions," you could serve your unsuspecting family "the most delicious dessert in the world" at a one o'clock dinner. She particularly enjoyed being able to surprise her husband. She wrote, "I have often laughed in my sleeve at seeing *my* John walk through the cellar in search of some mislaid basket or box, whistling carelessly, without a suspicion that his favorite delicacy was coolly working out its own solidification under the inverted barrel on which I chanced to be leaning at his entrance."[19] Harland's "self-freezing" method was popular enough to be reprinted in at least two other books, one of which, *Buckeye Cookery*, credited it to her.

In some families, the woman of the house made the ice cream mixture, and chipping the ice and churning the ice cream was the responsibility of the man and boys of the house. It was often one of a family's best-loved summer vacation traditions. Author Cornelius Weygandt, who was born in 1871, reminisced about making ice cream at his family's summer place in New Hampshire in his book *Philadelphia Folks*:

> The ritual is begun by digging out a cake of ice from the sawdust of the ice-house. I cut off a chunk the years have taught me is enough for freezing and packing the ice-cream. . . . I extract the six-pronged ice-pick from its lair behind the refrigerator, gather up the salt bucket and freezer from the buttery, and summon what man-power is about for the churning. . . . As the "agitating" process goes on, more ice and salt are supplied, the one who turns relieved, and these processes are repeated until by the stiffness of the turning it is evident that the ice-cream is sufficiently frozen.

Tasting the ice cream when the paddle was removed from the ice cream maker was an extremely important part of the ritual. Weygandt recalled:

> Such a ceremony I can remember from earliest childhood. Each member of the family is armed with a spoon and removes his or her infinitesimal dab of ice-cream from the paddle, at best no more than a taste. Cries of "delicious" or "not sweet enough" rise on the air, and appetites are whetted for the reappearance of the ice-cream at dinner's end. The top of the

can is corked and put back where it belongs, the tub repacked with ice and salt, and carried down into the cellar so the ice-cream shall ripen.[20]

At home in Philadelphia, he wrote, his family generally bought ice cream from confectioners. But on Sundays, when there were no deliveries, they sometimes made their own. Noting that his favorite flavors were coffee, chocolate, and bisque, he said, "I like all kinds of ice cream, strawberry and peach, vanilla and chocolate[;] . . . raspberry almost as much for its color of old rose as for its so-individual taste; black walnut because of its rich nuttiness, banana because of its smoothness; and pineapple because that flavor will rise to the occasion from its quietude in a can at seasons and in places when no other trustworthy fruit is attainable. It isn't everywhere you can get fresh strawberries or vanilla-bean and sherry."[21]

The Recipes

Early in the nineteenth century, most homemakers' cookbooks offered just a few recipes for ices and ice creams. By its end, they offered dozens. Several women published cookbooks on ice creams and other "frozen dainties." Recipes ranged from simple to sumptuous; the flavors, from strawberry to frozen pudding, from peach to pistachio. In addition to plain ices and ice creams, homemakers' cookbooks offered directions for more elaborate frozen desserts, including mousses, parfaits, sherbets, bombes, punches, and puddings. They included recipes for food colorings and directions for creating presentations that were nearly as stylish as a confectioner's.

There are just two ice cream recipes in Eliza Leslie's first cookbook, *Seventy-five Receipts for Pastry, Cakes, and Sweetmeats,* first published in 1828. Leslie, who later wrote *Directions for Cookery,* the most popular American cookbook of the nineteenth century, had learned how to cut corners when necessary. Just sixteen when her father died, she abandoned her hopes for a literary life and helped her mother run a boardinghouse to support the family.[22] After attending cooking school, she wrote *Seventy-five Receipts,* whose first ice cream recipe called for a "quart of rich cream," sugar, and either lemon juice, strawberries, or raspberries. The second was made with a combination of cream and milk thickened with a tablespoon of flour and two eggs. She said it was "inferior in richness" to the first, but more economical in "places where cream is not abundant."[23]

In 1847, when she was a successful and celebrated author, Leslie wrote *The Lady's Receipt-Book* for "families who possess the means and the inclination to keep an excellent table." There are no thrifty alternatives among the six recipes for water ices and three recipes for ice creams in this book. Her recipes call for "fine ripe plums," "the best chocolate," and "rich cream." Twentieth-century food writer James Beard called Leslie his favorite cook. "She had great recipes for ice cream and things like that before most people did," he said.[24] Here is one of her lush, flavorful ice creams:

PEACH ICE-CREAM

Take fine soft free-stone peaches, perfectly ripe. Pare them, and remove the stones. Crack about half the stones, and extract the kernels, which must be blanched by putting them into a bowl, and pouring on boiling water to loosen the skins. Then break them up, or pound them slightly; put them into a little sauce-pan, and boil the kernels in a small quantity of rich milk, till it is highly flavoured with them; keeping the sauce-pan covered.[25] Strain out the kernels and set the milk to cool. Cut up the peaches in a large, broad, shallow pan, or a flat dish, and chop them very small. Mix with the chopped peaches sufficient powdered loaf-sugar to make them very sweet, and then mash them to a smooth jam with a silver spoon. Measure the peach jam; and to each quart allow a pint of cream, and a pint of rich unskimmed milk. Mix the whole well together, and put it into the freezer; adding when the mixture is about half-frozen, the milk in which you boiled the kernels, and which will greatly improve the peach-flavour. When well-frozen, turn out the cream and serve it in a glass bowl. If you wish to have it in a shape, transfer it to a mould, and give it a second freezing.[26]

Writers frequently mentioned the high cost of making ice cream and the scarcity of cream. One noted that "ices are much cheaper than cream, though confectioners charge just as much for one as the other."[27] In recipes containing such money-saving substitutes for cream and eggs as cornstarch, gelatin, flour, or arrowroot, they used phrases like: "In places where cream is not abundant . . ." or "If cream cannot be obtained . . ."[28] One wrote, "*Mock Cream* may be made by mixing half a table-spoonful of flour with a pint of new milk, letting it simmer five minutes to take off the rawness of the flour."[29] The author of a frugal recipe for an ice cream made with milk and thickened with cornstarch rather plaintively added, "If to be extra nice, add a pint of rich cream."[30]

Some writers disapproved of the practice of making ice creams of lesser quality, but provided recipes or suggestions for those who were forced to do so. Lincoln wrote in *The Boston Cook Book*, "It is better to make sherbet, or fruit and water ices, than an inferior quality of ice-cream with milk,"[31] but she provided a recipe for a frozen custard made with milk in another of her books. Similarly, in her 1898 book, *Good Cooking*, Rorer wrote, "When making ice cream do not use gelatine, arrowroot, or other thickening substances. Good, pure cream, ripe fruit, or the best canned fruit in winter, and granulated sugar, make a perfect ice cream."[32] However, she also recognized that not everyone had access to such ingredients. In *Ice Creams, Water Ices, Frozen Puddings, Together with Refreshments for All Social Affairs*, she wrote, "In this book, Philadelphia Ice Creams, comprising the first group, are very palatable, but expensive. In many parts of the country it is quite difficult to get good cream. For that reason, I have given a group of creams, using part milk and part cream, but it must be remembered that it takes smart 'juggling' to make ice cream from milk. By far better use condensed milk, with enough water or milk to rinse out the cans."[33] She said that, by using condensed milk to make "ordinary fruit creams," the cost would be reduced to just fifteen cents a quart. She also suggested that, "in places where neither cream nor condensed milk can be purchased, a fair ice cream is made by adding two tablespoonfuls of olive oil to each quart of milk."[34]

However, she did not include any recipes actually calling for the olive oil and milk mixture.

One of the most parsimonious ice cream recipes was contributed to the 1877 edition of *Buckeye Cookery* by Louise Skinner of Battle Creek, Michigan. It makes a thin, sweet ice milk that is similar to today's soft-serve ice creams.

EGGLESS ICE-CREAM

Two quarts milk, one pound sugar, three heaping table-spoons corn starch; wet the starch with a little cold milk, scald the milk by putting it in a tin pail and setting it in a pot of boiling water, let boil and stir in the sugar and starch, strain, let cool, flavor and freeze.[35]

Just as wholesalers made ice cream of different quality levels for different markets, some writers offered basic ice cream recipes with different degrees of richness and cost. In *Frozen Dainties*, written for the White Mountain Freezer Company, Lincoln offered five "foundation" recipes for ice cream. Her Neapolitan ice cream contained four eggs, cream, sugar, and a flavoring. Philadelphia ice cream was made with cream, sugar, and a flavoring. "Ice-cream, with Gelatine," contained both milk and cream, as well as the gelatin, along with eight eggs, sugar, and salt. She recommended flavoring it "highly with lemon, wine, or any flavoring strong enough to disguise the taste of the gelatine." Her "Plain Ice-cream" was also made with milk and cream, sugar, salt, and a flavoring, but it contained just two eggs and was thickened with flour. "Frozen Custard" contained no cream. It was made with milk, six to eight egg yolks, sugar, salt, and a flavoring. She said that from these "one may select according to taste or means."[36]

In *The Book of Ices*, first published in 1885, England's Agnes Marshall also gave her readers different foundation ice cream recipes, along with titles that left no doubt as to their expense. The first, "Very Rich," was made with cream, sugar, and eight egg yolks. Number two, "Ordinary," was made with milk, sugar, and eight egg yolks. She said it could be improved by using half milk and half cream instead of all milk. Number three, "Common," was made with milk, sugar, two eggs, and gelatin. She did not suggest disguising the taste of the gelatin, possibly because she recommended that her own "Finest leaf gelatine" be used. Number four, "Cheap," was made with milk, sugar, and corn flour or arrowroot. The fifth, "Plain Cream Ice," was simply cream and sugar. Recipes using specific flavorings followed.[37]

Marshall was another exceptional woman. She wrote several cookbooks, ran a well-known London cooking school, gave lectures, and owned a kitchen equipment store where many of her own products were sold. Today, she would be called an entrepreneur and celebrated for her astute cross-promotion. Her recipes called for her gelatin, her baking powder, and her flavor extracts. Her ice creams were to be churned in her patented freezer, molded in any of the hundreds of molds she sold, and kept in her ice *cave* until ready to be served.

Marshall was also an innovator. She wrote about the possibility of using liquid nitrogen to freeze ice cream, although it is doubtful that she ever did so. She was one of the first to serve ice cream in cones, which she called cornets. Her recipes for ices and ice creams numbered more than a hundred and included a cinnamon ice cream made with lemon peel and a bay leaf. The combination of spice, citrus, and the faint resin flavor of the bay leaf makes a complex and very flavorful ice cream:

CINNAMON CREAM ICE (*CRÈME DE CANNELLE*)
Put 1 pint of milk or cream to boil with a finger-length of cinnamon, 1 bay leaf, and the peel of half a lemon; when well flavoured, mix it on to 8 raw yolks of eggs and 4 ounces of castor sugar; thicken over the fire. Add a little apricot yellow (p. 63); tammy, and finish as for other ices.[38]

Fannie Merritt Farmer was the most famous of the era's female cooks and authors. Born in Boston in 1857, she suffered ill health, possibly from polio, while young and was not able to finish high school. But she enrolled in the Boston Cooking School and in 1891 became its principal. Subsequently, she opened her own school, wrote several cookbooks, was a columnist for the *Women's Home Companion,* and lectured at Harvard Medical School. Known as the "mother of level measurements," she was dedicated to the scientific approach to cooking. *The Boston Cooking-School Cook Book,* her first book, was an immediate best-seller. Although much revised, it is still in print.[39]

Her chapter "Ices, Ice Creams, and Other Frozen Desserts" included more than three dozen recipes. Farmer's writing was clear, crisp, and concise. She listed the ingredients, in order of use, above the directions. She included detailed directions for freezing, molding, and unmolding the desserts. For the most part, her flavors were similar to those in other cookbooks of the day. They included everything from vanilla ice cream to frozen Nesselrode pudding. She used canned fruit for several ices, and included several recipes for the then-popular frozen punches. The following recipe brings to mind Mrs. Randolph's earlier recipe for oyster cream:

CLAM FRAPPÉ

20 clams.
½ cup cold water.

Wash clams thoroughly, changing water several times; put in stewpan with cold water, cover closely, and steam until shells open. Strain the liquor, cool, and freeze to a mush.[40]

Household cooks, like confectioners, went to the trouble of making food colorings to give their ice creams added visual appeal. Rorer supplied directions for making green food coloring from spinach and wrote, "If no spinach is at hand, clover or lawn grass may be used."[41] Elizabeth Ellicott Lea's 1869 book *Domestic Cookery* was intended to be "connected with the ordinary," but it included recipes for ice cream and food colorings. Lea said her pokeberry jelly was to be used to stain ices, and she made a preparation using cochineal and other ingredients and wrote of it: "Use as much of this infusion as will give the desired shade. This produces a brilliant pink color."[42] *Buckeye Cookery* also explained how to make food coloring with pokeberry juice and said that it "gives a very beautiful color to creams and ices."[43]

What's in a Name?

By the late 1800s, so many frozen desserts were being made that Lincoln and Farmer both provided glossaries in their works; other writers defined terms along with their recipes. But there were exceptions to every definition. The names and descriptions varied from author to author, from book to book, from table to table.

Take Philadelphia ice cream, for example. Traditionally, it was made with cream, sugar, and flavoring. It did not contain milk or eggs. Eleanor Parkinson had been adamant on the subject: "Use cream entirely, and on no account mingle the slightest quantity of milk, which detracts materially from the richness and smoothness of the ices." She called ice creams made with eggs "custard ices." Farmer defined Philadelphia ice cream as "thin cream, sweetened, flavored, and frozen," and "plain ice cream" as "custard foundation, thin cream, and flavoring." Although Lincoln's glossary in the *New England Kitchen* magazine did not mention Philadelphia ice cream, it defined ice cream as being made "mainly or entirely of cream" and said that it took "a specific name from the substance used for flavoring." However, the first ice cream recipe in *Mrs. Lincoln's Boston Cook Book*, titled "Ice-Cream, No. 1 (Philadelphia Ice Cream)," calls for both milk and cream.[44] Earlier, Beecher made Philadelphia ice cream with milk or "cream when you have it," along with arrowroot, eight egg whites, sugar, and a flavoring.[45] Rorer's *Philadelphia Cook Book* stated emphatically, "To make good Philadelphia ice cream, use only the best materials. Avoid gelatine, arrowroot, or any other thickening substance. Good, pure cream, ripe fruit, or the best canned in winter, and granulated sugar, make a perfect ice cream."[46] Another writer, Juliet Corson, author of *Miss Corson's Practical American Cookery and Household Management*, said, "Philadelphia ice-cream is pure cream over-sweetened, over-flavored, and then frozen."[47] Her definition probably was not intended to be as

1. In seventeenth-century Naples, the banquet table was a stage on which the brilliance of the finest confectioners shone. From *Lo scalco alla moderna* by Antonio Latini, Napoli, 1692–94.

2. An elegant dessert table featuring ices and other delicacies
from the 1717 edition of François Massialot's *Nouvelle instruction
pour les confitures, les liqueurs, et les fruits.*
COURTESY OF BARBARA KETCHAM WHEATON.

OPPOSITE PAGE:

3. Cherubs are making heavenly ice cream on the frontispiece
of M. Emy's *L'art de bien faire les glaces d'office* (1768).
COURTESY OF THE WINTERTHUR LIBRARY:
PRINTED BOOK AND PERIODICAL COLLECTION.

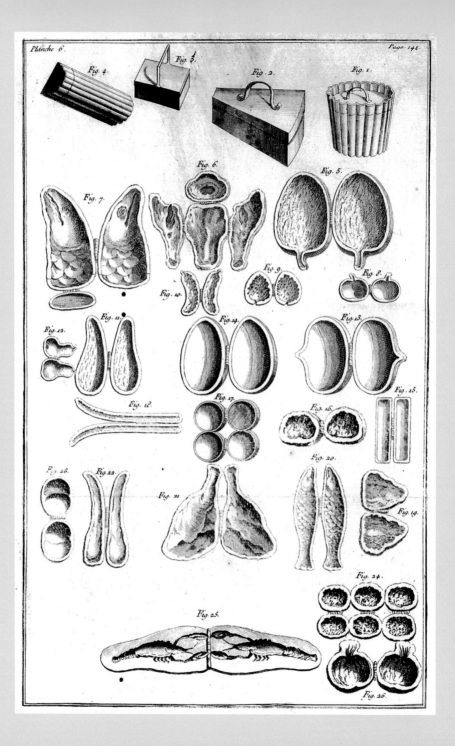

Fig. 4.

Fig. 3.

Fig. 2.

Fig. 1.

Fig. 6.

Fig. 5.

Fig. 7.

Fig. 9.

Fig. 10.

Fig. 8.

Fig. 12.

Fig. 11.

Fig. 14.

Fig. 13.

Fig. 18.

Fig. 17.

Fig. 16.

Fig. 15.

Fig. 28.

Fig. 22.

Fig. 21.

Fig. 20.

Fig. 19.

Fig. 24.

Fig. 25.

Fig. 26.

OPPOSITE PAGE:

4. Eighteenth-century ice cream
molds in the shape of everything
from fish heads to pickles.
From Joseph Gilliers's
Le Cannameliste français (1768).
COURTESY OF THE SCHLESINGER LIBRARY,
RADCLIFFE INSTITUTE, HARVARD UNIVERSITY.

—

THIS PAGE, ABOVE AND RIGHT:

5. A graceful swan made with vanilla,
lemon, and coffee ice creams and
surrounded by pulled sugar reeds
and rushes. From Charles Ranhofer's
The Epicurean (1920).
COURTESY OF THE SCHLESINGER LIBRARY,
RADCLIFFE INSTITUTE, HARVARD UNIVERSITY.

6. Agnes Marshall filled the body
of her pineapple mold with
pineapple ice and used pistachio ice
cream for the crown. From her
Fancy Ices (1894).
COURTESY OF BARBARA KETCHAM WHEATON.

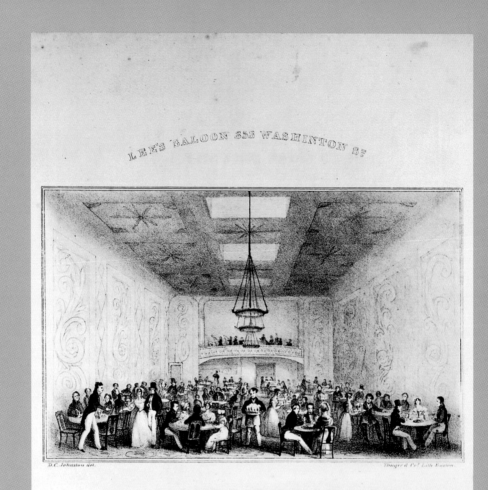

LEE'S SALOON 253 WASHINTON ST

D.C. Johnston del.   Thayer & Co? Lith. Boston.

THE ICE-CREAM QUICK STEP,

Composed and dedicated to

Mr WILLIAM LEE

as a token of respect for industry and enterprise by

J. R. GARCIA.

Price 25 cts Nett.

N.B. The Motive of this Quick Step was Suggested by Mr Lee's extreme celerity and apparent
ubiquity when in attendance upon his crowded Saloon 253 Washington St.

To be had at the Saloon and the principal Music Stores in Boston

Entered according to Act of Congress in the year 1841 by J.R. Garcia in the Clerk's office of the District Court of Massachusetts

11. A decorative Keystone soda water apparatus from the *Illustrated History of the Centennial Exhibition,* by James Dabney McCabe (1876).

OPPOSITE PAGE:

12. A small selection of the many fancy ice cream molds Agnes Marshall offered for sale. From *Fancy Ices* (1894).

12

Advertisements.

SPECIMENS FROM
THE BOOK OF MOULDS
Containing 68 pages of Illustrations, published by
MARSHALL'S SCHOOL OF COOKERY
And sent POST FREE on application.

FANCY ICE MOULDS IN PEWTER.

No. 43. SWAN.   No. 44. DOVE.   No. 42. DUCK.

2 pints, £1.   1¼ pints, 15s.   1 quart, £1. 2s.

No. 50.   No. 39G.
BASKET OF   No. 47. HEN.   FANCY MELON.
FLOWERS.

1 quart, £1. 4s.   1 quart, £1.   No. 1. 1½ pints, 15s.
                                        „   2. 1 quart, 19s.

No. 49.   No. 39I.
PINEAPPLE.   No. 48.   GIANT
                 FISH.   STRAWBERRY.

1 quart, 19s.   1 quart, £1.   1 quart, 18s.

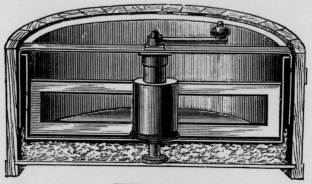

The Food Administration classifies
Ice Cream as an essential food
Eat it regularly—insisting upon

Crescent REGISTERED Pasteurized
ICE CREAM

16. During World War I, the U.S. government encouraged ice cream eating, and ice cream makers took full advantage of the fact in their advertising.
COURTESY OF THE MINNESOTA HISTORICAL SOCIETY.

OPPOSITE PAGE:

17. Making ice cream was simple and relaxing, according to this 1917 recipe pamphlet published by the makers of Auto Vacuum freezers.
AUTHOR'S COLLECTION.

18. Every ice cream lover's dream, as depicted in
"The Cream of Love" by Currier & Ives.
COURTESY OF THE LIBRARY OF CONGRESS,
PRINTS AND PHOTOGRAPHS DIVISION, LC-USZC2-2151.

negative as it sounds. She recommended oversweetening several of her ice creams, and seems to have meant that the mixture should taste a little too sweet before freezing in order for the flavor to come through in the ice cream.

Other names were equally arbitrary. Corson had a recipe for a rich ice cream made with cream, sugar, and the yolks of a dozen eggs, along with a vanilla bean; she called it "French Ice-Cream." *"Aunt Babette's" Cook Book* called a similar combination "New York Ice-Cream." In addition to her many Philadelphia ice creams, Rorer made "French Ice Creams" with cream and the yolks of from six to fourteen eggs. She cooked the mixtures for those ice creams, but her "English Ice Creams" were generally uncooked and contained no eggs.[48] Her "Neapolitan Ice Creams" were cooked custards made with cream, sugar, and six egg yolks, and she also added six stiffly whisked egg whites to the mixture. The term *Neapolitan* was generally used to refer to an ice cream brick layered with three flavors. Initially, strawberry, pistachio, and vanilla ice creams were used to represent the colors of the Italian flag, but over time vanilla, chocolate, and strawberry became more common. Every now and then, a writer describing a multiflavored brick mistakenly called it "metropolitan" ice cream. "Harlequin" was another name used for the same preparation. Rorer called the multilayered bricks "Neapolitan Blocks."[49]

Sherbet was a fluid term. Its usage to describe an ice, rather than the Middle Eastern drink, seems to have originated in America in the late nineteenth century. *Housekeeping in Old Virginia,* published in 1878 and consisting of recipes collected from "Two Hundred and Fifty Ladies in Virginia and her Sister States," had six sherbet recipes. Three called for cream, and one was made with milk. The remaining two—a lemon sherbet and an orange sherbet—were made with fruit juice, sugar, water, and egg whites.[50] Lincoln and Farmer both defined sherbet as a water ice with gelatin or egg whites added. In many cookbooks, the terms *sherbet, fruit ice,* and *water ice* were interchangeable. When the word *sorbet* was used, it meant a fruit or water ice.

Earlier, when Emy and others made them, the frozen desserts known as biscuits were so-called because grated biscuits, cookies, or macaroons were among the ingredients. But in the late 1800s, many biscuits were made without biscuits. Lincoln used the term *biscuit glacé* for combinations of an ice cream and a sherbet or mousse frozen in small paper cases like cupcake papers. She said they were sometimes covered with meringue and browned before serving.[51] Rorer's "Biscuit Tortoni" was ice cream flavored with sherry and maraschino liqueur. It did not contain biscuits, but it was frozen in paper cases.[52] A British confectioners' manual published at the beginning of the twentieth century said the term *biscuit glacé* was "a contentious subject, and a healthy fight might perhaps result in an authoritative ruling that would establish a universal standard." The authors said it was originally made with crushed biscuits or macaroons, but they explained the product had changed. Today, they wrote, "a rich, light sponginess is desired, and more often than not some form of iced soufflé is sent to table as a 'biscuit glacé.' "[53]

Homemade frozen puddings were also a popular dessert. Lincoln defined them as "any rich ice-cream highly flavored with wine, brandy, Jamaica rum or maraschino, and made quite thick with a variety of fruits, nuts, etc. and served with a cold, rich sauce." For the fruits, she recommended a pound of assorted French fruit (these would have been candied fruits); or a mix of raisins, currants, and citron; or figs and dates; or half fruits and half nuts; or half fruits and half crumbs of macaroons or cake. She offered two recipes for the sauce, a flavored whipped cream and a flavored custard.[54] Other cooks used a variety of different fruits and nuts; some added whipped cream to the ice cream just before freezing it. The recipe that Mrs. Governor J. B. McCreary of Kentucky contributed to *Buckeye Cookery* called for a pound of raisins and one pint of strawberry preserves. An unnamed contributor to *Housekeeping in Old Virginia* offered a recipe for "Plumbière" [*sic*] made with almonds, citron, and "brandy peaches." Three Nesselrode recipes were contributed to *The Blue Grass Cook Book*, two of which used chestnuts. The other used an assortment of fruits and fruit peel. *"Aunt Babette's" Cook Book* contained a most elaborate Nesselrode pudding including chestnuts that had been cooked in wine and "a quarter of a pound of the finest chocolate, grated." After it was frozen, it was layered in a mold with apricot marmalade, fig preserves, and candied fruit. Aunt Babette wrote, "In serving, dump on a platter, and pour a cold sauce over it, which is made of whipped cream flavored with Maraschina brandy and sweetened to taste."[55]

A simpler version is this one from Farmer's *Boston Cooking-School Cook Book:*

FROZEN PUDDING I

2½ cups milk.
1 cup sugar.
⅛ teaspoonful salt.
2 eggs.
1 cup heavy cream.
½ cup rum.
1 cup candied fruit, cherries, pineapples, pears, and apricots.

Cut fruit in pieces, and soak several hours in brandy to cover, which prevents fruit freezing; make custard of first four ingredients; strain, cool, add cream and rum, then freeze. Fill a brick mould with alternate layers of the cream and fruit; pack in salt and ice and let stand two hours.[56]

Recipes for iced punches also began to appear in the American household cookbooks late in the nineteenth century and were similar to those made by the English confectioners Jarrin and Jeanes. Most cooks started by making a lemon ice; then they added whipped egg whites and liquor and froze the mixture. The liquor was often rum, but brandy, champagne, and maraschino were also used. In fact, sometimes they were all used. Farmer made her Roman punch with rum, tea, and both lemon and orange juices. One of Rorer's Roman punch recipes was unique. She simply made a lemon water ice and spooned it into small punch glasses.

Then she made a small well in the center of each one and filled it with "good Jamaica rum."

The iced punches were frothy rather than frozen hard; the liquors would prevent them from freezing completely. Served as palate refreshers during a multicourse banquet, they were replaced later by sorbets. An etiquette book of the day referred to Roman punch as the best of the "provocatives of appetite . . . which, coming after the heavy roasts, prepares the palate and stomach for the canvas-back ducks or other game."[57]

Serving Suggestion

Ices and ice creams molded into all the elaborate shapes confectioners and caterers loved—bunches of asparagus, towering pillars, assorted fruits, flora, and fauna—could be purchased to serve at fancy dinner parties. One could serve ice cream molded into petite individual desserts or present a single large molded ice cream to dinner guests. By 1887 Minneapolis hostesses could buy ice cream molded into the shape of a large deer for five dollars or an elephant for six dollars. Each was intended to serve twelve guests.[58]

Mary F. Henderson, author of *Practical Cooking and Dinner Giving*, published in 1876, explained that the fancy molds were the purview of professionals, but that simpler ice creams could be served by anyone.

> The devices of form for creams served at handsome dinners in large cities are very beautiful; for instance, one sees a hen surrounded by her chickens; or a hen sitting on the side of a spun-glass nest, looking sideways at her eggs; or a fine collection of fruits in colors. One may see also a perfect imitation of asparagus with a cream-dressing, the asparagus being made of the *pistache* cream, and the dressing simply a whipped cream. These fancy displays are, of course, generally arranged by the confectioner. It is a convenience, of course, when giving dinner companies, to have the dessert or any other course made outside of the house; but for ordinary occasions, ices are no more troublesome to prepare than anything else, especially when they can be made early in the day, or even the day before serving.[59]

Ordinary people did find ways, often imaginative ones, to emulate the elaborate presentations of professionals. Molds in simple shapes like melons, spheres, or bricks were being stamped out of steel and sold at reasonable prices, so homemakers could serve prettily molded ice creams.[60] Lacking even one of those, the ice cream freezer itself could be used as a mold, Lincoln pointed out: "If we have not the elaborate moulds of the caterers, good effects can be gained by a little ingenuity. The freezer-can always gives a good shape if the cream is carefully packed in place after the dasher is removed. With care, the center may be filled with whipped cream of contrasting color and flavor, or with some preserved fruit; enough cream should be reserved to thoroughly cover this, and a surprise awaits the family when the apparently plain mound discloses its hidden treasures."[61]

Some molds had a removable centerpiece, called a pipe.[62] It allowed the confectioner to fill the mold with ice cream, then remove the pipe and fill the hollow space with a different ice or ice cream, with flavored or colored whipped cream, or with fresh fruit. Parloa achieved a similar result using the ice cream freezer rather than a mold. To make what she called "Strawberry Ice Cream à la Surprise," she first made strawberry ice cream, and then, taking the beaters out of the freezer, she filled the space with sugared strawberries. She topped the strawberries with some of the frozen ice cream and set it on ice for another hour. When she turned it out, she garnished it with more strawberries.[63] Mrs. J. C. P. of Stockbridge, Massachusetts, contributed a nearly identical recipe to *Buckeye Cookery*. She called it "Fruit Frappées" and used a mold rather than the ice cream freezer. She lined the mold with vanilla ice cream, filled the center with fresh berries or fruit cut in slices, covered it with ice cream, and put it back in the freezer for half an hour. She said, "The fruit must be chilled, but not frozen."[64]

Many of the recipes and serving ideas meant for home cooks reflected the influence of professional confectioners and chefs. To celebrate the purchase of Alaska by the United States in 1867, famed Delmonico's restaurant served individual desserts called "Alaska, Florida," better known today as baked Alaska. Chef Charles Ranhofer filled individual Savoy biscuits with apricot marmalade, then topped them with banana and vanilla ice creams molded into the shape of a pyramid. When it was time to serve them, he removed them from the freezing box, covered each one with meringue, and put them in a hot oven until they were a light golden brown.[65] Home cooks armed with Lincoln's *Frozen Dainties* could make something very similar. Lincoln called it "Ice-Cream en Deguiser" and used a sheet of sponge cake rather than individual biscuits. She did not use marmalade, nor did she specify the flavor of the ice cream. But just as Ranhofer did, she topped the cake with ice cream, covered it with meringue, and baked it "quickly in a hot oven." She said it was "recommended chiefly for its novelty."[66]

Like confectioners, home cooks also served ice cream in fruit shells—lemon ices or ice creams in scooped-out lemon halves; orange, in orange halves; banana, in banana skins. Aunt Babette suggested serving strawberry ice cream in "eggs made of meringue" or in small nests of spun sugar. She said the effect would be very pretty, then added, "Of course, this is meant for company only."[67] Lincoln also made meringue eggs filled with ice cream, and suggested tying the two halves together with a dainty ribbon.[68] Rorer cut a square cake in half, hollowed out the center, and filled it with ice cream. After replacing the top, she served it with cold brandy sauce poured around it.[69] She also suggested using baking powder cans as ice cream molds.[70] Henderson used a piece of pasteboard to divide a mold in half and filled one side with vanilla ice cream, the other with chocolate. She topped her pineapple ice cream with the reserved crown of fresh pineapple, much as Emy had more than a hundred years before.[71]

When ice cream was not molded into fanciful shapes, it might be brought to the table in a lovely porcelain glacier, or ice cream pail, in the same pattern as the family's best china service. The pails resembled wine pails, but they had lids with concave tops that were filled with ice to help keep the ice cream chilled. The ice cream was dished from the pails into individual ice cream dishes or handled cups and heaped up as high as possible.

At the end of the century, ices were served between dinner courses. Marshall specified that they should be presented after the fish course and before the roast. Rorer suggested that they accompany specific foods. For example, she said her apple ice should be served in lemonade glasses at dinner with roasted duck, goose, or pork. She served her mint sherbet with lamb. Her ginger water ice was "nice to serve with roasted or braised beef."[72] Most of these ices were as sweet as any dessert ice, but her cucumber sorbet was made with only a teaspoonful of sugar. As a result, it freezes to a rock-solid consistency. When it's only partially frozen, it tastes like cucumber slush and would perhaps be a pleasant first course on a hot summer evening.

CUCUMBER SORBET

2 large cucumbers
2 tart apples
1 pint of water
1 teaspoonful of sugar
½ teaspoonful of salt
1 tablespoonful of gelatin
1 saltspoonful of black pepper
Juice of one lemon

Peel the cucumbers, cut them into halves and remove the seeds. Dissolve the gelatin in a half cupful of hot water. Grate the flesh of the cucumbers; grate the apples, add them to the cucumbers, and add all the other ingredients. Freeze as you would ordinary sherbet.

Serve in tiny glasses, with boiled cod or halibut.

This will fill eight small stem glasses.[73]

Both American and British dinner tables featured serving pieces—bowls, vases, punch bowls, goblets, and cups—made of ice. To make them, water was poured into double molds similar to those used to make metal serving pieces, then the mold was covered with ice and salt and frozen. When the serving pieces were released from the molds, they were filled with sorbets, fruits, or drinks and set on the table. As soon as one started to melt and drip, a servant would whisk it away and replace it with another. Marshall presented most of her dinner sorbets in small cups made of ice, sometimes coloring the water before freezing it. The molds needed to make the cups were advertised for sale at the back of her book.[74]

Mark Twain called the end of the nineteenth century the "Gilded Age."[75] For some, it was a time of great wealth, elegant attire, and dinner tables gleaming with silver, crystal, and china, as well as ice. Etiquette books abounded, and eating properly was critical to one's social standing. This was a far cry from the scene Mrs. Basil Hall, an English traveler, described in 1828. She was at a dinner party in Washington when she observed a young lady "feeding herself with very much-melted ice-cream with a great steel knife!"[76] By the last quarter of the century, one did not eat with a knife at a dinner party. In fact, it seemed as if every food had its own specialized implement. Ice cream had several, including a three-pronged, slightly concave fork, which Mary Elizabeth Wilson Sherwood, author of *Manners and Social Usages,* referred to as "a queer little combination of fork and spoon, called an 'ice-spoon.'"[77] There were ice cream spoons for serving and ones for eating, some with squared-off ends that made them resemble miniature shovels. Specialized knives were used to slice molded ice creams. Since the knives were quite similar to fish knives, sometimes they did double duty. The fish course was served early in the meal, and molded ice cream at the close, so there was ample time to wash the knives before using them again.[78] There were also elegant silver ice cream hatchets for slicing and serving. Shaped rather like conventional hatchets, about twelve inches long and two and a half inches wide, they are now prized antiques. One made by Tiffany in sterling silver is valued at more than a thousand dollars today.

The ice cream scoop seems to have been a professional's implement at the time, not used in the home. Alfred L. Cralle, an African American living in Pittsburgh, received a patent for an ice cream scoop, which he called an "ice-cream mold and disher," in 1897. His application shows a cone-shaped scoop, but he explained that it could be made in any shape. Its advantages included the fact that it could be used with one hand. Cralle also said it was "strong, durable, effectual in its operation, and comparatively inexpensive to manufacture."[79]

Celebrating with Ice Cream

Whether it was bought from a confectioner or homemade, mixed from thin milk or heavy cream, served from fanciful molds or pottery bowls, ice cream added a sense of celebration to any occasion, from a simple supper to a grand gathering. Over the course of the nineteenth century, it gradually became the perfect dessert for everything from a child's birthday party to an exuberant Fourth of July observance. One of the earliest, and most unusual, events took place on the Oregon Trail in 1849. Charles Ross Parke, MD, was on his way to California to search for gold when he and his party stopped to celebrate "the nation's birthday." They were about to cross the Continental Divide at South Pass and decided to take advantage of nearby snowbanks to make ice cream. They lacked any sort of ice cream maker, but since they had two cows, they did have plenty of milk. Parke wrote in his diary:

> I determined to [do] something no other living man ever did in this place and on this sacred day of the year, and that was to make Ice Cream at the South Pass of the Rockies.
>
> I procured a small tin bucket which held about 2 quarts. This I sweetened and flavored with peppermint—had nothing else. This bucket was placed inside a wooden bucket, or Yankee Pale, and the top put on.
>
> Nature had supplied a huge bank of coarse snow, or hail, nearby, which was just the thing for this new factory. With alternate layers of this, and salt between the two buckets and aid of a clean stick to stir with, I soon produced the most delicious ice cream tasted in this place. In fact, the whole company so decided, and as a compliment drew up in front of our tent and fired a salute, bursting one gun but injuring no one.[80]

Soon less explosive Independence Day parties featured ice cream made under more practical conditions. Civic events, fairs, exhibitions, and other festive occasions all called for ice cream. In 1887, the dessert menu for the Ancient and Honorable Artillery Company banquet held at Faneuil Hall in Boston featured no less than nine different ices and ice creams.[81] Ice cream became a symbol of celebration. According to Weygandt, "Ice-cream was the *sine qua non* of Fourth of July and Thanksgiving and Christmas, of New Year's Day and Washington's Birthday and Decoration Day, the chief festivals of the year in the remote period of which I write."[82]

By the 1880s, summertime ice cream socials had become a favorite fundraiser for churches and community organizations. The women would make up the ice cream mixtures; the men and any boys they could coerce into participating did the churning in return for a chance to lick the dasher.[83] Ice cream went on picnics, too. Some carried it in an ice *cave* with a handle, made especially for such a purpose. Most just left the ice cream in the freezer after it was made, then packed it in more ice and salt, wrapped it up in an old carpet to keep the cold in, and carried it off to the picnic spot. Then, as now, a child's birthday party was incomplete unless ice cream was paired with the festive cake. By the turn of the twentieth century, *Godey's* declaration had finally come true. A party without ice cream had become unimaginable.

SEVEN

Modern Times

At the turn of the twentieth century, ice cream was one of the country's best-loved desserts, and the cone was about to become its constant partner. The ice cream cone had originated in the nineteenth century, but it didn't become a popular street food until after the 1904 World's Fair in Saint Louis. Many of the visitors to the fair ate an ice cream cone there for the first time and took a taste for the treat home with them afterward. They made the ice cream cone an American institution.

The fair, or as it was actually named, the Louisiana Purchase Exposition, belatedly celebrated the centennial of the 1803 Louisiana Purchase and welcomed in the twentieth century with great style. It was the biggest, most spectacular, most extravagant fair the country had ever known. The event was by all accounts a huge success and helped revitalize Saint Louis, which had been suffering the effects of the depression of the mid-1890s. Composed of 1,272 acres of exhibit halls, gardens, lagoons, and a mile-and-a-half-long midway called the Pike, it cost nearly fifty million dollars, more than the price of the Purchase itself.[1] In fact, one of its exhibits was the original Treasury draft of fifteen million dollars for the Louisiana Purchase. Other exhibits included everything from art from the Vatican's collection to Jefferson's original version of the Declaration of Independence. Some features were less exalted. There was a bear made from prunes, a palace made from corn, and an elephant made from almonds.[2] The states constructed buildings in local architectural styles. Maine's was a log cabin. California's was a mission-style building. Texas built a structure in the form of a five-pointed star. Sarah Tyson Rorer ran the main restaurant and sold her *World's Fair Souvenir Cook Book*. Ice cream cones were among the many refreshments sold at the fair, and there are many stories about its invention there.

The cone—but not the ice cream cone—dates back many centuries. It can be traced back at least to the ancient Greeks, who made flat cakes cooked between two hot metal plates and called them *obelios*. The French initially called them *oublies*, either after the Greek or from the Latin *oblata*, meaning "offering" or "unconsecrated host." A wafer-makers guild was established in France in the thirteenth century, and since its members also made hosts for the Catholic mass, they were supposed to be men of irreproachable character, not the sort who frequented prostitutes. They were so discreet that it was said lovers trusted them to deliver clandestine notes without arousing the suspicion of their spouses. The wafer makers sold their wares on the street, at fairs, and in front of churches on feast days. Some rolled their *oublies* into cornets and tucked them inside each other, selling five as a *main d'oublies*, or hand of wafers.[3]

The wafers were generally made with a batter that could be as simple as a flour-and-milk combination or as rich as a mixture of flour, eggs, cream, butter, sugar, and a flavoring. After the batter was mixed, it was cooked on two hot metal plates or irons that were hinged together. The wafer maker squeezed the plates together by the handles and held them over a fire until the wafers were cooked, then turned them out to dry. Other cooks baked wafers in ovens. Either way, the wafers were pliable before they dried, so they could be rolled into the shape of a cylinder, a cup, or a cone while still warm. As they cooled, they became crisp and held their shape.

In the 1734 edition of French chef François Massialot's *Nouvelle instruction pour les confitures, les liqueurs, et les fruits* (New Instruction for Jams, Liqueurs, and Fruits), a recipe for wafers concluded by noting that, when the wafer was ready, it should be rolled on a wooden implement made for the purpose, then put back in the stove to dry and crisp.[4] More than a century later, in his 1866 book *The Royal Confectioner: English and Foreign,*

Charles Elmé Francatelli included a recipe for chocolate wafers, which he called "Spanish Wafers." He wrote, "When done, curl them in the form of cornucopiæ, using a wooden form . . . upon which to shape the wafers. Such tools are obtainable at all turners.' "[5]

Made by home cooks as well as pastry chefs and street vendors, wafers were both dinner table desserts and street foods. After the French introduced wafers to the English, an official waferer was attached to the royal court. In medieval London, wafers and hippocras, a spiced wine, were considered the proper way to end a meal. The English also put slices of cheese into their wafers, making an early version of the grilled cheese sandwich. Wafers came to be called *gaufres*, or honeycombs, in thirteenth-century France when craftsmen made the metal plates with a honeycomb design. In the sixteenth century, street sellers often cried, "Voilà le plaisir, mesdames!" (Here's pleasure, ladies!) As a result, the wafers became known as *plaisirs*.[6] The Italians called wafers *cialde* or *pizzelle;* the Dutch, *waffels;* the Swedes, *krumkaga;* the Germans, *eiserkuchen*. The English and the Americans called them wafers, waffles, cornets, cornucopias, and, of course, cones.

In the nineteenth century, cooks and confectioners not only rolled wafers into cone shapes but also gave them all sorts of flavorings and flourishes. They added coffee, chocolate, cinnamon, cloves, orange flower water, lemon zest, vanilla, brandy, eau de vie, or Madeira to their batters. They mixed in currants, ground almonds, or pistachios and decorated the finished cones with orange-, lemon-, or vanilla-flavored sugars. They dipped the open end into royal icing, meringue, or caramel and rolled it in chopped and often colored nuts. They filled the cones with jams or fruits or whipped cream and berries and arranged them on elegant tiered dishes. When did they put ice cream in a cone? According to British food historian Robin Weir, the earliest illustration of an ice cream cone is an 1807 engraving of the scene at the fashionable Parisian café Frascati's. It shows a young lady seated at a table eating what appears to be ice cream from a cone.[7]

It was inevitable that someone would put ice cream into the cones, since wafers, whether left flat or rolled into cornets, were regularly served along with ice cream. They were natural companions. Carlo Gatti, the first ice cream wholesaler in England, got his start selling *gaufres* in Paris in the middle of the nineteenth century. Francatelli wrote that *gaufres* were "well adapted, from their lightness and crispness, to be handed round with ices."[8] Jarrin said that wafers were used "to garnish creams." The British food historian Ivan Day has pointed out that the first recipes specifically calling for ice cream to be put in cones were in *Francatelli's Modern Cook*, published in 1846.[9] Francatelli garnished several of his molded ice creams with tiny cones filled with ice cream. His "Iced Pudding à la Chesterfield" was typical. He lined a pyramid-shaped mold with pineapple ice cream and filled the middle with a cherry water ice blended with a mixture of red fruits such as cherries and strawberries. He made miniature, two-inch-diameter wafers and rolled them into cones. When it was time to send the ice cream pyramid to the table, he said, one should "turn it out of the mould on to its dish, ornament the dish with a kind of drooping feather, formed with green angelica cut in strips, and arranged as represented in the wood-cut; garnish the base with small *gauffres*, filled with some of the iced cream reserved for the purpose, place a strawberry on the top of each, and serve."[10] For his "Iced Pudding à la Duchess of Kent," he lined a mold with cherry water ice and filled it with filbert cream ice. After turning it out of the mold, he ringed it with cornets filled with filbert ice cream.[11]

The innovative Agnes Marshall also put ice cream into cones, but she gave them a starring rather than a supporting role. Her 1894 book, *Fancy Ices*, included a recipe for cornets that she baked in an oven rather than on a wafer iron. Hers were five inches in diameter, closer to today's size and much larger than Francatelli's. Marshall rolled them into cone shapes, piped icing around the opening and down the seam, and dipped them in finely chopped pistachio nuts. She filled the ones she called "Margaret Cornets" partly with ginger ice and partly with apple ice cream.[12] She filled her "Christina Cornets" with vanilla ice cream to which she had added whipped cream and "nice dried fruits, such as greengage, apricot, dried ginger, cherries, &c., that are cut into very tiny dice shapes, as much ground cinnamon as will cover a threepenny piece, the same quantity of ground ginger, and a tablespoonful of Marshall's Maraschino Syrup."[13] She arranged the filled cones in a pyramid on a doily-covered platter.

Clearly, these were silver-platter cornets, not ice cream cones meant to be licked outdoors on a sunny summer day. However, more down-to-earth versions of the cone were also being made. In 1901, Antonio Valvona, described in his U.S. patent application as "a subject of the King of Italy, residing at 96 Great Ancoats street, Manchester, in the county of Lancaster, England," invented an "apparatus for baking biscuit-cups for ice-cream." According to Valvona's application, they were intended to be "filled with ice-cream, which can then be sold by the venders of ice-cream in public thoroughfares or other places." His patent was granted in 1902.[14] In 1903, Italo Marchiony, "a citizen of the United States, residing in the borough of Manhattan," received a patent for a mold that made ten ice cream cups at a time.[15] His grandson, William Marchiony, reported that Italo Marchiony had started out by selling lemon ices from a pushcart on Wall Street. He had wrapped them in paper cones so he wouldn't have to wash out penny-lick glasses. Later, he experimented with making confectionary cones. They became so popular that he invented and patented a machine to make them in quantity.[16] Although Valvona's and Marchiony's cones had flat, not pointed, bottoms, and both patent applications used the word *cups* rather than *cones*, it is clear they were making a variation on what we think of as an ice cream cone.

All of which brings us to 1904 and the fair. As one story goes, an ice cream vendor at the fair couldn't wash his dishes fast enough to keep up with the demand. Ernest Hamwi, a Syrian native, was making wafers called *zalabia* at the next stand and noticed his neighbor's dilemma. He rolled one of his wafers into a cone shape and gave it to the ice cream vendor to fill. Before long, everyone was strolling along licking ice cream from a cone. Later Hamwi established the Missouri Cone Company. It's a charming story, and it may even be true. A similar story cast Abe Doumar, a Syrian immigrant who sold souvenirs at the fair by day and *zalabia* at night, as the person who introduced the cone at the fair. In this version, Doumar was inspired to roll up the cone the same way he rolled Syrian flatbread into a cone shape to make a sandwich. He is said to have shared the idea with other vendors, thus spreading it throughout the fair. He later opened ice cream stands at Coney Island and then in Norfolk, Virginia. There are other claimants as well.[17]

Although none of them invented the cone, it is possible that each of them came up with the idea of putting ice cream in it without knowing it had been done before. Perhaps each one was the first, as far as he knew, to think of it. It's unlikely that they had read Francatelli or Marshall or had dined at one of the fancy dinner parties where pyramids of frosted, decorated, ice-cream-filled cones were served. Possibly they did not know about the cones Valvona and Marchiony made. However, it does seem more likely, since ice cream cones were being sold on the streets of New York and Manchester, that the people who sold ice cream cones at the fair came prepared to do so. But even if they did, many of the people who were visiting the fair had never seen or heard of an ice cream cone before. For them, visiting the spectacular fair and tasting an ice cream cone for the very first time must have been an unforgettable experience.

Becoming a Business

The ice cream cone did wonders for the ice cream business. "Ever since the invention of the ice cream cone, demand for ice cream has increased," said L. J. Schumaker of Philadelphia's Crane Ice Cream Company when he addressed the annual ice cream convention in 1919: "If you can put an idea in the mind of a child, the idea will last for the lifetime of that child. . . . You are not talking to baldheaded people, but to a people with a long term of years before them. The first idea is to teach children to eat ice cream once a week, twice or three times a week. When he grows up, he is going to want ice cream in his family."[18] Schumaker was right. Annual per capita consumption had been about a quart in 1900. By 1915 it had quadrupled to a gallon.[19] The ice cream cone and the ice cream sandwich had made ice cream a treat for all ages and incomes. In addition, the temperance movement was gaining ground, and people were turning to ice cream as an alternative to alcohol. As early as 1909, the editor of the *Ice Cream Trade Journal*, Thomas D. Cutler, wrote, "As the anti-saloon craze is rolling on larger and larger, it would seem that the ice cream business throughout the country will enjoy a banner year. Even in New York the effect of the great moral craze is being noted. There are 800 fewer saloons in New York County this year than last, and ice cream parlors are springing up on all sides."[20]

Temperance and then Prohibition made ice cream more popular than ever as local barrooms and luxurious bars alike were turned into ice cream parlors. Brewers, including Anheuser-Busch, became ice cream manufacturers. A Brooklyn brewery sold ice cream at Coney Island during the summer of 1920 in the hopes that it would replace beer sales. At ice cream makers' conventions, attendees sang this popular song, to the tune of "Old Black Joe":

Gone are the days when Father was a souse.
Gone are the days of the weekly family rows,
Gone from this land since prohibition's here—
He brings a brick of ice cream home instead of a beer.
Chorus:
He's coming, he's coming; we can see him coming near—
He brings a brick of ice cream home instead of a beer.[21]

In the early years of the twentieth century, the ice cream business still depended on supplies of ice and salt. Manufacturers still made ice cream in small batch freezers that, except for using steam and then electric power to churn the ice cream, had not changed much in fifty years. They still delivered ice cream from horse-drawn wagons. Nevertheless, the business was thriving. Despite the antiquated methods, wholesalers turned out a range of ice cream products. In one factory, some workers made, molded, and wrapped multiflavored ice cream bricks while others produced richer, more expensive "French" ice creams. Still others made ornamental works in ice cream for banquets and private parties. After the various ice creams were made, they were packed in porcelain-lined iron cans, placed in wooden tubs packed with ice and salt, and loaded onto wagons to be delivered to local retail shops, drugstores, homes, and ice cream parlors. Once delivered, the ice creams had to be frequently repacked in a fresh ice-and-salt mixture to keep them frozen.[22]

In 1921, a five-gallon can of ice cream was shipped by railway express from Ohio to a convention in Seattle, Washington. The trip took six days and seven nights, and the ice cream had to be repacked in ice at all the stops along the way. It arrived in perfect condition, according to a contemporary report. The experiment was a success, but no one imagined such shipments would become a commonplace distribution method. The industry simply saw them as a convenience for well-to-do ice cream lovers. "In a few years from now it may be possible for eastern tourists to go to Sunny California to spend the winter and have their favorite brand of ice cream shipped from the east to grace their tables in the west," predicted the *Ice Cream Review*.[23]

National distribution was far in the future, but change was coming. After years with relatively few developments, ice cream production was beginning to modernize. Major advances in equipment and freezing techniques would soon transform the way ice cream was made, distributed, and sold. Mechanical refrigeration would do away with the need for ice and salt. And ice cream would become a year-round treat.

In 1902, Burr Walker, son of the owner of a Pennsylvania ice cream company, experimented with freezing ice cream with brine cooled by an ammonia compressor. His circulating brine freezer sped up the process and allowed for greatly increased production. It could freeze a forty-quart batch of ice cream in six to eight minutes. The finished ice cream was then put in cans and hardened in brine-filled storage tanks rather than packed in ice and salt. Trade publications called the circulating brine freezer a "major advance in manufacturing because it greatly shortened freezing time."[24] Many other innovations followed. In 1905, Emery Thompson, manager of an ice cream and soda fountain in a New York City department store, developed a gravity-fed vertical batch freezer. Thompson's freezer made production almost continuous. As soon as one batch of ice cream emerged from the bottom of the freezer into a can, a new batch could be poured into the top without having to stop the machine. By 1910, continuous-process freezers could produce from 60 to 150 gallons per hour.[25] The homogenizer, also known as a viscolizer, was introduced in 1905. This machine whipped the cream mixture to make it smooth and creamy and achieve consistent overrun.[26] *Overrun* is an industry term for the amount of air that is whipped into a mixture during freezing to make it swell in volume. Too much overrun and the mixture is too airy and light. Not enough and it is too heavy and thick. Until the homogenizer came into use, mixtures were inconsistent and ice cream was often lumpy.

To accommodate the new freezers and other equipment, companies began to build new plants and remodel old ones. They built hardening rooms, where just-made ice cream was stored to firm up before delivery. They added larger carriage houses to accommodate more delivery wagons. In 1912, the Wheat Ice Cream Company built a three-story brick plant in Buffalo, New York. Heavy equipment was housed in the basement. Ice cream was processed and shipped from the first floor. Offices and the laboratory were located on the top floor. The plant's tanks could hold 14,000 gallons of milk products. There were three 160-gallon mixers, three gelatin heaters, sixteen freezers, and nine hardening rooms, each of which could store up to 8,000 gallons. One room in the plant was reserved for making bricks and molded ice creams. Another was dedicated to washing and sterilizing the cans. Next to the building, a wagon room and stable housed one hundred horses. It was the country's "finest and most perfect ice cream factory," according to the *Ice Cream Trade*

Journal.[27] Mechanical refrigeration had not yet had its full impact on the business, but ice cream makers were becoming manufacturers.

From Recipe to Formula

Up until the twentieth century, most ice cream was either Philadelphia-style, consisting of cream, sugar, and a flavoring; or custard-style, made with cream or milk or both, egg yolks, sugar, and a flavoring. The recipes were similar whether the ice cream was being made by professionals or home cooks. Both added fillers such as gelatin, cornstarch, and flour occasionally, but as Mary Lincoln, Rorer, and others suggested, the additions made inferior ice creams. However, after the turn of the century, the use of such ingredients increased dramatically, particularly by manufacturers. They justified their use by citing the demands of the business, pointing out that the storage and distribution requirements of ice cream factories necessitated using ingredients that stabilized mixtures and allowed ice cream to keep better. "When large quantities of cream are made for a moderate-priced trade, gelatin is often used to help the cream 'stand up,' or retain its shape when shipped or held for several days," wrote H. E. Van Norman in the 1910 edition of the *Cyclopedia of American Agriculture.*[28] According to a 1913 edition of the *Confectioners' and Bakers' Gazette,* gelatin was necessary to prevent "coarse granulation or crystallization of the watery portion of the ice cream." It was also said to keep ice cream from softening or melting too fast when served and to aid in digestibility.[29]

At the beginning of the century, there were no mandated standards for ice cream, despite concerns about its content and safety. But after the passage of the Pure Food and Drug Act in 1906, Dr. Harvey Wiley of the Department of Agriculture required that ice cream manufactured for interstate commerce contain not less than 14 percent butterfat. This was not met with universal approval. The manufacturers found it difficult to meet new state and federal government requirements to achieve a consistent percentage of butterfat in their ice creams using traditional ingredients and traditional recipes. The *New York Times* wondered whether the new federal standards would restrict ice cream to the wealthy. The *Ice Cream Trade Journal* simply opposed them. Some states adopted the federal guidelines; others set their own standards, some higher, some lower. The Supreme Court upheld the federal standards in 1916, and the trade made an effort to meet them.[30] In 1924, a congressional committee proposed new standards: 12 percent butterfat, 20 percent milk solids, and 0.5 percent stabilizer. In addition, the committee specified that a gallon of ice cream should weigh at least four and three-quarter pounds. After much controversy and argument, the 1906 standards were rescinded. However, the new ones did not pass, and regulation was left to the states.[31]

Whether manufacturers made their ice cream to meet federal or state requirements or to meet business imperatives, the trade literature began publishing formulas designed to achieve specific percentages of butterfat and solids. The *Ice Cream Review* ran a regular column by Professor A. C. Baer of the University of Wisconsin in which he answered manufacturers' questions about their formulas and suggested adjustments to help them meet their goals. Some shipped samples of their ice cream to him for his analysis in the magazine.

It was not easy to make ice cream with a particular butterfat content as well as consistent quality while using fresh cream, according to industry experts. For one thing, cream was inconsistent, containing more or less fat from day to day. Moreover, most dairies were in the countryside, and the milk had to be collected and shipped to the cities, where the ice cream plants and their customers were located. In the days before mechanically refrigerated trucks and trains were available, milk and cream did not travel well. They often arrived at the ice cream plant sour, sullied with hay or manure, infused with an unpleasant off-flavor, or "infected by pathogenic bacteria," according to the authors of an industry book called *Ice Cream, Carbonated Beverages*.[32] The book was written and published in 1924 by the Warner-Jenkinson Manufacturing Company of Saint Louis, makers of Red Seal brand products used in the ice cream and soda fountain industries, including stabilizers, ripeners, extracts, syrups, and food colors. Warner-Jenkinson pointed out that, if the milk was bad, the cream would be bad and the ice cream would be bad. As they saw it, the solution to the problem was for large manufacturers to use a mixture of butter, water, and milk solids rather than fresh cream. The mixture could be reconverted into cream by using machines such as a viscolizer or emulsifier. According to the Warner-Jenkinson people, such a mixture made the manufacturer "independent of the ordinary supply of sweet cream, enabling him to work up sweet cream from butter at any time and in the exact quantities required." The authors said that it "yields a product that is smoother, of finer texture, and less liable to separate than ice cream made from non-viscolized cream."[33] The company's book contained ten tables or formulas that would produce an ice cream mixture with a specific butterfat content using various combinations of milk solids, butter, skim milk, evaporated milk, or cream. Table 1, the first and simplest, called for the following ingredients to make a hundred-pound mixture with an 8 percent butterfat content:

Sugar	Filler	Butter	Milk Powder	Water
14	1	10	12.5	62.5

To achieve 14 percent butterfat, the following mixture was recommended:

Sugar	Filler	Butter	Milk Powder	Water
13	1	17.5	10.5	58

The authors offered instructions on transforming one of these mixtures into a flavored ice cream. For chocolate ice cream: "Any ordinary vanilla mix can be converted into chocolate ice cream by addition of 1¼ to 2 lbs. of Red Seal Cocoa to every 45 or 50 lbs. of mix (Tables 1–10)." To make a bisque or marshmallow ice cream: "To 45 or 50 lbs. of ordinary vanilla mix, add 1 to 2 lbs. of chopped dry macaroons or chopped marshmallows. . . . One gallon of Red Seal Marshmallow will improve the product." Beyond noting the federal standards for butterfat mandated for ice cream used in interstate trade (14 percent for ice cream and 12 percent for ice cream containing fruit or nuts), the authors took no position on the ideal percentage, saying that it was a matter of personal judgment. "We suggest that the best ice cream for any manufacturer," they wrote, "is the one that produces for his concern the largest annual net profits."[34]

England was following America's lead, according to the British confectioner P. Michael, who studied and emulated American techniques. In his book, *Ices and Soda Fountain Drinks*, which was published in the early 1920s, he wrote, "The trade here is emerging from its elementary stages, as it did about twenty years ago in the States." Saying that it would be years before the British had the big ice cream factories of the Americans, he suggested that they should make a start. He explained that a cream containing 25 percent fat, which he called the best for ice cream making, was *"in every way* similar for our purposes" to a mixture of butter, milk powder, and water, and the mixture would cost *"much less."* The result, he wrote, was "more use of butter and powdered milk, and less of the costly fresh cream and milk." He called this the "whole secret of the transformation of the American trade into what it is now."[35]

The more the ice cream business expanded, the more manufacturers depended on ingredients other than milk, cream, sugar, and eggs. When cream was low in butterfat, fillers such as rice flour, cornstarch, sago (a thickener obtained from the sago palm), arrowroot, or gum tragacanth (a plant-derived thickener used in candies and icings for cake decorating, as well as in ice cream) were added to give it more body. Condensed milk and condensed skimmed milk added body and smoothness to cream. If cream was a bit on the sour side, baking soda might be added to neutralize it.[36] Egg whites helped make a more uniform product but had the disadvantages of being expensive and of tending to make the ice cream tough. If the cream or ice cream was actually too sour to use, it might be sold to a butter maker, who would add extra salt and turn it into second-rate butter.[37]

Before long, the industry began to use sugar stand-ins as well. Initially, this was necessitated by the scarcity and high price of sugar during World War I. According to the dairy industry historian Ralph Selitzer, the price of sugar increased 83 percent between 1916 and 1917. The U.S. Food Administration classified ice cream as an essential food, so it could be manufactured during the war. However, it had to be made with less sugar than previously. The Department of Agriculture concluded that a perfectly acceptable ice cream could be made by replacing up to 50 percent of its cane sugar with corn syrup and corn sugar. The department thought the consumer should be made aware of the substitution.[38] A 1917 issue of the *Ice Cream Review* suggested that ice cream be made with 10 percent less sugar, but that the sugar be reduced gradually so that customers would not notice the change.[39] The U.S. government prohibited the making of sherbets and water ices during the war because of the sugar shortages. Wheat was also restricted. In fact, Mondays and Wednesdays were wheatless days. In response, some manufacturers made ice cream cones from popcorn, but this innovation did not catch on. American ice cream manufacturers were fortunate; the British prohibited ice cream making completely during the war.

Substitutions, shortcuts, and timesavers continued to be used after the war ended, both in the United States and in England. Trade publications were filled with ads for such products as Americose, a substitute for cane sugar made with corn syrup, and "Aulocrystal, the Economical Sugar."[40] They ran ads for dried egg whites, soluble yolks, gums, margarine, "Egso, the natural egg yellow," and "Butter flavour. A most unique production. No confectioner should be without it."[41] A stabilizer called Textor was sold to make fruit ices that "will keep for weeks without a sign of icy crystals, or separation, or watering down."[42] A 1919 ad for Gumpert's Ice Cream Improver said it was not "gelatine or filler" but did not say what it was.[43] Artificial flavors were also gaining ground. Mapleine substituted for maple syrup. Van-vo-Lan took the place of vanilla. Caramala stood in for caramel. Cremilla was, according to its ads, better than vanilla.

Ice cream powders had been introduced at the beginning of the century, and were claimed to require only the addition of boiling milk to produce excellent ice creams. An ad for "Frostor, the wonderful preparation for making Fruit Frosts, Water Ices, Ice-Cream of all kinds, as smooth as pure

Cream," declared that "if Frostor is used it is impossible to have rough or gritty ices."[44] Merrills's patent ice-cream mixture was said to make "ices and custard of the best quality." Its custard powder was "a triumph."[45] Italia ice cream powder made "de-luxe" ice cream without sugar or eggs. The tops of the letters spelling *Italia* were drawn to look as if they were frosted with snow.[46] Rennet, in the form of tablets and sold under the brand name Junket Cream Tablets, was sold to the trade as early as 1905. The company said Junket Cream Tablets made ice cream for the soda fountain that was "Rich, Smooth, Velvety, Exquisitely Delicious and Relishable," at half the cost of ordinary ice cream.[47]

Some of the same products were being marketed to home cooks as well. The makers of Junket tablets promised consumers that their use would help them make ice cream at home quickly and easily.[48] The Jell-O Company sold ice cream powders for home use that were said to produce ice cream for a penny a plate. The powders were sold for thirteen cents a package, or two for twenty-five cents, and each package made about a quart and a half of ice cream. At the time, a quart of ice cream bought at an ice cream parlor or soda fountain would have cost as much as forty-five cents. One could choose vanilla, chocolate, strawberry, lemon, maple, or unflavored powders. Not merely economical, Jell-O ice cream powder was supposed to save time and labor. According to a 1922 ad insert, it "requires no sugar, no eggs, no flavoring, no cooking, no bother at all in order to make the most delicious ice cream. . . . Just Add Milk."[49]

In a 1933 trade book called *Practical Ice Cream Making and Practical Mix Tables*, Arthur D. Burke, who was the head of the Dairy Department at Alabama Polytechnic Institute, suggested that the quality of commercial ice creams was inconsistent. The problem, he said, was that "all too frequently the ice cream maker relies on his own judgment as to what constitutes an ideal product." His solution? "Sherbets and ices should be carefully standardized and made up on the basis of one hundred pounds just as an ice cream mix, for in that way only, can a standard article be prepared."[50]

Burke's book offered formulas to make mixtures containing 8, 10, 12, 14, or 16 percent butterfat. For each percentage, he offered ten different formulas made up of ingredients such as butter, milk, skim powder, sweetened condensed milk, and evaporated milk. In addition to the many formulas, the book covered the advantages and disadvantages of such ingredients as fresh or dried eggs, frozen cream, and fresh, frozen, and canned fruits. It discussed pasteurization, homogenization, storage, bacteria, and testing. It included a chapter on sweeteners and how to calculate quantities whether using cane or beet sugar or sweeteners made from corn, malt, or the mix of dextrose and fructose called "invert" sugar. Burke did believe flavor was important, and suggested that ice cream makers hold tastings to compare the flavor of ice creams made with different vanilla extracts, fruit syrups, or other flavorings. Since he believed women were more sensitive to flavor than men, he suggested asking "prominent women of the community" to participate in the taste tests.[51]

In addition to the ingredient formulas, trade publications offered methods for determining accurate costs of ingredients, ways to reduce operating costs, and guidance in figuring out profit percentages. Manufacturing ice cream had become a big business. The authors and editors of the trade publications wanted to make sure it was a profitable one.

Ice Cream, in Season

The quality of ice cream may have been dropping, but the quantity was going up dramatically. National ice cream production had been estimated at five million gallons in 1899. Over the next few years, new production methods, coupled with new products such as the ice cream cone, resulted in a giant leap forward for the business. In 1909, national production reached twenty-nine million gallons.[52] It hit seventy-two million gallons in 1914.[53] Still, the business was primarily local, and, in most areas, it was still seasonal. However, the meaning of seasonality had changed. In the eighteenth century, Emy and other confectioners thought it was imprudent to make ice cream in the winter. When they were required to do so by their employers, they flavored winter ice creams with chocolate or cinna-mon because the fresh strawberries or peaches they used in summer were unavailable. To early-twentieth-century ice cream manufacturers, season-ality meant just one thing: their customers did not eat enough ice cream in winter. As a result, they had only a few months to make a year's pay, partic-ularly if they did business in small towns. "You have five months in which the revenue from your business is at its height, three months in which it is an even break under the best of conditions, and four long months in which you starve," said one industry leader.[54]

To get the season off to a positive start, ice cream companies held pa-rades complete with marching bands. They decorated delivery wagons to look like ice cream cartons, gave fans to the ladies, and treated the crowds to free ice cream. On April 3, 1913, thousands eagerly lined up along the streets of Nashville, Tennessee, for the annual Union Ice Cream Company parade. The company celebrated the start of the season with decorated horse-drawn wagons, a twenty-piece band, a touring car full of executives, and, best of all, ten thousand free ice cream bricks for the crowd.[55] Even if a company did well early in the season, it could end the year in the red. A cool, wet summer could be disastrous. Winter was always difficult. To sur-vive, many companies produced other products during the cold months. One, called a charlotte russe, consisted of a piece of cake topped with whipped cream and a cherry, encased in a paper wrapper.[56] Soda fountain operators introduced "hot sodas" such as hot chocolate, hot malted milk, tea, coffee, and hot lemonade to attract off-season customers. Soon foun-tain operators added chowders, bouillons, and later, sandwiches to improve winter business.

The *Ice Cream Review* regularly offered its readers suggestions on how to improve winter sales. It recommended advertising more frequently, offering new flavors or syrups, and making ice cream available at local events. Ads also promoted new products as off-season sales ideas. A mince sundae—a fruit, wine, and brandy ice cream topping—was pro-posed, and its manufacturer offered retailers free window posters to publicize the new sundae. One ad promoted a "Yuletide" ice cream in the form of a three-flavor brick. The magazine frequently ran articles featuring wintertime success stories from innovative ice cream makers. One told of a Montana company that had expanded its business by selling ice cream at events, including the annual dance to benefit the fire department. Ice cream makers at a Spokane dairy found success by making fancy molded ice creams during the winter of 1920, according to another. They molded ice cream into the shapes of a hen and her chicks, Uncle Sam, Martha and George Washington, and a Santa Claus holding a toy Christmas tree with a tiny candle on top to be lit when the ice cream was served. The article stressed the high level of skill involved in the creations: "The old white hen sitting on her generous nest of downy spun-sugar, surrounded by a brood of life-like buff and brown chicks, looks like a permanent work of art—not a quart of ice cream surrounded by a few scoopfuls of the same material."[57] The *Confectioners' and Bakers' Gazette* recommended hosting ice cream parties and inviting theater or dancing groups to meet at the parlor for refreshments. It also suggested that "children may be offered some little inducement for visiting the parlor mornings."[58] Still, wintertime ice cream was a hard sell.

Then, in December 1921—success. The *Ice Cream Review* carried an ad for the Russell Stover Company that asked, "What is Eskimo Pie?" The ad explained how ice cream makers could obtain a license to manufacture the brand-new product, a chocolate-covered ice cream bar. Most important, it stressed that the Eskimo Pie would do wonders for winter ice cream sales.[59] It did. Just one month later, in the January 1922 issue, ice cream equipment companies ran ads promising to supply everything needed to make Eskimo Pies, "the latest ice cream confection." Soon there were ads for tinfoil wrappers, chocolate for coating the ice cream, chocolate warmers, dipping tables, pie formers, cutters, and containers in which to transport the pies. During the next few months, the ads increased and competition materialized. Chocolate-covered ice cream products were everywhere. There was a chocolate-coated ice cream baseball complete with seams.[60]

A "Sundae-ette," defined as "the Candy Way to eat Ice Cream," was a layer of brick ice cream sandwiched between two crisp, sweet wafers and covered with chocolate.[61] "Tri-A-Cone" was a factory-filled ice cream cone, dipped in chocolate, frozen, and packaged in a glassine bag.[62]

That April, the *Ice Cream Review* ran a forty-eight-page supplement filled with ads and articles on chocolate-coated ice cream products and the equipment used to make them. It called the Eskimo Pie a new sensation that was not actually new, and noted that Val Miller had published a recipe for chocolate-covered ice cream cannonballs in his 1907 book, *Thirty-six Years an Ice Cream Maker*. The editors were not criticizing the Eskimo Pie; they were questioning why no one had thought to put such a product on the market earlier. The editors noted that the winter of 1921–22 ended with profits instead of losses. Attributing much of the Eskimo Pie's success to advertising, they said it was good for the cocoa bean business, the chocolate-coating business, the tinfoil business, the equipment business, and the ice cream business. (Clearly, it was good for the trade magazine business as well.) In England, Michael wrote, "America went Eskimo Pie mad and purchased millions."[63] When the Eskimo Pie Corporation was admitted to trade on the New York Stock Exchange in 1927, it was valued at twenty-five million dollars.[64]

The creator of the Eskimo Pie was Christian K. Nelson of Iowa. The son of a dairyman, Nelson taught high school and also ran an ice cream parlor. According to the story, one spring day in 1919 a young boy arrived at Nelson's shop with just a nickel to spend. He couldn't decide between an ice cream sandwich and a chocolate bar. The boy's dilemma inspired Nelson to experiment with a chocolate-covered ice cream bar. He spent months experimenting, and eventually found success by dipping a solidly frozen stick of ice cream into chocolate heated to between 80 and 90 degrees, then placing it in a freezing container. He called his new treat a "Temptation I-Scream Bar," and began selling it locally. When he met Russell Stover, who was superintendent of an Omaha ice cream company, the two men decided to go into business together. Their handwritten agreement, dated July 13, 1921, noted that Nelson had applied for a patent on the invention and Stover had agreed to pay half the cost of the patent. It called for them to divide business profits equally. They also agreed that "because of his business experience & knowledge," Stover would "assume the management, consulting C. K. Nelson on any new development." Changing the name to "Eskimo Pie," they began selling the one-and-a-half-ounce bars in Des Moines for ten cents each. They were wildly successful. The partners decided to sell manufacturing rights to local ice cream companies for five hundred to a thousand dollars, plus royalties on each pie sold. According to company records, by the spring of 1922 they had twenty-seven hundred licensees and were selling a million Eskimo Pies a day.[65]

Nelson was awarded the patent in 1922, but it was so broadly written that other ice cream makers frequently challenged it, and the company lost money defending it. Stover sold his share of the company and devoted himself to what became the very successful Russell Stover Candies. Nelson sold the Eskimo Pie Company to the manufacturer of the foil the pies were wrapped in, United States Foil Company, later to become the Reynolds Metals Company. But he continued to be associated with the company and developed many new products. The patent was later declared invalid.

Despite the legal setbacks, the Eskimo Pie had succeeded in making ice cream a year-round treat. It also inspired a burst of creativity among other ice cream makers. Harry Burt of Youngstown, Ohio, had begun delivering ice cream from a motorized delivery wagon in 1902, a time when most companies still delivered by horse-drawn wagons. In 1920, he created a chocolate-covered ice cream bar and put a lollipop stick in it so it would be less messy to eat. He called it the Good Humor Ice Cream Sucker. Later it became the Good Humor Ice Cream Bar. To sell it, he painted one of his trucks white, equipped it with bells from the family bobsled, and put a driver in a pristine white uniform behind the wheel.[66] The Good Humor Ice Cream Company became hugely successful, and the Good Humor man became ubiquitous. Whether he sold from a pushcart, a truck, or a tricycle, the Good Humor man was always scrupulously clean and wholesome, the perfect symbol for the ice cream he sold. During the 1930s and 1940s, he appeared as a character in dozens of movies, including *The Good Humor Man*, with the popular actor Jack Carson in the title role.[67]

The Popsicle was the next big frozen novelty. Frank Epperson, its creator, said he had made his first one in 1905, when he was a boy of eleven. He had mixed a flavored drink powder with water and left it out on his back porch with the stirring stick still in it. That night, the temperature dropped and the liquid froze. The next morning, Epperson enjoyed the first-ever Popsicle. When he became an adult, he made the treats occasionally and called them Epsicles, apparently a combination of *Epperson* and *icicle*. His children called them Pop's Sicles, which became Popsicle. He formed a company in 1923, and began selling Popsicles at amusement parks and beaches. They were known as a "drink on a stick" and an "all-day sucker with a chill" and were an instant hit.[68] One Coney Island stand was said to have sold eight thousand on one summer day that year. In 1924, the company reported sales of 6.5 million Popsicles.[69]

Pies, popsicles, bricks, cones, and other novelties were replacing the elegant molded and painted ice creams made by confectioners. In a 1913 article titled "Then and Now," the *Confectioners' and Bakers' Gazette* described the superior workmanship of the previous century's confectioners. "Ice cream was made in the shape of fruit—apples, pears, plums, cherries, grapes, etc. and they were made so perfect in color, in shape and design that it was hard to distinguish them from the genuine article," it reported. The story went on to say, "This art is not altogether lost; there are still some chefs in some of the prominent hotels who know how to produce a piece of art of this kind." The article suggested that, if one were to show one of the early confectioners an ice cream brick and suggest it was in any way connected to his art, he'd walk away in disgust.[70] Despite the magazine's gloomy outlook, molded ice creams were still made, although perhaps they were not as artistically made as they had been.

Roaring for Ice Cream in the Twenties

Clearly by the 1920s, business was booming. Soda fountains were more popular than ever. Novelty ice creams were all the rage. As demand increased, production techniques improved to keep up. Most important of all, mechanical refrigeration finally became feasible.

Refrigeration technology had been developing throughout the nineteenth century, but it was not until after World War I that it had a substantial impact, first on business and then on the home. By 1920, ice cream plants that used ammonia-based refrigeration systems were being built. The newest ice cream freezers did not require ice, salt, or brine. They operated by simple ammonia expansion, and ads proclaimed they would be "a great money maker for the ice cream manufacturer."[71] Over the next few years, refrigeration systems switched to other, safer refrigerants as the industry continued to advance. In 1923, at the Twenty-third Annual Ice Cream Convention, the Nizer Cabinet Company (which later became the Kelvinator Company) unveiled its new automatic electric refrigeration cabinet for ice cream parlors, soda fountains, and other retail outlets. The vice president of the Arctic Ice Cream Company, Glen P. Cowan, reported that his company had tested the new cabinets in three hundred of its stores. The cost savings were stunning. Since the cabinets required no ice or salt, the delivery trucks had to carry only a small amount to keep the ice cream frozen until they arrived at the stores. Previously, it had taken forty-three pounds of ice to deliver one gallon of ice cream. Under the new system, it took but two pounds. This meant they used fewer trucks and employed fewer workers to deliver the same amount of ice cream. The new cabinets swept the industry.[72]

There were still few refrigerators in homes of the day, and those that did exist did not have freezers. The companies that became Kelvinator and Frigidaire were manufacturing refrigerators for home use by 1920, but there were only twenty thousand in use in 1923. That is hardly surprising, since the refrigerators cost about $900 at a time when a typical household's annual income was about $2,000 and the price of Ford's Model T had dropped to about $300.[73] The first home refrigerators looked very much like iceboxes with dark wood exteriors, but by 1935, streamlined white enamel refrigerators had replaced them. The price had dropped to an average of $170, and a million and a half were sold.[74] They did not have freezer compartments large enough to store more than a few ice cube trays, so storing ice cream was still a challenge. Whether a family made its own ice cream or bought it, it would have been eaten, if not immediately, then within a day or so. It was not until after World War II that the average household had a freezer in which to store its ice cream.

During the 1920s, many other advances in ice cream production occurred. Packaging was mechanized. The early machines could package twenty quarts per minute, or twelve hundred quarts per hour, ten times as many as by the manual method. Conveyor systems were installed in plants. An automatic brick-slicer was introduced. A machine run by two operators that could coat and wrap ninety dozen Eskimo Pies an hour was in use by 1923. It increased productivity so much that the price of the pies was cut in half, to five cents.[75] In 1928, Clarence Vogt of Louisville, Kentucky, invented the continuous process freezer. It froze the ice cream in a continuous stream, controlled overrun accurately, and allowed for the efficient use of fruit feeders and automatic packaging.[76] The large metal ice cream containers that manufacturers supplied to retail outlets were replaced by lighter-weight paper containers. Not only did the new containers weigh less, making transportation more economical, but they also did not rust and were more sanitary than metal containers.

Innovation followed innovation and made possible new products such as the Dixie cup. The idea of putting individual servings of ice cream into small paper cups was not a new one. But Dixie cups became a big hit when the Dixie Cup Company developed a two-and-a-half-ounce paper cup that could stand up to moisture, and the Mojonnier Brothers Company created a machine to fill it with two different flavors automatically. Usually one side was filled with vanilla, the other, with chocolate. A successful franchise program and extensive advertising made the five-cent novelty nationally known and a children's favorite. The company sponsored a radio show called the *Dixie*

Circus, and the undersides of Dixie cup lids were decorated with circus pictures. Kids could collect the lids and redeem them for a full-color, eight-by-eight-and-a-half-inch picture of their favorite *Dixie Circus* character. Later, movie stars and sports personalities were pictured on the lids.[77]

Despite the grumblings of the editors of the *Confectioners' and Bakers' Gazette,* molded ice creams made a comeback in the 1920s. Ice cream in the shape of turkeys, airplanes, dirigibles, and Uncle Sam began to be mass-produced, thanks to new metal-molding technology. Perhaps their quality would not have met with approval by someone such as Emy, but customers loved them.

Soda fountains were doing more ice cream business than ever. By 1929, 60 percent of the country's 58,258 drugstores had installed soda fountains. But they were hardly limited to drugstores. In his book *Soda Fountain and Luncheonette Management,* Joseph O. Dahl listed thirty different types of sites where he had seen them. They ranged from dining cars to airports, from tobacco shops to office buildings, from department stores to restaurants. As soda fountains became ubiquitous, sundaes multiplied. In the early days, there were just a handful, and they were named for their ingredients. They also required some explaining. According to the 1904 edition of *The Standard Manual of Soda and Other Beverages,* "The name of the sundae is derived from the syrup which is used; chocolate syrup makes chocolate sundae, vanilla syrup makes vanilla sundae, etc. These sundaes are usually served in what are known as sherbet cups or glasses with a sherbet spoon (which is smaller than an ice cream spoon). The nicest dispensers also serve a small glass of ice water with a sundae."[78]

Rorer introduced sundaes to home cooks with a recipe for vanilla ice cream with hot chocolate sauce in her 1905 edition of *Dainty Dishes for All the Year Round.* Explaining that the sauce must be made just before serving, she said that, when the hot sauce was poured over the ice cream, it "forms a sort of icing."[79]

By the 1920s, no explanations were needed. Everyone knew what sundaes were, and their names were no longer limited to the name of their syrup. There was a Bachelor sundae, a Boston Club sundae, a Delmonico, a Merry Widow, a Coney Island, a Theda Bara, an Easter Sundae, and more. A Hawaiian Special was made with vanilla ice cream, crushed orange and pineapple, and a topping of marshmallow.[80] The Aviation Glide was made in an oblong dish and consisted of banana halves flanking a scoop each of chocolate, vanilla, and strawberry ice creams. Nabisco wafers represented the forward and tail ends of the air ship, and a cherry atop the chocolate ice cream stood in for the pilot. Crushed cherries, pineapple, pecans, and whipped cream completed the sundae, which was said to be a big hit with university students. It sold for twenty cents.[81]

Sundaes, banana splits, sodas, milk shakes, parfaits, malteds, frappés, frosteds, and floats were all on the soda fountain menu. Ice cream sales were soaring. By 1930, the industry was producing 277 million gallons of ice cream annually, and Americans were eating nine quarts a year.[82] Yet another ice cream novelty was introduced at the beginning of the decade. The Drumstick combined two ice cream favorites, the sundae and the cone. The cone was filled with ice cream at the factory, hardened, hand-dipped in chocolate syrup, rolled in ground peanuts, and packaged in glassine bags. Its name was born when its creator, I. C. Parker, advertising manager of the Pangburn Candy and Ice Cream Company in Fort Worth, Texas, showed the new product to his wife. Jewel Parker said that it looked just like a chicken drumstick.[83]

The cone had journeyed from ancient Greece to medieval Paris, from Victorian London to the grand 1904 Louisiana Purchase Exposition in Saint Louis. It had been served on its own and then filled with fruits, creams, and finally ice creams. Then, in 1930, it was recreated in a factory in Texas to look like a chicken drumstick. Some might say this was a sorry fate for an esteemed confection. But it was an inevitable result of the industry's development. In the nineteenth century, confectioners had dipped cones in royal icing, sprinkled them with chopped nuts, and filled them with whipped cream. In the twentieth century, manufacturers filled cones with ice cream, dipped them in chocolate, and rolled them in chopped nuts. Wittingly or not, the manufacturers were carrying on a venerable tradition.

EIGHT

Ice Cream for Breakfast

When Howard Deering Johnson was a child in Quincy, Massachusetts, he loved the strawberry ice cream his mother made on Sunday afternoons in the summer. She used fresh cream from the family's cows and luscious ripe strawberries, and he never forgot the flavor. The years passed, and Johnson grew up. He served in France during World War I, came back, and worked as a salesman for his father's cigar business. In 1925, he bought a drugstore with a small soda fountain in Quincy's Wollaston neighborhood. Johnson started out by buying his ice cream from a local manufacturer. But he remembered good ice cream, and this was not good ice cream. "Every time we opened up a drum of vanilla in front of a customer, the fumes gave away the artificial flavoring," he recalled later. He decided to provide his customers with ice cream that was "as good as the homemade ice cream they all remembered."

His first batch was not a success. When he served it, one customer said it would be just great if he "could get the sand out of it." Johnson kept working on the mixture, and soon he was making a rich, high-butterfat, smooth ice cream. Before long, people were lining up for Howard Johnson's ice cream. Since the soda fountain seated only ten people, he decided to expand by opening an ice cream stand at nearby Wollaston Beach during the summer. To attract attention, he painted the stand orange. Whether it was the bright color or the quality of the ice cream, the stand drew crowds. On one hot August day, Johnson sold fourteen thousand ice cream cones. He packed the ice cream in drums at the drugstore and delivered it to the beach in a taxicab. When the ice cream ran out, he'd send back to the store for more and call out to the crowd, "Stand by, everybody. More ice cream on its way."[1] By 1929, business could hardly have been better. Then the Depression hit.

The Depression of the 1930s and the repeal of Prohibition in 1933 were devastating for the ice cream business. Opinions vary as to which was more to blame, but the combination hit the business hard. As one industry magazine put it, "The dime that went for soda now frequently goes for beer."[2] Ice cream had been one of the nation's fastest-growing industries. In 1929, Americans were eating nine quarts of ice cream per person annually, and production was more than 277 million gallons. In 1933, ice cream production dropped below 162 million gallons, its lowest level since 1919, and annual per-person consumption dropped to just over five quarts.[3] Trade magazines, previously one hundred or more pages long, shrank to sixty pages or fewer. Many in the industry had never experienced bad times and were at a loss for a solution as the numbers spiraled downward. In 1933, the president of the International Association of Ice Cream Manufacturers, G. G. Kindervater, described the situation in uncompromising terms:

Everything was wonderful while we were riding the crest of the wave.

Then suddenly and without warning something happened—the wave flattened out and we found ourselves gasping for breath and struggling to get our feet on solid ground. And, we are still engaged in that struggle.

If, after reflecting upon the course of events in the past four years, we will make an appraisal we must reach the conclusion that we were not the sound, sagacious business men we pretended to be.

We were carried away with the fantastic notion that because handsome profits were being made in the industry a miracle, for which we were responsible, was being performed.

In the light of our knowledge today we realize fully that these same handsome profits acted as a powerful drug that lulled us to sleep.[4]

Fortunately, the industry had taken some steps that kept it in good stead when the bad times arrived. Mechanization and refrigeration had helped to modernize the business. In addition, the mergers and consolidations that had taken place in the industry, as they had in so many others during the 1920s, created efficiencies. But the problems were severe and not easily overcome. Ice cream had turned back into a luxury for many, and ice cream sellers faced more competition. A new generation of street peddlers was selling second-rate ice cream, often made under less-than-sanitary conditions. These were not pristine Good Humor men, but members of the army of the unemployed who also sold apples, pencils, and anything else they could manage. To compete, some retailers added the "cheap package," a lower-quality, lower-priced ice cream, to their lines. In Los Angeles, the standard pint sold for twenty cents; the lesser one was fifteen. In Boston, the standard pint sold for fifteen to thirty cents while the cheaper one was ten to fifteen cents.[5] When customers complained that the ice cream was full of air, some states passed laws prohibiting more than 100 percent overrun or requiring a minimum weight per package.[6]

The Depression also gave rise to ice cream bootleggers. They provided lesser-grade ice cream to retailers who sold it from refrigerator cabinets bearing the brand name of reputable manufacturers. A 1933 issue of *Business Week* provided a succinct definition of a bootlegger: "A small, often a hole-in-wall, manufacturer who makes ice cream after his own standards—which may or may not be those prescribed by state laws—and sells it to dealers for less than the popular advertised brands cost them. His chief sin in the eyes of his big competitors is that he frequently tempts their dealers to let him put his 40-quart cans in the shiny refrigerated cabinets that they furnish for the exclusive use of their own product."[7]

According to the *Ice Cream Trade Journal*, bootleg ice cream sold for as little as ten cents a package. It reported that "certain foreign fats, reprocessed butter, or the like are often found to be used for ingredients."[8] If customers complained that the ice cream didn't taste the same or, worse, if it made them ill, they blamed the brand advertised on the cabinet. The retailers couldn't admit they had put the bootleggers' brand X ice cream in brand A's cabinet, because the practice of selling one manufacturer's ice cream under another's name was illegal. Some bootleggers were prosecuted. In fact, according to dairy industry historian Ralph Selitzer, 899 bootleggers were convicted in New York City between March 1 and April 21, 1933.[9] But the problem was not solved until economic conditions improved.

Scapegoats and Competitors

In their anxiety over the state of the business, some manufacturers even blamed home cooks for their problems. In 1933, the *Ice Cream Review* called homemade ice cream "make shift" and wrote that comparing it to manufactured ice cream was like comparing a stagecoach to a steam railroad. Without stating exactly who would deliver the message or how, the *Review* said the housewife needed to be told that her ice cream was not good. In fact, it was an embarrassment to serve to her guests, and they would talk about her behind her back if she did so. Referring to bread and soap as well as ice cream, the editors stated flatly, "Technically trained men . . . have learned how to make these things in a better way."[10]

At the time, those few housewives who could afford new mechanical refrigerators were learning how to make the most of them. Appliance manufacturers published pamphlets, booklets, and even hardcover books explaining how to make everything from refrigerator cookies to chilled soups, from ice cubes (plain, colored, or with rosebuds or mint leaves frozen in them) to ice creams. "The electric refrigerator is yet a new invention and the total sum of its usefulness has not in any way been discovered," wrote Alice Bradley in *Electric Refrigerator Menus and Recipes,* a book whose subtitle was "Recipes prepared especially for the General Electric Refrigerator." It was published in 1927. "It remains for the users of electric refrigerators to find new ways to make it serve them."[11]

Making ice cream in the new refrigerators was simpler than using an ice cream freezer, because it did not require mixing ice and salt or churning the mixture. The cooks just poured the ice cream mixture into a tray and put it in the coldest section of the refrigerator. When it began to freeze around the edges, they took it out, mixed it with an eggbeater or a new electric mixer, and put it back in the "chilling unit." The process would be repeated once or twice to make the ice cream freeze relatively smoothly. Lacking an eggbeater or mixer, one could simply stir it with a spoon, but that required more frequent mixing and was less satisfactory. Ice cream recipes did have to be adjusted to the new method, however, and even the writers of the refrigerator company publications admitted that the ice creams were not perfect. Bradley wrote, "Sherbets and ice creams may be frozen but are not as smooth as though frozen in an ice cream freezer. They must be stirred or beaten occasionally while freezing. The addition of gelatine or flour to thicken, and of corn syrup in place of part of the sugar, insures a smoother mixture than is secured with ordinary recipes. The more cream used the richer and smoother the mixture will be."[12]

Bradley's recipe for chocolate ice cream is a good example of how she compensated for the challenges of the new method. However, it makes a thin, icy ice cream without much flavor.

CHOCOLATE ICE CREAM

In top of double boiler melt
1½ squares of chocolate, add
½ cup sugar or ¼ cup sugar and
¼ cup corn syrup;

mix well, add slowly
1 teaspoon gelatine soaked in
1 cup evaporated milk. Scald and stir until blended.
Chill, add
1 cup water and freeze. Beat with egg beater once during the freezing.
Serve with or without Marshmallow Sauce, No. 63, flavored with ½
    teaspoon vanilla in place of peppermint.[13]

When it was ready, the ice cream was turned out of the freezing tray onto a serving platter and sliced or cut into squares, or it was simply scooped or spooned from the tray into cups or bowls.

Most of the publications also included recipes for frozen desserts such as mousses, which did not require mixing during the freezing process. And they included recipes for such soda fountain specialties as ice cream sodas, floats, and syrups for sundaes. The caption under a picture of ice cream sundaes in Bradley's book asked, "Why go out to the soda fountain when you can have a chocolate or maple nut sundae at an instant's notice by visiting your own refrigerator[?]"[14] The refrigerator company publications, and all-purpose cookbooks as well, also featured recipes for frozen salads. Frozen salads—tomato salads, chicken salads, pear and ginger ale salads—were as popular at soda fountains and luncheonettes as at home. One of the best liked of the group was a fruit salad. Generally, it called for a mixture of fruits, which could include canned pineapple, maraschino cherries, pears, peaches, or apricots, combined with mayonnaise and whipped cream. Some recipes also added cream cheese or American cheese. Everything was mixed together, poured into a freezer tray, and frozen. Then the salad was sliced and served on lettuce leaves. One recipe called for sprinkling it with paprika before serving. If a housewife did not want to make her own salad, she could buy it at a soda fountain, either as an individual serving to enjoy there or by the quart to take home to serve. According to the *Ice Cream Trade Journal*, "The frozen salad is sliced and served on a lettuce leaf with sandwiches or crackers. A topping of mayonnaise is desirable. This frozen dessert is very popular as a serving at bridge parties because of its extreme palatability and food value. The product usually sells for about $1.00 a quart."[15]

It is unlikely that the housewife's frozen salads and ice creams were a threat to ice cream manufacturers. But manufacturers did face a new source of competition from small retailers operating roadside stands like Howard Johnson's. Called "wayside stands" by the *Ice Cream Trade Journal*, they had begun cropping up to serve the increasing numbers of new car owners who enjoyed driving just for the sake of driving. The stands sold sandwiches, cigars, cold drinks, baked beans, homemade pies, and invariably, ice cream. In addition, dairy farms were opening small roadside outlets called dairy bars, where they sold farm-fresh milk, butter, and ice cream.

The ice cream stands and dairy bars relied on a new small, self-contained ice cream freezer that used mechanical refrigeration. Called a counter freezer, it did not require ice and salt or hand-cranking, made five to ten gallons of ice cream at a time, and was small enough to sit on a counter. In fact, some soda fountain operators also began using the new freezers to make their ice cream. The counter freezer was developed in 1926 by Charles Taylor of Buffalo, New York, but did not have a substantial impact on the business until the 1930s, when it became more affordable.

The retailers who used counter freezers called their ice cream "homemade" and often made it in full view of the customers. However, the term was deceptive. Certainly some of them took pride in making their ice cream mixture from scratch and had every right to call it homemade. But most simply bought an ice cream mixture from a large commercial maker and poured it into the freezer. In fact, the *Ice Cream Trade Journal* wrote that the counter freezer was designed "so that retailers could manufacture their own ice cream from previously purchased mix and ingredients."[16]

The purchased mixture consisted of cream, milk, evaporated milk, or butter; milk solids; sugar; and a stabilizer or binder such as gelatin or vegetable gum. Some mixes also included dried eggs or egg yolk powder. The butterfat content could range from a low of 7 percent all the way up to 20 percent. If retailers bought a high-quality mixture and added, for example, fresh fruit or pralined nuts or rich chocolate, as many did, the quality of the ice cream would probably be quite good, maybe as good as homemade. However, if they bought a lower-quality, preflavored mix and simply froze it, calling it homemade stretched the meaning of the word considerably. The same practice occurs today.

During the 1930s, trade books and magazines provided small retailers with all the information they needed to set up a business. They offered detailed information on the composition of the manufacturers' ice cream mixtures and explained the function of the raw materials. They described how to set up a small retail operation, calculate costs, control quality, and freeze ice cream in the new counter freezers. They also provided a plethora of recipes for turning a plain mix into any flavor, from banana nut to cherry-vanilla. They offered instructions for making specials such as ice cream hearts and slippers for wedding parties, ice cream mushrooms to ornament a Yule log cake, ice cream rolls with shamrock-shaped centers for Saint Patrick's Day, and individually molded ice cream hearts, clubs, spades, and diamonds for the local bridge club. Although small retailers could purchase these ready-made from large commercial manufacturers, they could also create their own specialties by starting with a basic mixture and some molds and following the instructions provided by the trade publications.

Surviving the Depression

Business publications were filled with suggestions for improving sales during the Depression, not all of which were effective. Editors urged patience and stressed the value of continuing to advertise and merchandise. The *Ice Cream Review* encouraged its readers to think positively and avoid compromising quality. Its ideas for surviving ranged from giving calendars away to customers to providing insulated bags for take-home ice cream. Individual ice cream makers came up with a variety of imaginative ways to compete for the consumer's business. Some dairies began delivering ice cream along with milk on their regular home delivery routes. After Prohibition was repealed, it was only natural to add alcohol to ice creams. New products included Milanaise Pudding, which combined brandy-flavored whipped cream with cherry ice and vanilla ice cream. Pineapple Pudding added pineapples soaked in sauterne to vanilla ice cream. Molded Walnut Bisquit was flavored with rum, sherry, or brandy.

The industry also tried to increase sales by encouraging people to enjoy ice cream at different times of day. The Hydrox Corporation advertised "Ice Cream for Breakfast!—well, why not?" The ad copy suggested serving the company's ice cream atop cereal instead of cream, since "IT IS cream, you know . . ." A Hendlers Ice Cream Company ad claimed that the British custom of drinking tea at four o'clock was giving way to eating ice cream. "Both tea and ice cream are a whip to flagging spirits," it reported, "and Baltimoreans will do well to adopt a plate of ice cream daily to combat that four-o'clock fag."[17]

One of the more ingenious suggestions came from the author of *Practical Ice Cream Making and Practical Mix Tables.* Arthur D. Burke said winter was a good time to increase sales, because ice cream helped fortify the body against the common cold. "Wheezes and winter are synonymous, and there's an opportunity!" he wrote. "Why not fight winter wheezes with ice cream—the protective food in a concentrated form?" Burke also made more constructive suggestions including co-op advertising, weekly ice cream specials, radio advertising, and balloons given to children when they bought a dish of ice cream. He also suggested packaging ice cream in containers that would fit in "the ice cube compartments of mechanical refrigerators."[18] In fact, a Detroit company was already producing a flattened brick that did just that, but it was not immediately successful.

J. O. Dahl, author of *Soda Fountain and Luncheonette Management,* recommended attracting new business by naming a soda fountain special after a local ball player or college hero. He thought "Reducing Diet Sundaes" made with fresh, seasonal fruits and just a taste of ice cream would attract dieters. He also suggested topping children's sundaes with gumdrops. "Catch the children's fancy," he noted, "and their trade is loyal—and profitable."[19]

To control portions and cut costs, the industry experimented with factory-filled packages for sale at soda fountains and other retail outlets. One such package, called a Kleen Kup, was a factory-filled paper ice cream cup that was designed to allow the retailer to push the ice cream out onto a plate for service.[20] Another, the Twinkle-Cup, was a paper cone filled with ice cream. The retailer would remove the paper from the ice cream and slide it into a pastry cone for the customer. With its flat top, it contained roughly the same amount as a scooped cone, but it gave the illusion of more because the ice cream filled the cone all the way to its tip.[21] Because they controlled portion size, the factory-filled packages made economic sense for the business. Soda jerks too often scooped a little extra into a cone or cup, especially when they were waiting on friends.

The most successful strategy was offering the consumer a bargain. Howard Johnson sold a large ice cream cone for a dime, but it cost him eight and a half cents to produce. "Not what you'd call a great profit," he said, "but it made me and that shop and that ice cream famous."[22] A nickel product was better still. In an article in the *Ice Cream Trade Journal*, Burr Walker, the man who pioneered the circulating brine freezer, recommended selling a four-ounce ice cream cone for a nickel. It was not profitable, he said, but it was worth it to bring in customers.[23] Isaly's, the company known for the Klondike, a chocolate-covered ice cream bar, sold a unique ice cream cone that was eventually dubbed the Skyscraper. The company's clerks were trained to scoop ice cream into an inverted cone shape that towered above the pastry cone. The four-ounce cone sold for a nickel. Recalling those years, one Isaly's employee said the tall cone was the "first thing in the depression years where somebody was giving you something better than your money's worth."[24]

Even during the Depression, many customers were able to spend a nickel on ice cream, and the industry found success not only with five-cent cones but also with nickel novelties. They included a Side-Walk Sundae, described as the "syrup-center nickel sensation"; the Cho-Cho, a chocolate-malted ice cream on a stick; and the Twin Popsicle,[25] which allowed kids to split a Popsicle if they could not afford one each. Good Humor's new chocolate-covered ice milk bar sold for a nickel and was a big hit. The novelties were inexpensive and tasty. Even more important during those hard times, they were fun. They were among the attractions as well as the refreshments at the 1939 World's Fair in New York. Fairgoers visiting the Borden's exhibit lined up for the "milking merry-go-round," where they could watch cows being milked, and they watched as an ice cream novelty called a Mel-O-Rol was made. "Spectators could see how it came out in long rolls, was cut to size, packaged, sealed, weighed and put in freezers to be sold later at the Milk Bar and restaurant," according to Selitzer.[26]

The novelties, along with business consolidations, were responsible for most of the renewed growth of the ice cream business. By 1939, Americans were eating more than nine quarts of ice cream per person per year, and production had surpassed 319 million gallons. Happy days were here again.

Happy Days

The ice cream business had come back, and soda fountains were bigger than ever. Literally and figuratively. In 1937, Walgreens built a five-story, air-conditioned drugstore in Miami. In addition to its own ice cream plant, the store featured an eighty-foot-long, streamlined, stainless steel soda fountain. During the 1930s and 1940s, Hollywood cast the soda fountain in dozens of films, and every star from Mickey Rooney to Judy Garland to Elizabeth Taylor ate ice cream at one side of the counter or dished it out from the other. Lana Turner was not discovered sipping an ice cream soda at Schwab's drugstore on Hollywood and Vine, but the story was so good it triumphed over the facts. Celebrities from the worlds of sports, politics, and the arts were photographed eating ice cream, often at soda fountains. Even Snow White and the Seven Dwarfs were ice cream fans.

The roadside rivals to the soda fountains had kept growing during the Depression. The roadside stands were economical to build and operate, since they required less space and fewer furnishings than a conventional restaurant. As a result, they could charge less. The ones that specialized in ice cream were able to compete with drugstore soda fountains by also offering more variety and larger portions. In addition, the owners of roadside stands did not merely wait for customers to drive in. Some attracted drivers' attention by painting their stands bright colors, like that of

Howard Johnson's orange roofs. Others turned to imaginative, even out-landish, architecture. Families could pull up to an oversized root beer bar-rel for some root beer, drive to a building that looked like a bowl of chili to buy chili, and stop at a building that looked like an ice cream carton or an igloo to have some ice cream. The famed Brown Derby restaurant in Los Angeles was built in the shape of a hat because owner Herbert Somborn said that, as long as the food was good, a restaurant could look like any-thing at all.[27]

Although the roadside ice cream stands accompanied the growth of the automobile industry, they had antecedents in the preautomobile era. At the beginning of the nineteenth century, at places such as Tortoni's in Paris and Gunter's in London, waiters often served ices and ice creams to patrons as they sat outside in their elegant carriages. Later, American drugstore owners would sometimes send a clerk out to the curb to deliver an ice cream or soda to a customer sitting in a carriage or a wagon. In the 1920s, Americans began eating in their automobiles. At some roadside stands or drive-ins, customers parked their cars and walked up to the take-out window to order their food. Others used "tray boys" or "tray girls," later called carhops, to serve customers in their cars.[28] Some of the most famous names in the ice cream business started out operating simple roadside stands and, within a relatively short period of time, were running large chains. Although his first enterprise was a conventional drugstore soda fountain, Howard Johnson found success with his beach and road-side ice cream stands before he expanded into roadside restaurants and, later, hotels.

Johnson was well known for the high quality of his ice cream and his fa-mous twenty-eight flavors when, in 1935, he decided to open a full-service restaurant in the Cape Cod town of Orleans. Lacking the money to finance it himself, he used a business method that was common in other indus-tries but not in the restaurant business—franchising. He proposed that his friend Reginald Sprague would build and operate the restaurant; but it would bear Johnson's name, be built to his specifications, and be topped with a bright orange roof. Johnson would supply the ice cream and other foods, as well as the excellent reputation he'd established. Sprague agreed. They went into business together, and the restaurant was a success. By 1940, there were more than 130 Howard Johnson's restaurants located from Maine to Florida. Ice cream was such an important part of the business that the restaurants had a separate counter area for ice cream, desserts, and simple meals. In the early years, the counters were furnished with moveable stools. Customers could sit down for lunch, but afterward the stools were removed to make room for all the people who lined up for Howard Johnson's ice cream in the afternoon.[29]

Another successful ice cream entrepreneur, a contemporary of Howard Johnson, was born Thomas Carvelas in Greece and brought to the United States by his parents when he was a boy. In 1929, when he was twenty-three years old, the young man who called himself Tom Carvel began selling ice cream from the back of a truck. According to company lore, the truck broke down in Hartsdale, New York, on Memorial Day weekend in 1934, so he had to sell all his ice cream quickly before it melted.[30] The site became the location of the first ice cream store of what would become a national chain. Ever the innovator, over the years Carvel pioneered such concepts as "Buy one, get one free" promotions, gift certificates, round ice cream sandwiches called Flying Saucers, kosher ice cream products, and, in 1939, soft-serve ice cream.

Carvel was not the only one experimenting with soft-serve ice cream at that time. J. F. McCullough of Green River, Illinois, began making and selling ice cream in 1927 and soon started to experiment with ways to serve a softer, less frozen product. Like so many who remembered how good homemade ice cream tasted when they licked it off the dasher, McCullough liked ice cream best when it was freshly made, before it was hardened. He wanted to sell such ice cream to his retail store customers. However, before investing in the equipment he knew would be required to produce such a product consistently, McCullough and his son Alex decided to test customer interest. One of their best retailers, Sherb Noble, agreed to hold a soft ice cream promotion with them. On August 4, 1938, they offered customers "All the Ice Cream You Can Eat for 10 Cents." They went through sixteen hundred servings in two hours. Apparently no one questioned whether it was the price or the softness of the ice cream that the customers found more appealing. In any event, they began looking into machines that would make and serve soft ice cream effectively. Alex McCullough discovered a Chicago street vendor who was selling a soft frozen custard out of a small freezer. They signed an agreement with the freezer's designer, Harry Oltz, despite the fact that the freezer did not work very well. But they made some adjustments to it, and, in 1940, Noble opened the first store to dispense the McCulloughs' new soft ice cream. McCullough called the product Dairy Queen because he thought it was the "queen" of dairy products.[31] The company's typical store was a simple white building topped with a blue Dairy Queen sign featuring a tilted cone of swirled soft-serve ice cream. Dairy Queen soon became known as the cone with the curl on top.

Before the soft-serve chains could develop further, World War II intervened. Ice cream equipment manufacturers switched to building airplane parts and other military supplies. Perfecting soft-serve ice cream makers would have to wait.

Ice Cream Goes to War

During World War II, ice cream was a morale builder overseas and a symbol of patriotism at home. Americans were fortunate. The English banned ice cream during the war (although they allowed some ersatz products). Mussolini outlawed ice cream in Italy. The emperor of Japan ordered ice cream to be priced so low that it was impossible for manufacturers to produce it. But in America, despite some shortages and compromises in its quality, both civilians and members of the military continued to enjoy ice cream throughout the war years.

This was no accident. The industry lobbied hard to have ice cream included on the government's official "Basic Seven Foods Chart." Thanks to the combined efforts of the International Association of Ice Cream Manufacturers and the National Dairy Council, the government reversed a 1941 decision and declared ice cream an essential food. In 1942, the War Production Board asked (but did not require) ice cream manufacturers to make no more than twenty varieties—ten flavors of the manufacturer's choice in each of two grades. The board requested that ice cream novelties be limited to five varieties per month and that just two flavors of ices and sherbets be made. The goal was not only to use less sugar but also to cut down on containers, labor, and transportation. *Time* magazine reported that the United States had plenty of milk, but "ice cream—childhood's caviar, poor man's pheasant, fat lady's tempter—has the demerit of needing sugar as well as milk." The report concluded, "Although some big, inventive ice-cream makers have been turning out a total of 28 flavors, ten seemed plenty."[32]

The armed forces had fewer flavors, but they did have ice cream. The industry at home supplied them with freezers, soda fountain equipment, and expertise. In 1943, the U.S. Armed Forces, with its capacity to produce eight hundred million gallons a year, became the world's largest ice cream manufacturer. Refrigeration barges sailed to Pacific battlefronts equipped with cold storage facilities and ice cream plants. Nicknamed "Ice Cream Ships," they could carry a thousand tons of food and make five hundred gallons of ice cream a day. In 1945, the navy built a barge that was a floating ice cream parlor, at a cost of one million dollars.[33]

Since ice cream ingredients such as fresh cream and eggs were not available on jungle islands and far-flung bases, the military supplied the troops with packaged ice cream mixes. Distributed in four-and-a-quarter-pound packages, each one made two and a half gallons of ice cream. Best of all, they were so simple to use that anyone could make ice cream with them. The mixes consisted of dried whole milk solids, a stabilizer, sugar, flavoring, and occasionally dried eggs. They did not require refrigeration and were designed to stay dry through any kind of shipping or weather conditions. They were "packed in hermetically sealed cans from which the air had been exhausted and an inert gas substituted to insure keeping qualities in storage," according to Selitzer.[34] Flavors such as peach, coffee, maple, and pineapple were provided, and the troops sometimes crushed hard candy and mixed it into their ice cream.

When the armed forces could not provide the troops with the equipment they needed to make ice cream, they found creative ways to supply themselves. On one Pacific island, Seabees (Navy construction brigades) built an ice cream freezer from "the tubing of an airplane, gears from a Japanese engine, a Japanese airplane starter, Japanese shell cases, and miscellaneous vehicle parts, machined to fit the purpose," Selitzer reported. "The freezer was powered by a small gasoline motor."[35]

At home, the ice cream business was prospering despite rationing and shortages. Soda fountains and luncheonettes were busier than ever as a result of full employment and good wages. The business did have to accommodate the war effort, but as they said at the time, people made do. Manufacturers substituted corn syrup for a portion of rationed sugar. Vanilla was in short supply because the British had blockaded Madagascar, where vanilla beans were grown, so other flavors substituted. Butterfat was not rationed, but there were some restrictions on its use, and many states lowered their ice cream butterfat standards. Before the war, quality ice cream was made with about 14 percent butterfat. During the war, it went down to 10 percent. Sherbet, made with milk rather than cream, gained a larger share of the market, and servings of half sherbet and half ice cream became popular. In addition, businesses cut down on deliveries to save on gas and rubber-tire wear and tear. When the government ordered milk companies to switch to every-other-day delivery, many consumers became accustomed to buying milk at their local markets rather than from the milkman. Toward the end of the war years, ice cream making equipment began showing signs of age and breaking down, but manufacturing new equipment had to wait until the war was over. Despite all that, between 1940 and 1945, production of ice cream products rose from a little more than 339 million gallons to more than 560 million gallons.[36]

During the war years, eating ice cream acquired a decidedly patriotic flavor, due in large part to the efforts of the Ice Cream Merchandising Institute. The institute, led by George Hennerich, had been influential in helping the industry recover during the Depression. Working at the soda fountain laboratory at the institute's Washington, D.C., headquarters, Hennerich had created many successful promotions during those difficult years. When the war began, he devised a promotion to help the war effort as well as the ice cream business. It was called the Victory Sundae. Using the slogan "Keep 'em buying Victory Sundaes to keep 'em flying," Hennerich proposed that the soda fountain operator choose a sundae, advertise it as a Victory Sundae, and serve it accompanied by a ten-cent defense savings stamp. The stamps, like war bonds, helped raise money for the war. In 1942, the *Ice Cream Review* estimated that the promotion could raise more than four million dollars. The cost of the stamp was not borne by the soda fountain operator; it was added to the price of the sundae. So if a strawberry sundae selling for fifteen cents was designated a Victory Sundae, it would be priced at twenty-five cents.[37]

Other ice cream treats were also associated with the war. An Iowa City ice cream maker advertised a Hitler sundae that was tagged "half nuts."[38] Children still collected Dixie cup lids, but now the lids pictured tanks, planes, and battleships instead of circuses or movie stars. Since so many men were serving in the armed forces, young women began taking their places as soda jerks. In Syracuse, New York, an ice cream maker opened a Soda & Sundae School to train them. To graduate, the women had to make a MacArthur sundae successfully. Named after the famous general, the sundae consisted of vanilla ice cream, blueberry and strawberry sauces, toasted coconut, and whipped cream. It was served topped off with a tiny American flag.[39]

During the war, families adapted to rationing, found ways to consume less meat and sugar, and planted victory gardens. The 1944 edition of *The Good Housekeeping Cook Book* included the section "Food Stretchers and Alternates," describing techniques such as mixing butter with gelatin and evaporated milk to make butter go further. A 1942 cookbook titled *What Do We Eat Now?* by Helen Robertson, Sarah MacLeod, and Frances Preston had a section called "Patriotic Economy," which suggested ways of using cooking fuel wisely and taking care of appliances such as refrigerators so they would last longer. Most of the dessert recipes used fruits since, the authors said, "the rich and luscious desserts we have known in the past . . . are giving way to simpler dishes." They did include some recipes for ice creams and other frozen desserts, although they pointed out the challenges of making them: "Frozen desserts made at home these days are limited to those which do not make too heavy demands on cream, upon sugar, or spices. Thus, the selection simmers down to sherbets and creams with custard foundation[s]."[40]

During the war years, many vanilla ice cream recipes called for "vanilla or other flavoring," because vanilla was so scarce. Like manufacturers, home cooks made milk and buttermilk sherbets, which did not require cream. They learned that evaporated milk would whip better if they added gelatin to it. They substituted sweetened condensed milk, which was not subject to sugar rationing, for sugar and cream. Honey, maple syrup, molasses, jelly, or corn syrup all stood in for or supplemented sugar and helped home cooks save their sugar rations.

Marshmallow did the same. Made with gelatin, sugar, corn syrup, and often egg whites, marshmallow was used as a sweetener and as a stabilizer by the trade before the war. In the early 1920s, Red Seal Marshmallow was advertised to manufacturers as a product that "improves ice cream, ices and sherbets" and "gives added smoothness."[41] Soon commercially made marshmallows were popping up for home use in everything from salads to gelatin desserts and, of course, ice creams. William Dreyer, founder of the Grand Ice Cream Company in Oakland, California, was said to have created Rocky Road ice cream in 1929, when he cut up some marshmallows with his wife's sewing shears and added them to his chocolate ice cream along with some walnuts. The name was intended to be a humorous way of addressing the Depression, according to company lore.[42]

Recipes for ice cream made with melted marshmallows appeared frequently both in cookbooks and in articles and ads in magazines such as *Ladies' Home Journal* and *Woman's Day*. Since the marshmallows were sweet, the ice cream made with them required little or no added sugar, a big advantage during the war. Generally, the recipes called for whole marshmallows to be melted in heated cream or evaporated milk. Then fruit or flavoring was added. Whipped cream or beaten egg whites could also be stirred in after the mixture cooled. Some of these recipes had simple titles like "Marshmallow Pineapple Ice Cream" or "Marshmallow Pistachio Ice Cream," but others used such words as *marlobet, mallobet, mallow,* or *marlow*. The following recipe appeared in *What Do We Eat Now?*

STRAWBERRY MALLOBET

21 marshmallows
½ cup water
1⅓ cups crushed strawberries
1 tablespoon lemon juice
2 tablespoons orange juice
3 egg whites
Few grains salt
2 tablespoons sugar

Melt marshmallows with water in the top part of a double boiler. Remove from heat. Add berries and fruit juices. Cool until mixture starts to congeal. Beat egg whites stiff with salt. Add sugar gradually, beating it in. Fold into strawberry and marshmallow mixture. Turn into freezing tray of refrigerator and freeze, stirring several times.

Other fruits may be used in place of strawberries.[43]

The dessert that results is thin and foamy, more like an ice milk than an ice cream, and very sweet. As the recipe directs, it is necessary to stir it several times during freezing, because the ingredients separate during the early stages.

The authors of *What Do We Eat Now?* froze a few of their ice creams in a traditional crank freezer, but made many more using the refrigerator method. Many other recipes of the era used the refrigerator method as well. Refrigerator company publications had been successful at introducing the method, and by the late 1930s, cookbooks and magazines regularly featured recipes using it. Ads for Karo Syrup, A&P markets, Campfire Marshmallows, and a canned ice cream mixture called "Ten-B-Low, concentrated *real* ice cream" regularly featured recipes using the method. Chef Louis DeGouy included dozens of "refrigerator tray" ice creams in his 1938 book *Ice Cream and Ice Cream Desserts*, as did the 1940 edition of *America's Cook Book*, compiled by editors of the *New York Herald Tribune*. Even the British author and ice cream purist Elizabeth David used it. Although no one suggested the refrigerator method made better ice cream, it was faster and easier than the cranked method. As more households acquired refrigerators, it became the norm. In addition to ice creams, frozen desserts such as mousses, biscuit Tortoni, and frozen puddings became popular since they did not require an ice cream maker, and they could be frozen in the refrigerator without being taken out and stirred during the freezing process.

Another option during wartime was simply buying ice cream instead of making it. Although *The Good Housekeeping Cook Book* included recipes for ice creams, it also suggested that women buy ice cream and other sweets instead of making them, since that way they would not have to use their sugar rations. In effect, it gave store-bought ice cream the Good Housekeeping seal of approval.

Peacetime Pleasures

When the war ended, a new and prosperous era began. Switching from a wartime economy to a peacetime one, the United States built new homes and highways, cars and household appliances. In 1949 alone, Americans bought more than six million cars and trucks and began construction of more than a million new houses. When they moved in, they drove to supermarkets and filled their new refrigerators and freezers with all the foods they had done without during the war.

As we have seen, ice cream was not among the foods they had done without. Per capita consumption, just over ten quarts in 1940, reached a high of nearly seventeen quarts by 1945. Nevertheless, Americans were hungry for more. In 1946, they each gobbled up a record-setting twenty one and one-third quarts.[44] That was an anomaly. Consumption went back down to the teens in 1947 and stayed there until 1956, when it reached twenty quarts. Ever since, consumption has ranged between twenty and twenty-two quarts per person.[45]

The end of gas rationing was a boon for drive-in and roadside restaurants. Business picked up dramatically, and restaurants such as Howard Johnson's, which had been forced to close many outlets during the war, prospered. Soft-serve shops were able to make long-delayed equipment purchases, and soft-serve ice cream came back stronger than ever. Carvel and Dairy Queen, along with newcomers to the business such as Tastee-Freez, opened thousands of new stores. The drive-ins also benefited from the postwar baby boom. Families with young children enjoyed eating in the informal environment of a roadside stand or in the family car. For the most part, hard-serve ice cream was sold indoors at ice cream shops or soda fountains, where eating required a bit of decorum. Soft-serve was a casual, outdoor ice cream, and drive-ins were the kid-friendly choice.

Soda fountains were hurt by the soft-serve chains, but they were dealt a death blow by supermarkets and home freezers. Before the war, most ice cream was scooped at drugstore soda fountains and ice cream shops. The amount of packaged ice cream sold in grocery stores was small, simply because both stores and homes lacked freezers. After the war, supermarkets with frozen food departments largely replaced local grocery stores. As soon as appliance manufacturers got out of the defense business and back into producing equipment for the home, families bought refrigerators with freezing compartments, as well as stand-alone freezers. For the first time, it was easy and convenient to buy and store frozen foods, including packaged ice creams. In 1948, half-gallon packages of ice cream were introduced; by 1950, the Breyers Ice Cream Company was selling two million a year.[46] Bigger was better. Half-pints were a thing of the past; half-gallons became the norm. Supermarkets also began to sell novelties in multipacks. Families got into the habit of picking up a box of factory-filled ice cream cups or popsicles to keep in the freezer for treats anytime. By 1951, supermarkets accounted for about 30 percent of sales, and drugstores had slipped to 18 percent.[47] As packaged ice cream sales grew, soda fountain sales continued to shrink. Although the soda fountain continued to be a presence for a few more years, its demise was inevitable.

At the same time, both the quantity and quality of homemade ice cream declined. The refrigerator-tray method was flourishing, and cranked ice cream, like the soda fountain, was viewed with nostalgia after the war. In the 1948 edition of *Toll House Tried and True Recipes*, author Ruth Wakefield reminisced, "Few of the younger generation own ice cream freezers so common before automatic refrigeration. Those of us who can look back on the happy days of 'licking the dasher' are fortunate. Homemade freezer ice cream was indeed a marvelous Sunday treat!"[48] Despite her enthusiasm for the old method, Wakefield froze her ices and ice creams in the refrigerator tray. Although a few publications (notably *The Joy of Cooking*) still included recipes for ice cream made in a crank freezer as well, the refrigerator method had become the norm. Over the course of the 1940s, the ice cream recipes in *Woman's Day* made the transition from the crank freezer to the refrigerator method. In many publications, recipes for crank-freezer ice cream were labeled as such as if to underline their uniqueness. Cookbooks of the 1950s and 1960s such as *The American Everyday Cookbook, The Complete Book of Home Freezing, Better Homes & Gardens New Cook Book*, and the *Culinary Arts Institute Encyclopedic Cookbook* all featured refrigerator-style ice creams and frozen desserts that did not need churning. In addition, convenience foods abounded in recipes. Instant coffee, canned fruit, frozen orange juice concentrate, canned cranberry jelly, packaged puddings, marshmallows, and even a "cola beverage" found their way into refrigerator-tray ice creams. *Quick and Easy Desserts*, the title of a 1965 book, summed up the cooking style of the day.[49]

Of course, some people made good, old-fashioned ice cream on a summer weekend or for a special occasion, just as some still made their own jam or holiday fruit cakes, but their numbers were dwindling. If a housewife wanted to make ice cream in a traditional freezer, she had to wait for the refrigerator to produce enough ice, which took a long time. Or she would have to go out and buy ice, because home delivery of ice had ceased.

Even refrigerator-method ice cream took planning and work, and often the results were not worth the effort. Neither option was ideal. Increasingly, people bought rather than made their ice cream. Supermarket ice cream was not as good as old-fashioned soda fountain and homemade ice cream, but the younger generation hardly remembered them, and others had become used to the lesser quality. In England, the ersatz ice cream made during the war with frozen, whipped vegetable fat rather than cream or milk continued to be popular after the war. In fact, it is still sold today. Moreover, supermarket ice cream was convenient and affordable. It could be kept in the freezer and taken out at a moment's notice.

As more people bought supermarket ice cream, magazines and cookbooks began to feature recipes for turning it into a company dessert. Wakefield wrote, " 'Store' ice cream also has interesting possibilities. Broken bits of fruitcake may be stirred into vanilla ice cream which is then hardened and ripened in the tray of an automatic refrigerator. Or you can add broken chocolate mint wafers, Nestlé's Semi-Sweet Chocolate Morsels, or such a fruit as banana. . . . This is an easy way to have unusual and delicious kinds of ice cream."[50]

Baked Alaska, a trend-setting dessert in the 1950s and 1960s, was generally made with a brick of store-bought ice cream. In fact, the cake used in the dessert was often store-bought as well. Many cookbooks included recipes for *coupes*, also known as sundaes, made with store-bought ice cream topped with such sophisticated items as canned mandarin oranges, canned chestnuts in brandy, or crème de menthe. Peg Bracken, author of a 1960 best-seller, the *I Hate to Cook Book*, was not about to make old-fashioned ice cream. Rather, she came up with these suggestions for dressing up purchased ice cream:

> Here are some uncomplicated Things to Do with ICE CREAM:
>
> You can mix two-thirds of a cup of mincemeat and two ounces of brandy or bourbon with a quart of vanilla ice cream, then spread it in ice-cube trays (with dividers removed, of course), and refreeze.
>
> You can do the same thing with almond toffee, coarsely broken, but skip the whisky. You needn't buy a whole box of toffee—just pick up some nickel bars at the candy stand.
>
> Ditto with peanut brittle.[51]

Ice cream quality had taken a downturn during World War II because of ingredient shortages and the demands of rationing, but that was predictable. What was less expected was that the ice cream manufacturers, for the most part, did not go back to fundamentals after the war. They continued to use dried milk powders and artificial flavorings. They continued to make high-overrun ice cream. Butterfat content remained at 10 percent or less, rather than the prewar norm of 14 percent. Quality took a backseat to quantity, as consumers bought bigger packages rather than better ice cream. Art Hayward, the owner of a farm stand in New Hampshire who took pride in making his own ice cream, said, "From the late '50s till the early '80s selling a quality ice cream was very difficult. People thought the size of their serving made it good."[52]

As packages grew larger, so did the size, though not the number, of ice cream plants. Fewer plants made more ice cream than ever. Companies consolidated, and plants were automated as equipment manufacturers came up with new, more efficient machinery to speed and simplify production. New forms of refrigerated transport allowed ice cream makers to ship their products from centrally located plants to every corner of the country.

Most retailers bought packaged ice cream from one of the large wholesalers. Some bought a mix and froze it themselves, occasionally personalizing it through packaging or serving style. But speed, efficiency, and economy were more important than quality or taste. A 1958 *Time* magazine report on recently issued government standards revealed just how fraught the ice cream situation had become:

> Last week the Food and Drug Administration finally issued a code to regulate everything from quality "French" to the "ice milk" sold at roadside stands.
>
> Some minimum standards: At least 10% milk fat and 20% milk solids for all ice cream. 2% to 7% milk fat for ice milk, both higher than some current brands. A weight of 4.5 lbs. per gallon to hold down the amount of air manufacturers whip into their product. A minimum of 1.6 lbs. of solid substance per gallon to avoid too much water and not enough cream. Real fruit flavors for sherbets and water ices. Artificially colored products must be clearly labeled.
>
> Most important, the new rules clamp down hard on the numerous additives used in mass ice-cream making. FDA approves the continued use of such lump-preventing stabilizers as gelatin, locust-bean gum, sodium alginate, guar-seed gum and extract of Irish peat moss. But it frowns on any further use of alkaline neutralizers, e.g., baking soda, which some producers use to sweeten up sour milk and cream, make it palatable. Totally banned: certain acid emulsifiers that make ice cream smooth by breaking down the barrier between fat and water. While approving chemicals that occur naturally in food, FDA rejected all synthetic emulsifiers (monoesters of polyoxyethylene sorbitan, monoesters of polyoxyethylene glycols, etc.), which have long since been excluded from salad dressings and bread but are still being used in ice cream. In animal experiments, scientists found that such synthetics have dubious effects, including diarrhea and kidney stones.[53]

There were exceptions to the postwar downturn in quality, and Baskin-Robbins ice cream was one. The California-based chain had begun in the late 1940s as separate ice cream stores run by brothers-in-law Irvine Robbins and Burton Baskin. They joined forces as Baskin-Robbins and made old-fashioned, real-cream ice cream. In 1953, they introduced the idea of featuring thirty-one different flavors, one for every day of even the longest months.

Another firm, the Häagen-Dazs company, was launched in 1959 by Reuben Mattus, who had grown up in the ice cream business. He got his start by peddling his mother's lemon ice in the Bronx. When he and his wife, Rose, launched their own business, they created a high-butterfat, low-overrun ice cream made with cream and egg yolks rather than the dried milk solids and fillers of many supermarket ice creams. They made just three flavors: vanilla, chocolate, and coffee. The Häagen-Dazs name, which has no meaning, was meant to suggest the quality and tradition of the Old World. Since Mattus thought it sounded vaguely Danish, he put a map of Scandinavia on the package. By the early 1970s, Häagen-Dazs was being distributed in supermarkets throughout the country.

By then, the quality tide was turning, both in the marketplace and at home. Thin, airy ice cream was out; rich, creamy ice cream was in. Newcomers to the business were making top-quality ice cream and selling it in scoop shops, the ice cream parlors of the day. The latest model ice cream freezers made it easier to produce good ice cream at home, and publications began promoting ice cream cranked the old-fashioned way, albeit with electric ice cream makers. Ice cream made in an ice cube tray was old hat. No less an authority than James Beard, writing in the July 1970 edition of *Gourmet* magazine, said, "Although most people today make ice cream in an electric freezer, there is also a great deal of freezing done in refrigerator ice trays. It is my feeling, however, that the finished product seldom equals that made in the freezer."[54]

A month later, *McCall's* magazine ran an article explaining how to make a lime and peach bombe, noting that "we nostalgically returned to the old-fashioned, fun-for-the-whole-family method, and used a hand-cranked freezer. . . . Electric models . . . are available for the less ambitious."[55]

There was no mention of the refrigerator-tray method. *The Complete Book of Homemade Ice Cream, Milk Sherbet, & Sherbet* by Carolyn Anderson, which was published in 1972, included brief directions for making refrigerator-tray ice cream. However, nearly all her ice cream recipes called for churn-freezing. She noted, "In most cases, churn-freezing, if possible, will create a better product."[56]

Just as Häagen-Dazs was becoming well known, in 1973 a scoop shop called Steve's Ice Cream opened in Somerville, Massachusetts, a few miles outside Boston. Owner Steve Herrell made his own 14-percent-butterfat ice cream in a five-gallon motorized White Mountain freezer he had modified himself. It was so good that customers happily waited their turn in lines that were often several blocks long. Herrell pioneered the practice of mixing M&Ms, nuts, crushed candy bars, chunks of Oreo cookies, and other goodies into scoops of ice cream. It was an idea many others would imitate. *Entrepreneur Magazine* credited him with inspiring a wave of "new, home-grown, superpremium ice cream shops that emphasized fun and indulgence. . . . He virtually invented the homemade ice cream craze in America."[57]

Following Herrell's example, a pair of entrepreneurs named Ben Cohen and Jerry Greenfield founded Ben & Jerry's. They began their company in 1978 with a scoop shop in Burlington, Vermont. In just a few years, their brand became famous for rich ice creams with chunky additions and funky names like "New York Super Fudge Chunk" and "Cherry Garcia."

In the 1980s, scoop shops, also known as dipping stores, opened and thrived in towns, particularly college towns, all over the country. Each one claimed to sell the world's best ice cream. They charged up to an attention-getting seven dollars for a hand-packed quart, and customers were happy to pay it. In 1981, *Time* pronounced ice cream America's "drug of choice, and butterfat . . . the occasion of our guiltiest and most delicious sin." According to *Time*, America produced 829,798,000 gallons of ice cream in 1980, the equivalent of "ten single-scoop cones for every human being on earth."[58]

By the end of the century, ice cream had risen to gourmet status, and famous chefs were playing with ice cream. Thomas Keller, chef and owner of the French Laundry in California, reversed the trompe l'oeil ruse of the eighteenth-century confectioners and created an *amuse-bouche* that looked like a tray of tiny strawberry ice cream cones. Actually, they were miniature cornets filled with salmon *tartare* and crème fraîche. Chefs put house-made ice creams on their dessert menus, often creating anew some flavors Emy and Gilliers would have recognized, such as Parmesan, artichoke, and truffle. They arranged precious little scoops of ice cream in miniature cones and served a trio for dessert. They even brought back midmeal sorbets.

Home cooks also experimented with ice cream making. New easy-to-use ice cream makers and a plethora of recipes in magazines, newspaper food pages, and cookbooks encouraged home cooks to take it up, if only as an occasional pursuit. A sampling of recipes from end-of-the-century publications shows how many and varied the recipes were. They included wildflower honey ice cream, blue martini ice pops, gingersnap ice cream, Champagne lavender sorbet, strawberry cheesecake ice cream, Parmesan ice cream sandwiches, cantaloupe and ginger sherbet, pear-verbena sorbet, white pepper ice cream, peach gelato, oatmeal ice cream, *fromage blanc*—lemongrass sorbet, chestnut ice cream with chocolate Grand Marnier sauce, sweet corn ice cream, mochaccino frozen yogurt, and, of course, the flavor that people overwhelmingly choose as their favorite year after year—vanilla.

Industry and Artistry

Today, the ice cream business is a vast global enterprise. In fact, it's so big that it's not called the ice cream business anymore. It's the frozen dessert business. It includes ice creams, low-fat and nonfat desserts (formerly known as ice milks), water ices, sherbets, sorbets, frozen juice bars, frozen yogurts, gelati, and more. Multinational corporations such as Unilever, Nestlé, and General Mills own most of the major brands, including Ben & Jerry's, Breyers, Dreyer's, Good Humor, Klondike, Popsicle, and Häagen-Dazs. They market the ice creams in nearly every country in the world, changing flavors and packaging to respond to local market demands and tastes. They are continually upgrading their freezing and packaging technologies, coming up with new branding strategies, and looking for new growth opportunities and markets. The Asian market is, of course, potentially huge. In China, for example, Häagen-Dazs is now a prestigious brand and sells for about ten dollars a pint. The green tea flavor is especially popular, as it is in Japan.

The manufacturers are trying to increase their presence in the American market as well. Americans eat roughly twenty-two quarts of frozen desserts (let's call it all ice cream for simplicity's sake) a year. Only New Zealanders, who consume an impressive twenty-seven quarts per person, eat more.[1] Yet consumption in the United States has remained stuck at the twenty-or-so-quart level since the 1960s.

Some attribute the lack of growth to the eating less, eating better phenomenon. In other words, rather than buy a half gallon of inexpensive, lesser-quality ice cream, many consumers buy a quart of superpremium or go out to a scoop shop and have a dish of rich, house-made ice cream. In addition, competition for the customer's time, money, and calorie allotment continues to increase. There's a coffee shop on every corner these days; and while coffee may not seem like an ice cream alternative, a flavored coffee topped with whipped cream and caramel syrup is. Of course, ice cream is fattening, and it's possible that some people are pushing back from the table without it. Or it could simply be that we have reached our limit. Maybe twenty quarts is enough, even for a true ice cream lover.

Manufacturers don't want to hear that we're having enough ice cream, though. They want to increase sales, and they think diet-friendly ice cream is one way to do it. They've discovered an ice-structuring protein in the blood of a particular type of fish, the ocean pout, that is said to replace fat while maintaining flavor. Unilever has come up with a way to make it without involving the fish. The protein is produced in the lab by altering the genetic structure of a strain of yeast. It is now being used in some light ice creams and novelties both in the United States and in Great Britain.

Ice cream makers are also developing cellulose-based ingredients to try to cut fat in ice cream. They're trying to get rid of sugar, corn syrup, and other sweeteners, too. Supermarket freezers are full of low-sugar, sugar-free, low-carb, and, from Ben & Jerry's, "Carb Karma" ice creams. And more are popping up every day.

Cutting ice cream calories is not a new idea. Back in June 1967, an article in the *Ice Cream Field & Trade Journal* asked, "Is the future of the ice cream business behind us?" Bemoaning the lack of growth in the business, the article suggested that developing a flavorful low-calorie ice cream might rescue the industry, since 60 percent of Americans said they were either on a diet or planning to go on one.[2] That was just before superpremium ice creams made their splash in the market and the new scoop shops made their debut. In other words, just before richer, higher-fat ice cream—not diet ice cream—transformed the business.

Shortcuts always appeal to people, and making ice cream by simply mixing a powder with milk or water is an idea that keeps coming back. At the beginning of the twentieth century, ice cream powders were introduced with claims that they would make ice cream of "a very high standard of purity and excellence of manufacture." Today, the claim is that powders make ice cream "with the physical and sensory characteristics of a premium product." The language is a bit different, but the idea is the same. Ice cream powders for commercial use are now sold everywhere, from Australia to America—even in Italy. There, they call it *gelato industriale*, or "industrial gelato," as opposed to *gelato artiginale*, or "artisanal gelato." At least one Italian company, Fabbri, sells a gelato mix that you simply blend with water or milk and freeze, and, presto, gelato. Or so it claims. According to the company's U.S. sales agency, the product allows shopkeepers who don't "want to get involved with all the traditional way of measuring and weighing stuff" to put gelato into their stores.[3]

Also back for a return engagement are mix-ins. In 1973, when Steve Herrell introduced the idea of mixing brand-name candies and cookies into ice cream as the customer watched, mix-ins were a fun accompaniment to seriously good ice cream. Herrell is still making ice cream in Massachusetts; he has four stores under the Herrell's name, as well as a thriving wholesale business. And he still mixes goodies—now called "smoosh-ins"—into ice cream.

Now at some national chains, mix-ins are primary and ice cream is secondary. The updated concept features an ice-cold counter where personable young servers mash all manner of ice creams, cookies, nuts, fruits, and candies together. However, the servers don't just scoop and mash; they sing. They burst into song at the slightest provocation—like being given a tip. In fact, at Cold Stone Creamery, you don't apply for a job. You audition. Although many ice cream aficionados say the extras that get folded into the ice cream are there to disguise its poor quality, these shops have been extremely successful so far.

Freezing ice cream is a science as well as an art. We are indebted to those who first added salt to ice and made it all possible. Over time, others perfected freezing techniques and made it ever easier to produce, ship, and store ice cream. Now science is bringing us ice cream flash-frozen into tiny beads or kernels by means of liquid nitrogen. These are often dispensed from vending machines. They are fun, especially the first time you have them, and even more so for children. However, they don't have the mouth-feel of *real* ice cream. They're a novelty item for kids. Also, ice creams frozen with liquid nitrogen require subzero storage, so you can't take them home and store them. However, food scientists are experimenting with the technique, so liquid nitrogen ice cream may make it to your home freezer one day.

Actually the liquid nitrogen freezing method, although attracting more attention lately, has been around for years. At the end of the nineteenth century, Agnes Marshall thought freezing ice cream at the dinner table with liquid nitrogen would be entertaining, and so do some of today's chefs. They mix up a small batch of, say, tarragon-lime sorbet and freeze it *à la minute* at the table with the same fanfare that used to accompany flaming desserts. The result may well be delicious, but few of us can afford to enjoy such rarefied pleasures often.

Another ice cream trend has its origins in immigration patterns. Traditionally, immigrants played a significant role in the development of ice cream. In the eighteenth century, French and Italian confectioners introduced high-quality ices and ice creams to England and the United States. Later, unskilled immigrants, often from Italy, operated pushcarts and peddled penny-licks, hokeypokeys, and ice cream sandwiches. Against all odds, some of them went on to open their own ice cream shops and became very successful. Today, immigration's impact is mostly on the flavors of ice cream that are coming into the marketplace. A few years back, Häagen-Dazs had a huge hit with its *dulce de leche* ice cream. The caramelized milk flavor was intended for the Latin market, but it turned out to appeal to everyone. Now it's available everywhere Häagen-Dazs is sold, which is pretty much everywhere except, oddly enough, Denmark. And other manufacturers are bringing new, ethnically diverse flavors to market.

A California-based company, Palapa Azul, is selling Mexican-style ice creams and sorbets in supermarkets, and not just in ethnic neighborhoods. Their flavors include corn, mango, flan, and Mexican chocolate. They also make frozen fruit bars in such flavors as Mexican papaya, cucumber-chile, and mango-chile. Popsicles have long appealed to children, but not to most adults. Maybe these more sophisticated frozen ice pops will expand the market.

The Artisans of Ice Cream

Owners of some neighborhood ice cream shops have been offering ethnically diverse flavors for many years. Gus Rancatore, owner of Toscanini's Ice Cream in Cambridge, Massachusetts, and an alumnus of Steve's Ice Cream, has been in the business for more than twenty-five years. He says his area's international student population has always given him the leeway to develop flavors that might not have made it in the mass market. For example, he makes his own *khulfee*, an adaptation of a traditional Indian ice cream, with cardamom, almonds, and pistachios. Rancatore's menu changes all the time, but he has made saffron ice cream, five spice, ginger, *gianduia* (Italian for a hazelnut-and-chocolate flavor combination), stout (yes, the beer), and many more.

Stephanie Reitano, owner with her husband, John, of Capogiro in Philadelphia, says that, as soon as ethnic restaurants move into a neighborhood, unusual ingredients become easier to find. And she starts making gelato or *sorbetto* with them. Sometimes it takes a while for a flavor to catch on, but customers love trying her latest experiments. "Avocado is old hat" for her customers, she says. Lately, they've been tasting persimmon, carambola, and lychee nut.

Customers are developing more adventurous palates, according to ice cream makers. Amy Miller, another Steve's alum, owner of Amy's Ice Cream shops in Texas, says that, when she started out twenty-something years ago, she couldn't offer her customers the range of flavors Gus Rancatore was featuring. But today Texans are more ethnically diverse and more daring. Now her menu includes such flavors as hibiscus, amaretto peach, and chipotle peanut butter. Torrance Kopfer, owner of Cold Fusion Gelato in Newport, Rhode Island, also says he's seen a big increase in flavor acceptance in the last ten years. He cites black sesame ice cream as an example of the change. Others mention flavors like garam masala and curry leaf. Adzuki bean and green tea ice creams, previously limited to Japanese neighborhoods, are gaining popularity beyond their borders.

I hear echoes of Emy as I talk to these hands-on ice cream makers. Whether they're new to the business or experts, they're all full of enthusiasm about ice cream. After more than thirty years in the business, Herrell still speaks lovingly about spooning up the last puddle of melting ice cream at the bottom of his hot fudge sundae. He's optimistic about the future of ice cream, because, he says, eating ice cream is part of our culture and our consciousness.

The others are equally upbeat. When they talk about their business, there's no mention of fish protein, instant powders, or cellulose. They talk about the quality of their ingredients, about finding local sources for the best cream and the freshest fruits. They get excited about buying eggs with bright, golden yolks. Some even make their ice cream seasonally, with fresh local ingredients.

Gabrielle Carbone, co-owner with her husband, Matt Errico, of the Bent Spoon, an ice cream shop in Princeton, New Jersey, animatedly describes making autumn ice creams with locally grown pumpkins or apples, and talks about the strawberry and mint sorbet she makes when both plants are at their absolute peak of ripeness. Capogiro's Reitano says simply, "If it grows in Pennsylvania, we buy it in Pennsylvania." In winter, that means Lancaster County bosc pear with Wild Turkey bourbon; spring brings rhubarb; summer, black raspberry; autumn, heirloom apple cider with clove. Emy would approve.

These ice cream makers are particular about their ingredients. Kopfer says his current favorite flavor is chocolate curry ice cream. But he doesn't simply buy curry powder to make it. He mixes his own spice blend. Reitano caramelizes her hazelnuts before chopping them up and blending them into chocolate and hazelnut gelato to make her *bacio* flavor. *Bacio,* also the name of a chocolate and hazelnut candy, is Italian for "kiss."

They all love to experiment. Gus Rancatore mentions that he welcomes the January slowdown because it gives him time to dream up new flavors. Years ago, he says, he created Grape-Nuts ice cream and later was disappointed to discover that others had done it before him. But he says he's come up with some four hundred flavors so far, and it's clear he has more in his future. He's still experimenting after all these years. So is Miller, who says she's up to three hundred so far.

Herrell is still experimenting too. With vanilla. It's his personal favorite, and he has at least five different kinds of vanilla on his flavor board at any one time—vanilla, malted vanilla, vanilla fudge ripple, high-definition vanilla, and private stock. "We need more types of vanilla," he says, "because it is the most popular flavor." He's exploring a combination of two vanillas now, but won't say more because he hasn't perfected the flavor yet.

Personally, I hope the tradition of making ice cream at home comes back. Granted, it was never an everyday occurrence, because of the difficulties around ice and cranking. But today's ice cream freezers make it simple. Anyone who has memories of homemade ice cream talks about it lovingly, and I think that at the very least it's a summer ritual worth reviving. Even if you make ice cream only a few times a season, you'll have fun. With just a little practice, you'll make wonderful ice cream, and you'll know exactly what's in it—the freshest cream, the ripest strawberries, the lushest mangoes. You can create your own flavors. If you've always wondered what lemon-raspberry ice cream would taste like, make some. When you do, I guarantee that your family and friends will be impressed far out of proportion to the effort you've made. One day, you, like Emy, can make ice cream that's *parfait.*

NOTES

PREFACE

1. Alberto Capatti and Massimo Montanari, *Italian Cuisine: A Cultural History* (New York: Columbia University Press, 1999), 106–111; Gillian Riley, *The Oxford Companion to Italian Food* (New York: Oxford University Press, 2007), 318–319.
2. W. S. Stallings Jr., "Ice Cream and Water Ices in 17th and 18th Century England," *Petits Propos Culinaires* 3 (1979): S1–7.

ONE. EARLY ICES AND ICED CREAMS

1. Tom Shachtman, *Absolute Zero and the Conquest of Cold* (Boston: Houghton Mifflin, 1999), 17.
2. Elizabeth David, *Harvest of the Cold Months* (New York: Viking Penguin, 1995), xii–xvii.
3. Giambattista della Porta, *Natural Magick*, bk. 14, chap. 11, "Of Diverse Confections of Wines," 1658, http://homepages.tscnet.com/omard1/jportac14.html #bk14X1, accessed July 23, 2008. The original was published in Naples in 1558, and it was followed, in 1589, by a much-expanded version. The latter has information about wine freezing in glasses. The online translation is based on an English edition published in London in 1658.
4. David, *Harvest of the Cold Months*, 71–72.
5. Ibid., 60.
6. Alan Davidson, *The Oxford Companion to Food* (Oxford: Oxford University Press, 1999), 314.
7. Hippocrates, *Aphorisms*, sec. 5, no. 24.
8. Anthimus, *On the Observance of Foods*, trans. and ed. Mark Grant (Totnes, U.K.: Prospect Books, 1996), 47.
9. Jean-Louis Flandrin, *Food: A Culinary History from Antiquity to the Present* (New York: Columbia University Press, 1999), 419.

10. David, *Harvest of the Cold Months*, 68.

11. Ibid., 1.

12. John Evelyn, *The Diary of John Evelyn*, ed. E. S. de Beer (London: Oxford University Press, 1959), 239.

13. Fannie Merritt Farmer, *The Boston Cooking-School Cook Book* (Boston: Little, Brown, 1896), 365.

14. Sir Thomas Herbert, *Travels in Persia, 1627–1629*, abridged and edited by Sir William Foster (New York: Robert M. McBride, 1929), 45, 260.

15. James Morier, *The Adventures of Hajji Baba of Ispahan* (1824; reprint, New York: Hart, 1976), 152.

16. Jean Chardin, *Travels in Persia, 1673–1677* (New York: Dover, 1988).

17. Fredrick Nutt, *The Complete Confectioner*, 4th ed. (1789; reprint, London: Richard Scott, 1807), 48, 60.

18. Today, in England, *sherbet* is also the name of a sweet, fizzy powder that children suck through a straw or a stick of licorice. Oddly, in Australia, *sherbet* is a nickname for beer.

19. Iranians make *bastani-e gol-o bolbol*, a flavorful saffron and rosewater ice cream with tiny cubes of plain frozen cream blended into it for added texture. *Paludeh-ye shirazi* is an unusual rice-stick sorbet that they serve with sour cherry syrup. The many and varied ices and ice creams of the Middle East are delightful, but the story of their evolution is beyond the scope of this book.

20. C. Anne Wilson, *Food and Drink in Britain* (Chicago: Academy Chicago Publishers, 1991), 169.

21. Bartolomeo Stefani, *L'Arte de ben cucinare* (1662; reprint, Sala Bolognese, Italy: A. Forni, 1983), 73.

22. Robert May, *The Accomplisht Cook* (London: printed for Obadiah Blagrave, 1685), 277–290.

23. Davidson, *Oxford Companion to Food*, 237.

24. Antonio Latini, *Lo scalco alla moderna* (Napoli: Parrino & Mutii, 1692, 1694; reprint, Milano: Appunti di Gastronomia, 1993).

25. Alberto Capatti and Massimo Montanari, *Italian Cuisine: A Cultural History* (New York: Columbia University Press, 1999), 213–215.

26. Alfred W. Crosby Jr., *The Columbian Exchange: Biological and Cultural Consequences of 1492* (Westport, CT: Greenwood Press, 1972), 182.

27. Stefano Milioni, *Columbus Menu: Italian Cuisine after the First Voyage of Christopher Columbus* (New York: Italian Trade Commission, 1992), 13–16.

28. David, *Harvest of the Cold Months,* 146–147.

29. This information comes from A. Th. Kupffer, *Travaux de la Commission pour fixer les mesures et les poids de l'Empire de Russie* (St. Petersburg, Russia: Imprimerie de l'Expedition de la Confection des Papiers de la Couronne, 1841), 63. Cited in "Caraffa," Units and Systems of Units, 2001, Sizes, www.sizes .com/units/caraffa.htm, accessed July 21, 2008.

30. Sophie D. Coe and Michael D. Coe, *The True History of Chocolate* (London: Thames and Hudson, 1996), 125–138.

31. Herbert, *Travels in Persia,* 45. According to a footnote in the book, "*Bun* is the Abyssinian name for the coffee plant and its berry; while *kahwah* (when both 'coho' and 'choava') is the Arabic equivalent." *Mussulmans* are Muslims.

32. Dominique Kassel, "Tout va très bien Madame la marquise," June 2005, Ordre National des Pharmaciens, Documents de référence, Histoire et art pharmaceutique, www.ordre.pharmacien.fr, accessed July 22, 2008.

33. David, *Harvest of the Cold Months,* 111–128; Alfred Fierro, *Histoire et dictionnaire de Paris* (Paris: Éditions Robert Laffont, S.A., 1996), 742–743; Barbara Ketcham Wheaton, *Savouring the Past: The French Kitchen and Table from 1300 to 1789* (London: Chatto & Windus, Hogarth Press, 1983), 92–93.

34. Le Procope is still located on the Rue de l'Ancienne Comédie, but the Comédie Française is now in the first arrondissement—near the Palais Royal.

35. Nicolas Audiger, *La maison réglée* (Paris: Librairie Plon, 1692). Reprinted in Alfred Franklin, *La vie privée d'autrefois* (Paris: Librairie Plon, 1898), 131.

36. Elizabeth David writes, in *Harvest of the Cold Months,* that the date was actually 1661, since the king was not in Paris on the date Audiger cites.

37. Wheaton, *Savouring the Past,* 104–106.

38. At the time, a *pinte* was 1.005 U.S. quarts, according to Stephen Naft, *International Conversion Tables,* expanded and revised by Ralph de Sola (New York: Duell, Sloan and Pearce, 1961), 328.

39. In the days before lead poisoning was known, lead containers were commonly used to freeze and also to mold ice cream.

40. Naft, *International Conversion Tables.*

41. David, *Harvest of the Cold Months,* 387–388.

42. Ibid., 387–388.

43. David Potter, "Icy Cream," *Petits Propos Culinaires* 72 (2003): 45. Published by Prospect Books, London. The article refers to a manuscript by Lady Anne Fanshawe, 1651–1678, folio 158.

44. Mary Eales, *Mrs. Mary Eales's Receipts* (London: Prospect Books, 1985), 88–93. Facsimile of the 1733 edition; originally published in 1718; distributed in the United States by the University Press of Virginia.

TWO. CRÈME DE LA CREAM

1. Mark Kurlansky, *Salt: A World History* (New York: Walker, 2002), 144.
2. Pellegrino Artusi, *Science in the Kitchen and the Art of Eating Well*, trans. Murtha Baca and Stephen Sartarelli (Toronto: University of Toronto Press, 2004), 545.
3. François Massialot, *Nouvelle instruction pour les confitures, les liqueurs, et les fruits* (Paris: Chez Claude Prudhomme, 1716), 1–8.
4. Karen Hess, *Martha Washington's Booke of Cookery* (New York: Columbia University Press, 1981), 227.
5. Massialot, *Nouvelle instruction*, 1734 edition, 236.
6. Massialot, *Nouvelle instruction*, 1716 edition, 286.
7. John Pinkerton, *Recollections of Paris, in the Years 1802–3–4–5* (London: Longman, Hurst, Rees & Orme, 1806), 209.
8. François Menon, *The Art of Modern Cookery Displayed* [Les soupers de la cour] (London: R. Davis, 1767), 576–577.
9. The *office*, or cold kitchen, later called the *garde manger*, was where salads, pastries, ices, distilled liquors, marzipans, jellies, and other confections were prepared. The *cannelon* is a mold shaped like a series of tubes or cinnamon sticks. *Cannelle* is French for "cinnamon."
10. M. Emy, *L'Art de bien faire les glaces d'office* (Paris: Chez le Clerc, 1768), 59, ii.
11. Ibid., 143–146.
12. Alan Davidson, *The Oxford Companion to Food* (Oxford: Oxford University Press, 1999), 820–821.
13. Emy, *L'Art de bien faire les glaces d'office*, 191.
14. Menon, *Art of Modern Cookery Displayed*, 423.
15. Mr. Borella, *The Court and Country Confectioner: Or, the House-Keeper's Guide* (London: printed for G. Riley . . . J. Bell . . . J. Wheble . . . and C. Etherington, 1772), 96–97.
16. Menon, *Art of Modern Cookery Displayed*, 575–576.
17. "The Court Dessert in Eighteenth Century France," 2003, Historic Food: The Website of Food Historian Ivan Day, http://www.historicfood.com, accessed July 23, 2008.
18. Menon, *Art of Modern Cookery Displayed*, 409–410.

19. Patrick Brydone, *A Tour Through Sicily & Malta, In a series of letters to William Beckford, Esq.* (London: T. Cadell and W. Davies, 1806), 223–225.

20. John Moore, *A View of Society and Manners in Italy* (Dublin: Printed for W. Gilbert, W. Wilson, J. Moore, W. Jones and J. Rice, 1792), 3:108–109.

THREE. INGENIOUS FOREIGNERS AND OTHERS

1. Filippo Baldini, *De sorbetti* (Bologna, Italy: Arnaldo Forni Editore, 1979); reprint of the 1784 edition.

2. Vincenzo Corrado, *Il credenziere di buon gusto* (Naples: Nella Stamperia Raimondiana, 1778; reprint, Sala Bolognese: A. Forni, 1991). Introduction by Claudio Benporat.

3. Elizabeth David, *Harvest of the Cold Months* (New York: Viking Penguin, 1995), 176–179.

4. Corrado, *Il credenziere di buon gusto*, 13.

5. The measurements are based on the twelve-ounce pound in use at the time.

6. Barbara Ketcham Wheaton, *Savouring the Past: The French Kitchen & Table from 1300–1789* (London: Chatto & Windus, Hogarth Press, 1983), 98–99.

7. Hannah Glasse, *The Art of Cookery Made Plain and Easy* (London, 1796; reprint, Hamden, CT: Archon Books, 1971), v.

8. Hannah Glasse, *The Compleat Confectioner* (Dublin: printed by John Exshaw, 1762), 140.

9. Ibid., 91.

10. Elizabeth Raffald, *The Experienced English Housekeeper* (1769; reprint, Lewes, U.K.: Southover Press, 1997), 126.

11. Mr. Borella, *The Court and Country Confectioner: Or, the House-Keeper's Guide* (London: printed for G. Riley . . . J. Bell . . . J. Wheble . . . and C. Etherington, 1772), i–3.

12. Ibid., 88–89.

13. Ibid., 90–95.

14. Ibid., 87.

15. Ivan Day, "Which Compleat Confectioner?" *Petits Propos Culinaire* 59 (1998): 44–53. Published by Prospect Books, London.

16. G. A. Jarrin, *The Italian Confectioner* (London: John Harding, 1823), vii.

17. Laura Mason, "William Alexis Jarrin: An Italian Confectioner in London," *Gastronomica* (Spring 2001): 50–64; "Georgian Ices," 2003, Historic Food: The Website of Food Historian Ivan Day, http://www.historicfood.com, accessed July 23, 2008.

18. Ben Weinreb and Christopher Hibbert, eds., *The London Encyclopedia* (London: Macmillan, 1983), 346–347.

19. Rees Howell Gronow, *The Reminiscences and Recollections of Captain Gronow: 1810–1860* (London: John C. Nimmo, 1892), 2:283–287.

20. George Augustus Sala, *Twice Round the Clock; or the Hours of the Day and Night in London* (London: Houlston and Wright, 1859), 317.

21. Pamela Haines, *Tea at Gunter's* (London: Heinemann, 1974).

22. William Gunter, *Gunter's Confectioner's Oracle* (London: Alfred Miller, 1830), 68.

23. Frederick Nutt, *The Complete Confectioner*, 4th ed. (1789; reprint, London: Richard Scott, 1807), introductory page labeled "Advertisement."

24. Mason, "William Alexis Jarrin," 50–64.

25. Jarrin, *Italian Confectioner*, viii.

26. Ibid., vii–viii.

27. William Jeanes, *The Modern Confectioner* (London: John Camden Hotten, 1861), iii–v.

28. Jarrin, *Italian Confectioner*, 123.

29. Jeanes, *Modern Confectioner*, 85.

30. Jarrin, *Italian Confectioner*, 124.

31. Jeanes, *Modern Confectioner*, 87–88, emphasis in the original.

32. A gill is a unit of measurement equal to one-quarter of a pint.

33. Nutt, *Complete Confectioner*, 153.

34. Jeanes, *Modern Confectioner*, 108.

35. Jarrin, *Italian Confectioner*, 125.

36. Jeanes, *Modern Confectioner*, 94–95.

37. Jarrin, *Italian Confectioner*, 132.

38. Sarah Garland, *The Complete Book of Herbs & Spices* (London: Frances Lincoln, 1989), 100–101.

39. Barbara K. Wheaton, *Victorian Ices & Ice Cream* (New York: Metropolitan Museum of Art, Charles Scribner's Sons, 1976), xvii.

40. Alice Arndt, *Seasoning Savvy* (New York: Haworth Herbal Press, 1999), 243.

41. Ivan Day, "A Natural History of the Ice Pudding," *Petits Propos Culinaire* 74 (2003): 24–38.

42. Jarrin, *Italian Confectioner*, 131.

43. Theodore Francis Garrett, ed., *The Encyclopædia of Practical Cookery* (London: Upcott Gill, [1890?]), 166.

44. Gronow, *Reminiscences and Recollections*, 287.

45. Jules Janin, *The American in Paris* (London: Longman, Brown, Green, and Longmans, 1843), 169.

46. Theodore Child, "Characteristic Parisian Cafés," *Harper's New Monthly Magazine* 78, no. 467 (April 1889): 687–703.

47. Honoré de Balzac, *A Harlot High and Low* [Splendeurs et misères des courtisanes], translated and with an introduction by Rayner Heppenstall (Harmondsworth, U.K.: Penguin Books, 1970), italics in the original. In *A Harlot High and Low*, *plombière* is translated as "sundae." When the French original was published, in 1839, there was no such thing as a sundae. Although there is no official birth date, the sundae is believed to have been introduced in the early 1890s.

48. Henry G. Harris and S. P. Borella, *All about Ices, Jellies, and Creams* (London: Kegan Paul, 2002), 40. Reprint of the 1926 edition.

49. Stoddard Dewey, "The End of Tortoni's," *Atlantic Monthly* 73, no. 440 (June 1894).

FOUR. THE LAND OF ICE CREAM

1. Anne Cooper Funderburg, *Chocolate, Strawberry, and Vanilla: A History of American Ice Cream* (Bowling Green, OH: Bowling Green State University Popular Press, 1995), 3.

2. "Ice Cream Recipe," n.d., Food and Cooking, Thomas Jefferson's Monticello, www.monticello.org, accessed July 23, 2008.

3. Mary Randolph, *The Virginia House-Wife* (Columbia: University of South Carolina Press, 1984), 144. Facsimile of the 1824 edition.

4. Ibid., 176.

5. Ibid., 178–179.

6. Jean Anthelme Brillat-Savarin, *The Physiology of Taste* (San Francisco: North Point Press, 1986), 377.

7. Abram C. Dayton, *Last Days of Knickerbocker Life in New York* (New York: George W. Harlan, 1882), 116–117.

8. Lately Thomas, *Delmonico's: A Century of Splendor* (Boston: Houghton Mifflin, 1967), 8–9.

9. "Eleanor Parkinson Biography" and introduction to *The Complete Confectioner, Pastry-Cook, and Baker*, February 2005, Feeding America: The Historic American Cookbook Project, Michigan State University Library, http://digital.lib.msu.edu/projects/cookbooks/html/project.html, accessed July 23, 2008. The Michigan State University Library and the Michigan State University

Museum have partnered to created an online collection of some of the most influential and important American cookbooks from the late eighteenth to the early twentieth centuries.

10. Eleanor Parkinson, *The Complete Confectioner, Pastry-Cook, and Baker* (1884; reprint, Philadelphia: J. B. Lippincott & Co., 1864), 69–70.

11. Ibid., 73.

12. Chas. H. Haswell, *Reminiscences of an Octogenarian of the City of New York (1816 to 1860)* (New York: Harper & Brothers, 1896), 60.

13. George G. Foster, *New York by Gas-Light and Other Urban Sketches*, edited and with an introduction by Stuart M. Blumin (1850; reprint, Berkeley: University of California Press, 1990), 138.

14. Dayton, *Last Days of Knickerbocker Life*, 140.

15. John Lambert, *Travels through Canada, and the United States of North America in the Years 1806, 1807, 1808* (London: Baldwin, Cradock, and Joy, 1816), excerpted in Kenneth T. Jackson and David S. Dunbar, eds., *Empire City: New York through the Centuries* (New York: Columbia University Press, 2002), 111.

16. Thomas A. Janvier, *In Old New York* (New York: Harper & Brothers, 1894), 261–262.

17. Dayton, *Last Days of Knickerbocker Life*, 125.

18. Marvin McAllister, *White People Do Not Know How to Behave at Entertainments Designed for Ladies and Gentlemen of Colour: William Brown's African and American Theater* (Chapel Hill: University of North Carolina Press, 2003).

19. "A History of Ice Cream in Philadelphia," 2008, Chilly Philly Ice Cream, www.chillyphilly.com, accessed July 23, 2008.

20. Heath Schenker, "Pleasure Gardens, Theme Parks, and the Picturesque," in *Theme Park Landscapes: Antecedents and Variations*, ed. Terence Young and Robert Riley (Washington, DC: Dumbarton Oaks Research Library and Collection, 2002), 80.

21. *New York Herald*, March 24, 1856, quoted in Schenker, "Pleasure Gardens, Theme Parks, and the Picturesque," 80.

22. Ibid., 88.

23. Ibid., 69.

24. Ibid., 84.

25. Foster, *New York by Gas-Light*, 133.

26. Ibid., 138.

27. George G. Foster, *New York in Slices: By an Experienced Carver: Being the Original Slices Published in the N.Y. Tribune* (New York: W. H. Graham, 1849), 72.

28. Foster, *New York by Gas-Light*, 139.

29. "Ice House," n.d., Food and Cooking, Thomas Jefferson's Monticello, www .monticello.org, accessed July 23, 2008.

30. William Jeanes, *The Modern Confectioner: A Practical Guide* (London: John Camden Hotten, 1861), 90–92.

31. Joseph C. Jones Jr., *America's Icemen* (Humble, TX: Jobeco Books, 1984), 15–20.

32. Gavin Weightman, *The Frozen-Water Trade: A True Story* (New York: Hyperion, 2003), 39.

33. Ibid., 40.

34. Ibid., 142.

35. Richard O. Cummings, *The American Ice Harvests: A Historical Study in Technology, 1800–1918* (Berkeley: University of California Press, 1949), 67–68.

36. Jennie G. Everson, *Tidewater Ice of the Kennebec River* (Freeport, ME: Bond Wheelwright, for the Maine State Museum by the Co., 1970), 107.

37. Chauncey M. Depew, *One Hundred Years of American Commerce* (New York: D. O. Haynes, 1895), 467–468.

38. Elizabeth David, *Harvest of the Cold Months* (New York: Viking, 1995), 278.

39. Robert Maclay, "The Ice Industry," in *One Hundred Years of American Commerce*, ed. Chauncey M. Depew (New York: D. O. Haynes, 1895), 469.

40. Mary Lincoln, "Ice and Ices," *New England Kitchen* 1, no. 4 (August 1894): 238–242.

41. Jones, *America's Icemen*, 159.

42. Elizabeth Ellicott Lea, *Domestic Cookery, Useful Receipts, and Hints to Young Housekeepers* (Baltimore, MD: Cushings and Bailey, 1869), 126.

43. Eliza Leslie, *Seventy-Five Receipts for Pastry, Cakes, and Sweetmeats* (Boston: Munroe and Francis, 1832), 85.

44. Catharine Esther Beecher, *Miss Beecher's Domestic Receipt Book: Designed as a Supplement to Her Treatise on Domestic Economy* (New York: Harper & Brothers, 1850), 219–220.

45. Sidney W. Mintz, *Sweetness and Power: The Place of Sugar in Modern History* (New York: Viking, 1985), 67.

46. Ibid., 144.

47. Wendy A. Woloson, *Refined Tastes: Sugar, Confectionery, and Consumers in Nineteenth-Century America* (Baltimore, MD: Johns Hopkins University Press, 2002), 5.

48. Mintz, *Sweetness and Power*, 143.

49. Woloson, *Refined Tastes*, 31.

50. *American Kitchen Magazine* (March 1898): xiv.

51. William Woys Weaver, "Ice Cream," in *Encyclopedia of Food and Culture*, ed. Solomon H. Katz (New York: Charles Scribner's Sons, 2003), 239.

52. Thomas Masters, *The Ice Book* (London: Simpkin, Marshall, 1844), xi.

53. Ibid., 161.

54. Ibid., 172.

55. Henry G. Harris and S. P. Borella, *All about Ices, Jellies, and Creams* (London: Kegan Paul, 2002), 2. Reprint of the 1926 edition.

56. Ralph Selitzer, *The Dairy Industry in America* (New York: Dairy & Ice Cream Field and Books for Industry, 1976), 101.

57. Ibid., 103.

58. Funderburg, *Chocolate, Strawberry, and Vanilla*, 55.

59. H. C. G. Matthew and Brian Harrison, eds., *Oxford Dictionary of National Biography* (New York: Oxford University Press, 2004), 641–643.

60. P. Michael, *Ices and Soda Fountain Drinks* (London: Maclaren & Sons [1925?]), 42.

61. Pellegrino Artusi, *Science in the Kitchen and the Art of Eating Well*, trans. Murtha Baca and Stephen Sartarelli (Toronto: University of Toronto Press, 2004), 545.

62. Alberto Capatti and Massimo Montanari, *Italian Cuisine: A Cultural History* (New York: Columbia University Press, 2003), 259.

63. Selitzer, *Dairy Industry in America*, 99.

FIVE. SCREAMING FOR ICE CREAM

1. An Observer, *City Cries, or, a Peep at Scenes in Town* (Philadelphia: George S. Appleton, 1850), 65–66.

2. Peter Quennell, editor, *Mayhew's London: Being Selections from 'London Labour and the London Poor,' by Henry Mayhew* (1851; reprint, London: Pilot, 1949), 136.

3. Ibid., 219.

4. Michael A. Musmanno, *The Story of the Italians in America* (New York: Doubleday, 1965), 103, 101.

5. Thomas Bailey Aldrich, *Unguarded Gates and Other Poems* (Boston: Houghton, Mifflin, 1895), 13–17.

6. Erik Amfitheatrof, *The Children of Columbus: An Informal History of the Italians in the New World* (Boston: Little, Brown, 1973), 170.

7. Harvey Levenstein, *Revolution at the Table* (New York: Oxford University Press, 1988), 157.

8. Kenneth T. Jackson and David S. Dunbar, eds., *Empire City: New York through the Centuries* (New York: Columbia University Press, 2002), 433.

9. Terri Colpi, *The Italian Factor: The Italian Community in Great Britain* (Edinburgh: Mainstream, 1991), 36.

10. Ibid., 34.

11. Grace M. Mayer, *Once upon a City* (New York: Macmillan, 1958), 382.

12. Junius Henri Browne, *The Great Metropolis: A Mirror of New York* (Hartford, CT: American Publishing, 1869), 99.

13. P. Michael, *Ices and Soda Fountain Drinks* (London: Maclaren & Sons [1925?]), 99.

14. Ibid., 100.

15. Autumn Stanley, *Mothers and Daughters of Invention* (New Brunswick, NJ: Rutgers University Press, 1995), 50–52.

16. Mary Sherman, "Manufacturing of Foods in the Tenements," 1906, Tenant Net: Tenants' and Renters' Rights, New York City, www.tenant.net/community/les, accessed July 23, 2008.

17. Ralph Selitzer, *The Dairy Industry in America* (New York: Dairy & Ice Cream Field and Books for Industry, 1976), 244–245.

18. Mayer, *Once upon a City*, 79.

19. James W. Parkinson, "Letter from Paris," *Confectioners' Journal* 4, no. 40 (May 1878): 19. Published by Journal Publishing Company, Philadelphia.

20. Frederick T. Vine, *Ices: Plain and Decorated* (London: Offices of the British Baker and Confectioner, and Hotel Guide and Caterers' Journal [1900?]), 6.

21. Andrew W. Tuer, *Old London Street Cries* (London: Field & Tuer, Leadenhall Press, 1885), 59–60.

22. Michael, *Ices and Soda Fountain Drinks*, 48.

23. Ibid., 48–49.

24. *Soda Fountain, the Trade Magazine*, comp., *Dispenser's Formulary*, 4th ed. (New York: Soda Fountain Publications, 1925), 171.

25. Selitzer, *Dairy Industry in America*, 245.

26. Michael, *Ices and Soda Fountain Drinks*, 70.

27. Ibid., 43.

28. Val Miller, *Thirty-six Years an Ice Cream Maker* (Davenport, IA: n.p., 1907), 51–54.

29. Michael, *Ices and Soda Fountain Drinks*, 105.

30. *American Kitchen Magazine* (March 1901): xxxiv.

31. Selitzer, *Dairy Industry in America*, 245.

32. "Ice Cream Sandwiches: All Wall Street Buying Them Nowadays to the Profit of the Inventor," *New York Sun*, August 19, 1900, p. 7.

33. Ibid.

34. Barbara Haber, *From Hardtack to Home Fries* (New York: Free Press, 2002), 62–68.

35. Charles Herman Senn, *Ices, and How to Make Them* (London: Universal Cookery and Food Association, 1900), 69.

36. *Soda Fountain, the Trade Magazine,* comp., *Dispenser's Formulary,* 148.

37. James W. Parkinson, "Ice Cream and Ice Cream Machinery, Ancient and Modern," *Confectioners' Journal* 2, no. 15 (March 1876): 11.

38. John J. Riley, *A History of the American Soft Drink Industry, Bottled Carbonated Beverages, 1805–1957* (New York: Arno, 1972), 5–6.

39. Harvey Wickes Felter, MD, and John Uri Lloyd, Phr.M., PhD, *King's American Dispensatory* (Cincinnati: Ohio Valley Company, 1898).

40. Riley, *History of the American Soft Drink Industry,* 49.

41. Ibid., 49.

42. Ibid., 50.

43. Ibid., 54.

44. See, for example, Anne Cooper Funderburg, *Sundae Best: A History of Soda Fountains* (Bowling Green, OH: Bowling Green State University Popular Press, 2002), 19; Riley, *History of the American Soft Drink Industry,* 3–21.

45. Funderburg, *Sundae Best,* 35–37.

46. James W. Tufts, "Soda-Fountains," in *One Hundred Years of American Commerce, 1795–1895,* ed. Chauncey M. Depew (New York: D. O. Hayes, 1895), 472.

47. James Dabney McCabe, *The Illustrated History of the Centennial Exhibition* (Philadelphia: National, 1876), 309–310.

48. Riley, *History of the American Soft Drink Industry,* 8–9.

49. Ibid., 9.

50. Ibid.

51. Ibid., 10.

52. E. F. White, *The Spatula Soda Water Guide* (Boston: Spatula Publishing, 1905), 115.

53. Ibid., 58.

54. Riley, *History of the American Soft Drink Industry,* 114.

55. Funderburg, *Sundae Best,* 52–59.
56. White, *Spatula Soda Water Guide,* 70.
57. Mayer, *Once upon a City,* 395.
58. Funderburg, *Sundae Best,* 62–64.
59. Michael Turback, *A Month of Sundaes* (New York: Red Rock Press, 2002), 30–32.
60. White, *Spatula Soda Water Guide,* 71.
61. Ibid.
62. Mayer, *Once upon a City,* 396–397.
63. Selitzer, *Dairy Industry in America,* 246.

SIX. WOMEN'S WORK

1. "Masser's Self-Acting Patent Ice-Cream Freezer and Beater," *Godey's Lady's Book* (Philadelphia) 41 (August 1850): 124.
2. Marjorie Kreidberg, *Food on the Frontier: Minnesota Cooking from 1850 to 1900, with Selected Recipes* (St. Paul: Minnesota Historical Society Press, 1975), 147.
3. Jennie G. Everson, *Tidewater Ice of the Kennebec River* (Freeport, ME: Bond Wheelwright, for the Maine State Museum, 1970), 124.
4. "Sarah Tyson Rorer Biography," February 2005, Feeding America: The Historic American Cookbook Project, Michigan State University Library, http://digital .lib.msu.edu/projects/cookbooks/html/project.html, accessed July 23, 2008.
5. Laura Shapiro, *Perfection Salad: Women and Cooking at the Turn of the Century* (New York: Modern Library, 2001), 4–7.
6. Catharine Esther Beecher, *Miss Beecher's Domestic Receipt Book: Designed as a Supplement to Her Treatise on Domestic Economy* (New York: Harper & Brothers, 1850), 166–167.
7. Agnes B. Marshall, *Fancy Ices* (London: Marshall's School of Cookery and Simpkin, Marshall, Hamilton, Kent, 1894), 117.
8. Maria Parloa, *Miss Parloa's New Cookbook: A Guide to Marketing and Cooking* (New York: C. T. Dillingham, 1882), 66–81.
9. Sarah Tyson Rorer, *Mrs. Rorer's Philadelphia Cook Book* (Philadelphia: Arnold, 1886), 546–548.
10. Mrs. D. A. Lincoln, *Mrs. Lincoln's Boston Cook Book* (Boston: Roberts Brothers, 1884), 361.
11. Janice Bluestein Longone, "Mary J. Lincoln," in *Culinary Biographies,* ed. Alice Arndt (Houston, TX: Yes Press, 2006), 243–245.

12. Mary Lincoln, "Ice and Ices," *New England Kitchen* 1, no. 4 (August 1894): 238–242.

13. Parloa, *Miss Parloa's New Cookbook*, 69.

14. Aunt Babette, *"Aunt Babette's" Cook Book* (Cincinnati, OH: Block Publishing and Print Company, 1889), 365.

15. Sarah Rorer, *Good Cooking* (Philadelphia: Curtis; New York: Doubleday & McClure, 1898), 88.

16. Estelle Woods Wilcox, *Buckeye Cookery and Practical Housekeeping: Compiled from Original Recipes* (Minneapolis, MN: Buckeye, 1877), 147.

17. Ibid., 398–399.

18. Aunt Babette, *"Aunt Babette's" Cook Book*, 365.

19. Marion Harland [Mary Virginia Terhune], *Common Sense in the Household: A Manual of Practical Housewifery* (New York: Scribner, Armstrong, 1873), 443–446.

20. Cornelius Weygandt, *Philadelphia Folks: Ways and Institutions in and about the Quaker City* (New York: D. Appleton–Century Company, 1938), 18–20.

21. Ibid., 23.

22. Susan MacDuff Wood, "Eliza Leslie," in *Culinary Biographies*, ed. Alice Arndt (Houston, TX: Yes Press, 2006), 239–240.

23. Eliza Leslie, *Seventy-Five Receipts for Pastry, Cakes, and Sweetmeats* (1828; reprint, Boston: Munroe and Francis, 1832), 37–39.

24. Florence Fabricant, "James Beard's American Favorites," *Food & Wine* (July 1981): 25–28.

25. At that time, confectioners and cooks often flavored ice creams and custards with fruit stones and leaves. However, they do contain a small amount of cyanide. As a result, the practice is not recommended today, particularly if the dessert is going to be served to children, the ill, or the elderly.

26. Eliza Leslie, *The Lady's Receipt-Book; a Useful Companion for Large or Small Families* (Philadelphia: Carey and Hart, 1847), 160.

27. Aunt Babette, *"Aunt Babette's" Cook Book*, 366.

28. Leslie, *Seventy-Five Receipts*, 39; Lincoln, *Boston Cook Book*, 363.

29. Elizabeth Fries Ellet, *Practical Housekeeper: A Cyclopaedia of Domestic Economy* (New York: Stringer and Townsend, 1857), 490.

30. Wilcox, *Buckeye Cookery*, 151.

31. Lincoln, *Boston Cook Book*, 363.

32. Rorer, *Good Cooking*, 87–88.

33. Sarah Tyson Rorer, *Ice Creams, Water Ices, Frozen Puddings, Together with Refreshments for All Social Affairs* (Philadelphia: Arnold, 1913; reprint, Whitefish, MT: Kessinger, n.d.), 2.

34. Ibid., 2.

35. Wilcox, *Buckeye Cookery*, 151.

36. Mrs. D. A. Lincoln, *Frozen Dainties* (Nashua, NH: White Mountain Freezer Company, 1889; reprint, Bedford, MA: Applewood Books, 2001), 5–8.

37. Barbara Ketcham Wheaton, *Victorian Ices & Ice Cream* (New York: Metropolitan Museum of Art, Charles Scribner's Sons, 1976), 6–7. Original recipes from Agnes B. Marshall, *The Book of Ices* (London: Marshall's School of Cookery and Simpkin, Marshall, Hamilton, Kent & Co., 1885).

38. Ibid., 13. Castor sugar was finely ground sugar. An ad for her "Pure Harmless Vegetable Colours for Colouring Ices, Creams, Jellies, Etc." appeared on page 63 of Marshall's *The Book of Ices*. A tammy was a fine strainer.

39. Alice Ross, "Fannie Merritt Farmer," in *Culinary Biographies*, ed. Alice Arndt (Houston, TX: Yes Press, 2006), 159–160.

40. Fannie Merritt Farmer, *The Boston Cooking-School Cook Book* (Boston: Little, Brown, 1896), 370.

41. Rorer, *Philadelphia Cook Book*, 451.

42. Elizabeth Ellicott Lea, *Domestic Cookery, Useful Receipts, and Hints to Young Housekeepers* (Baltimore, MD: Cushings and Bailey, 1869), 108–109.

43. Wilcox, *Buckeye Cookery*, 150.

44. Lincoln, *Boston Cook Book*, 362.

45. Beecher, *Miss Beecher's Domestic Receipt Book*, 167.

46. Rorer, *Philadelphia Cook Book*, 445.

47. Juliet Corson, *Miss Corson's Practical American Cookery and Household Management* (New York: Dodd, Mead, 1886), 527.

48. Sarah Tyson Rorer, *Dainty Dishes for All the Year Round* (Philadelphia: North Brothers Mfg., 1905), 23.

49. Rorer, *Ice Creams*, 14–16.

50. Marion Fontaine Cabell Tyree, *Housekeeping in Old Virginia* (Richmond, VA: J. W. Randolph & English, 1878), 439–440.

51. Lincoln, *Frozen Dainties*, 22–23.

52. Rorer, *Ice Creams*, 25.

53. Henry G. Harris and S. P. Borella, *All about Ices, Jellies, and Creams* (London: Kegan Paul, 2002), 39. Reprint of the 1926 edition published in London by Maclaren & Sons.

54. Lincoln, *Frozen Dainties*, 20–21.

55. Aunt Babette, *"Aunt Babette's" Cook Book*, 376.

56. Farmer, *Boston Cooking-School Cook Book*, 376.

57. Mary Elizabeth Wilson Sherwood, *Manners and Social Usages* (New York: Harper & Brothers, 1887), 275.

58. Kreidberg, *Food on the Frontier*, 187.

59. Mary F. Henderson, *Practical Cooking and Dinner Giving* (New York: Harper & Brothers, 1876), 306.

60. Kathryn Grover, ed., *Dining in America, 1850–1900* (Amherst: University of Massachusetts Press, 1987), 64–69.

61. Lincoln, "Ice and Ices," 242.

62. Robin Weir et al., *Mrs. Marshall: The Greatest Victorian Ice Cream Maker* (Otley, U.K.: Smith Settle, 1998), 54.

63. Parloa, *Miss Parloa's New Cookbook*, 294.

64. Wilcox, *Buckeye Cookery*, 151.

65. Charles Ranhofer, *The Epicurean* (New York: Charles Ranhofer, 1894), 1007.

66. Lincoln, *Frozen Dainties*, 23.

67. Aunt Babette, *"Aunt Babette's" Cook Book*, 377.

68. Lincoln, *Frozen Dainties*, 23.

69. Rorer, *Philadelphia Cook Book*, 456.

70. Rorer, *Dainty Dishes*, 48.

71. Henderson, *Practical Cooking*, 308–310.

72. Rorer, *Dainty Dishes*, 43.

73. Rorer, *Ice Creams*, 41–48.

74. Marshall, *Fancy Ices*, 13.

75. Mark Twain and Charles Dudley Warner, *The Gilded Age: A Tale of To-day* (Hartford, CT: American Publishing, 1874).

76. Una Pope-Hennessy, ed., *The Aristocratic Journey: Being the Outspoken Letters of Mrs. Basil Hall Written during a Fourteen Months' Sojourn in America, 1827–1828* (New York: G. P. Putnam's Sons, 1931), 182.

77. Sherwood, *Manners and Social Usage*, 361.

78. D. Albert Soeffing, "A Nineteenth-Century American Silver Flatware Service," *Antiques* (September 1999): 327–328.

79. Alfred L. Cralle, Ice Cream Mold and Disher, patented February 2, 1897, U.S. Patent No. 576,395.

80. Charles Ross Parke, *Dreams to Dust: A Diary of the California Gold Rush, 1849–1850*, ed. James E. Davis (Lincoln: University of Nebraska Press, 1989), 46–47.
81. Susan Williams, *Savory Suppers and Fashionable Feasts: Dining in Victorian America* (New York: Pantheon, 1985), 182.
82. Weygandt, *Philadelphia Folks*, 20.
83. Sandra L. Oliver, *Saltwater Foodways* (Mystic, CT: Mystic Seaport Museum, 1995), 316–318.

SEVEN. MODERN TIMES

1. Robert W. Rydell, John E. Findling, and Kimberly D. Pelle, *Fair America* (Washington, DC: Smithsonian Institution Press, 2000), 52–57.
2. Pamela J. Vaccaro, *Beyond the Ice Cream Cone* (St. Louis, MO: Enid Press, 2004), 92–98.
3. Jenifer Harvey Lang, ed., *Larousse gastronomique* (New York: Crown, 1990), 750–751 and 1143–1145.
4. François Massialot, *Nouvelle instruction pour les confitures, les liqueurs, et les fruits* (Amsterdam: Aux Depens de la Compagnie, 1734), 151.
5. Charles Elmé Francatelli, *The Royal Confectioner: English and Foreign* (London: Chapman and Hall, 1866), 181.
6. Lang, *Larousse gastronomique*, 750.
7. Robert J. Weir, "An 1807 Ice Cream Cone: Discovery and Evidence," *Food History News* 16, no. 2 (2004): 1–6.
8. Francatelli, *Royal Confectioner*, 181.
9. "Wafer Making," 2003, Historic Food: The Website of Food Historian Ivan Day, http://www.historicfood.com, accessed July 23, 2008.
10. Charles Elmé Francatelli, *Francatelli's Modern Cook* (Philadelphia: T. B. Peterson & Brothers, 1846), 468.
11. Ibid., 469–470.
12. Agnes B. Marshall, *Fancy Ices* (London: Marshall's School of Cookery and Simpkin, Marshall, Hamilton, Kent, 1894), 135.
13. Ibid., 116–117.
14. Antonio Valvona, Apparatus for Baking Biscuit-Cups for Ice-Cream, patented June 3, 1902, U.S. Patent No. 701,776, June 3, 1902.
15. I. Marchiony, Mold, patented December 15, 1903, U.S. Patent No. 746,971, December 15, 1903.

16. William Marchiony, "You Scream, I Scream, We All Scream for Ice Cream," *National Ice Cream Retailers Association Newsletter, NICRA Bulletin* (August 1984): 3.

17. Vaccaro, *Beyond the Ice Cream Cone,* 123–127; and Jack Marlowe, "Zalabia and the First Ice-Cream Cone," *Saudi Aramco World* (July–August 2003): 2–5.

18. Ralph Selitzer, *The Dairy Industry in America* (New York: Dairy & Ice Cream Field and Books for Industry, 1976), 243.

19. Al Reynolds, "IAICV Memories: The History of Ice Cream," 1998. International Association of Ice Cream Vendors, Philadelphia, www.iaicv.org, accessed July 23, 2008.

20. Selitzer, *Dairy Industry in America,* 247.

21. Ibid., 285.

22. Ibid., 106.

23. *Ice Cream Review* (December 1921): 83. Published by Olsen Publishing, Milwaukee, WI.

24. Selitzer, *Dairy Industry in America,* 235.

25. H. E. Van Norman, "Manufacture of Ice-Cream and Other Frozen Products," in *Cyclopedia of American Agriculture,* ed. Liberty Hyde Bailey (New York: Macmillan, 1910), 195–198.

26. Selitzer, *Dairy Industry in America,* 258.

27. Ibid., 238–239.

28. Van Norman, "Manufacture of Ice-Cream," 195.

29. "Gelatine Aids Digestion," *Confectioners' and Bakers' Gazette* (June 1913): 22. Published by H. B. Winton, New York.

30. Selitzer, *Dairy Industry in America,* 260–261.

31. Ibid., 284–285.

32. Warner-Jenkinson Manufacturing Company, *Ice Cream, Carbonated Beverages* (St. Louis, MO: Warner-Jenkinson Mfg., 1924), 1–2.

33. Ibid., 5.

34. Ibid., 18–37.

35. P. Michael, *Ices and Soda Fountain Drinks* (London: Maclaren & Sons [1925?]), 67–68, emphasis in the original.

36. Van Norman, "Manufacture of Ice-Cream," 196.

37. Selitzer, *Dairy Industry in America,* 258.

38. Ibid., 258–259.

39. *Ice Cream Review* (December 1917): 2.

40. *Ice Cream Review* (February 1919): 35; (September 1919): 18.

41. T. Percy Lewis and A. G. Bromley, *The Victorian Book of Cakes* (New York: Portland House, 1991), 142.

42. *Ice Cream Review* (May 1921): 99.

43. *Ice Cream Review* (September 1919): 18.

44. Lewis and Bromley, *Victorian Book of Cakes,* 20.

45. Ibid., 74.

46. Michael, *Ices and Soda Fountain Drinks,* 177.

47. E. F. White, *The Spatula Soda Water Guide* (Boston: Spatula Publishing, 1905), 133.

48. Junket rennet tablets and Junket ice cream mix are still sold. The latter is available in strawberry, Dutch chocolate, or vanilla flavors. The company Web site is www.junketdesserts.com.

49. "Jell-O: America's Most Famous Dessert," n.d., Duke University Libraries Digital Collections, http://library.duke.edu/digitalcollections/eaa.ck0050, accessed July 22, 2008; Carolyn Wyman, *Jell-O: A Biography* (New York: Harcourt, 2001), 16.

50. Arthur D. Burke, *Practical Ice Cream Making and Practical Mix Tables* (Milwaukee, WI: Olsen, 1933), 60–97.

51. Ibid., 104–105.

52. Reynolds, "IAICV Memories."

53. Selitzer, *Dairy Industry in America,* 285.

54. Ibid., 249–250.

55. Ibid., 248.

56. Ibid., 248–249.

57. William Bliss Stoddard, "How a Big Spokane Dairy Has Solved the Winter Ice Cream Problem," *Ice Cream Review* (August 1920): 78.

58. E. C. Beynon, "A Big Ice Cream Season," *Confectioners' and Bakers' Gazette* (May 1913): 24–25.

59. *Ice Cream Review* (December 1921): 145.

60. *Ice Cream Review* (February 1922): 179.

61. Ibid., 127.

62. *Ice Cream Review* (April 1922): 141.

63. Michael, *Ices and Soda Fountain Drinks,* 49.

64. "Cold Pie," *Time,* March 28, 1927.

65. Maurita Baldock, "Eskimo Pie Corporation Records, 1921–1926, #553," 1998, Smithsonian National Museum of American History, Archives Center.

Advertising, Marketing, and Commercial Imagery Collections, http://am
ericanhistory.si.edu/archives, accessed July 23, 2008.

66. Funderburg, *Chocolate, Strawberry, and Vanilla,* 129–130.

67. Selitzer, *Dairy Industry in America,* 264–266.

68. Ibid., 266–267.

69. Jefferson M. Moak, "The Frozen Sucker War: Good Humor v. Popsicle,"
Prologue Magazine (Spring 2005), U.S. National Archives and Records
Administration, www.archives.gov/publications/prologue/2005/spring/pop
sicle, accessed July 23, 2008.

70. F. W. Rueckheim, "Confectionery—Then and Now," *Confectioners' and Bakers'
Gazette* (March 10, 1913): 19.

71. *Ice Cream Review* (August 20, 1920): 1.

72. Selitzer, *Dairy Industry in America,* 276.

73. Siegfried Giedion, *Mechanization Takes Command* (New York: Oxford University Press, 1948), 602; Sylvia Lovegren, "Refrigerators," in *The Oxford Encyclopedia of Food and Drink in America,* ed. Andrew F. Smith (New York: Oxford
University Press, 2004), 351–352; Consumer Guide, the Auto Editors, "1923–
1927 Ford Model T," September 18, 2007, HowStuffWorks.com, http://auto
.howstuffworks/1923-1927-ford-model-t.htm, accessed July 29, 2008.

74. Lovegren, "Refrigerators," 351.

75. Selitzer, *Dairy Industry in America,* 264.

76. Ibid., 276.

77. "Company History," 1995, Hugh Moore Dixie Cup Company Collection,
1905–1986, compiled by Anke Voss-Hubbard, Lafayette College Libraries,
Easton, PA, ww2.lafayette.edu/~library/special/dixie/dixie.html, accessed July
22, 2008.

78. A. Emil Hiss, *The Standard Manual of Soda and Other Beverages: A Treatise
Especially Adapted to the Requirements of Druggists and Confectioners* (Chicago:
G. P. Engelhard, 1904), 233.

79. Sarah Tyson Rorer, *Dainty Dishes for All the Year Round* (Philadelphia: North
Brothers Mfg., 1905), 47.

80. Joseph Oliver Dahl, *Soda Fountain and Luncheonette Management* (New York:
Harper & Brothers, 1930), 217.

81. *Soda Fountain, the Trade Magazine,* comp., *Dispenser's Formulary,* 4th ed. (New
York: Soda Fountain Publications, 1925), 132.

82. Selitzer, *Dairy Industry in America,* 285.

83. Ibid., 269–270.

EIGHT. ICE CREAM FOR BREAKFAST

1. *Howard Johnson's Presents Old Time Ice Cream Soda Fountain Recipes, or How to Make a Soda Fountain Pay* (New York: Winter House, 1971), 16–18.

2. Ralph Selitzer, *The Dairy Industry in America* (New York: Dairy & Ice Cream Field and Books for Industry, 1976), 288.

3. Wendell Sherwood Arbuckle, *Ice Cream* (Westport, CT: Avi, 1966), 6–7.

4. Selitzer, *Dairy Industry in America*, 288–289.

5. Ibid., 291.

6. *A 50-Year History of the Ice Cream Industry, 1905–1955* (New York: Trade Paper Division, Reuben H. Donnelley Corporation, 1955), 128.

7. Selitzer, *Dairy Industry in America*, 289–290.

8. Malcolm Parks, "An Open Letter to My Manufacturer," *Ice Cream Trade Journal* 33 (August 1937): 30. Published by the Trade Papers Division of the Reuben H. Donnelley Corporation, New York.

9. Selitzer, *Dairy Industry in America*, 290.

10. "Some Suggestions on Methods of Meeting Mechanical Household Refrigeration Competition," *Ice Cream Review* (May 1933): 32. Published by Olsen Publishing, Milwaukee, WI.

11. Alice Bradley, *Electric Refrigerator Menus and Recipes: Recipes prepared especially for the General Electric Refrigerator* (Cleveland, OH: General Electric, 1927), 40.

12. Ibid., 37.

13. Ibid., 93.

14. Ibid., 94.

15. P. H. Tracy, "Questions and Answers," *Ice Cream Trade Journal* (November 1937): 33.

16. *A 50-Year History*, 129.

17. Selitzer, *Dairy Industry in America*, 288–289.

18. Arthur D. Burke, *Practical Ice Cream Making and Practical Mix Tables* (Milwaukee: Olsen, 1933), 203–206.

19. Joseph Oliver Dahl, *Soda Fountain and Luncheonette Management* (New York: Harper & Brothers, 1933), 10–12.

20. *Ice Cream Review* (November 1932): 19.

21. *Ice Cream Trade Journal* (July 1937): 9.

22. *Howard Johnson's Presents*, 19.

23. "Walker's Insures Its Business with Quality," *Ice Cream Trade Journal* (July 1937): 22.

24. Brian Butko, *Klondikes, Chipped Ham & Skyscraper Cones: The Story of Isaly's* (Mechanicsburg, PA: Stackpole Books, 2001), 1.

25. Selitzer, *Dairy Industry in America*, 291–292.

26. Ibid., 292.

27. Philip Langdon, *Orange Roofs, Golden Arches: The Architecture of American Chain Restaurants* (New York: Alfred A. Knopf, 1986), 43.

28. Ibid., 64.

29. Ibid., 50.

30. Ibid., 69.

31. Marcy Norton, "Dairy Queen History Curls through Area," 1998, Progress '98: 300 Things That Make the Quad-Cities Great, http://qconline.com/progress98/business, accessed July 23, 2008.

32. "I'll Take Vanilla," *Time* (May 11, 1942), Time Archive, 1923 to the Present, www.time.com/time/archive, accessed July 23, 2008.

33. Selitzer, *Dairy Industry in America*, 337–338.

34. Ibid., 338.

35. Ibid., 337.

36. Arbuckle, *Ice Cream*, 6–7.

37. "Victory Sundaes," *Ice Cream Review* (March 1942): 24–25.

38. Selitzer, *Dairy Industry in America*, 338.

39. "Patterns," *Time* (June 15, 1942), Time Archive, 1923 to the Present, www.time.com/time/archive, accessed July 23, 2008.

40. Helen Robertson, Sarah MacLeod, and Frances Preston, *What Do We Eat Now? A Guide to Wartime Housekeeping* (Philadelphia: J. B. Lippincott, 1942), 290.

41. Warner-Jenkinson Manufacturing Company, *Ice Cream, Carbonated Beverages* (St. Louis: Warner-Jenkinson Mfg., 1924), 34.

42. "About Dreyer's: Dreyer's Historic Headlines," n.d., Dreyer's Grand Ice Cream, www.dreyersinc.com, accessed July 22, 2008.

43. Robertson, MacLeod, and Preston, *What Do We Eat Now?* 297.

44. Arbuckle, *Ice Cream*, 6–7.

45. Robert T. Marshall, H. Douglas Goff, and Richard W. Hartel, *Ice Cream* (New York: Kluwer Academic/Plenum, 2003), 8.

46. *A 50-Year History*, 143.

47. Ibid., 144.

48. Ruth Graves Wakefield, *Toll House Tried and True Recipes* (New York: M. Barrows, 1948), 216.

49. William I. Kaufman, *Quick and Easy Desserts* (New York: Pyramid Publications, 1965).

50. Wakefield, *Toll House Tried and True Recipes*, 217.

51. Peg Bracken, *The I Hate to Cook Book* (Greenwich, CT: Fawcett Publications, 1960), 97.

52. Will Anderson, *Lost Diners and Roadside Restaurants of New England and New York* (Bath, ME: Anderson & Sons' Publishing, 1987), 92.

53. "Real Scoop," *Time* (April 7, 1958), Time Archive, 1923 to the Present, www.time.com/time/archive, accessed July 23, 2008.

54. James Beard, "Cooking with James Beard, Ice Cream," *Gourmet* (July 1970): 50.

55. "A Bang-Up Finish: Peach Bombe," *McCall's* (August 1970): 57.

56. Carolyn Anderson, *The Complete Book of Homemade Ice Cream, Milk Sherbet & Sherbet* (New York: Saturday Review Press, 1972), 23.

57. "Herrell's in the Media," quoting *Entrepreneur Magazine* (March 1987), Herrell's Ice Cream, www.herrells.com, accessed July 23, 2008.

58. John Skow, "They All Scream for It," *Time* (August 10, 1981), Time Archive, 1923 to the Present, www.time.com/time/archive, accessed July 23, 2008.

EPILOGUE

1. Robert T. Marshall, H. Douglas Goff, and Richard W. Hartel, *Ice Cream* (New York: Kluwer Academic/Plenum, 2003), 7.

2. G. O. Heck, "The Future of the Ice Cream Business," *Ice Cream Field & Trade Journal* (June 1967): 70–77.

3. Chris Ryan, "An Old Favorite Gets New Attention," *Fresh Cup Specialty Coffee & Tea Trade Magazine* (July 2005), www.freshcup.com, accessed July 2008.

BIBLIOGRAPHY

BOOKS

Albala, Ken. *Eating Right in the Renaissance*. Berkeley: University of California Press, 2002.

Amfitheatrof, Erik. *The Children of Columbus: An Informal History of the Italians in the New World*. Boston: Little, Brown, 1973.

Anderson, Carolyn. *The Complete Book of Homemade Ice Cream, Milk Sherbet & Sherbet*. New York: Saturday Review Press, 1972.

Anderson, Will. *Lost Diners and Roadside Restaurants of New England and New York*. Bath, ME: Anderson & Sons' Publishing, 1987.

Anthimus. *On the Observance of Foods*. Translated and edited by Mark Grant. Totnes, U.K.: Prospect Books, 1996.

Arbuckle, Wendell Sherwood. *Ice Cream*. Westport, CT: Avi, 1966.

Arndt, Alice, ed. *Culinary Biographies*. Houston, TX: Yes Press, 2006.

————. *Seasoning Savvy*. New York: Haworth Herbal Press, 1999.

Arnold, Arthur. *Through Persia by Caravan*. New York: Harper & Brothers, 1877.

Aron, Jean-Paul. *The Art of Eating in France*. Translated by Nina Rootes. New York: Harper & Row, 1973.

Artusi, Pellegrino. *Science in the Kitchen and the Art of Eating Well*. Translated by Murtha Baca and Stephen Sartarelli. Toronto: University of Toronto Press, 2004.

Audiger, Nicolas. *La maison réglée*. Paris: Librairie Plon, 1692. Reprinted in Alfred Franklin, *La vie privée d'autrefois*. Paris: Librairie Plon, 1898.

Babette, Aunt. *"Aunt Babette's" Cook Book*. Cincinnati, OH: Block Publishing and Print Company, 1889.

Bailey, Liberty Hyde, ed. *Cyclopedia of American Agriculture*. New York: Macmillan, 1910.

Baldini, Filippo. *De sorbetti*. Bologna, Italy: Arnaldo Forni Editore, 1979. Reprint of the 1784 edition.

Balzac, Honoré de. *A Harlot High and Low* [Splendeurs et misères des courtisanes]. Translated and with an introduction by Rayner Heppenstall. Harmondsworth, U.K.: Penguin Books, 1970.

———. *Splendeurs et misères des courtisanes.* 1839. Reprint, Paris: Éditions Gallimard, 1973.

Batchelder, Ann. *New Delineator Recipes.* Chicago: Butterick, 1930.

Batterberry, Michael, and Ariane Batterberry. *On the Town in New York: A History of Eating, Drinking, and Entertainments from 1776 to the Present.* New York: Charles Scribner's Sons, 1973.

Beecher, Catharine Esther. *Miss Beecher's Domestic Receipt Book: Designed as a Supplement to Her Treatise on Domestic Economy.* New York: Harper & Brothers, 1850.

Belden, Louise Conway. *The Festive Tradition: Table Decoration and Desserts in America, 1650–1900.* New York: W. W. Norton, 1983.

Bernardi. *L'Art de donner des bals et soirées, ou le glacier royal.* Bruxelles: Société Typographique Belge, 1844.

Berolzheimer, Ruth. *Culinary Arts Institute Encyclopedic Cookbook.* New York: Grosset & Dunlap, 1965.

Better Homes & Gardens Dessert Cook Book. New York: Meredith, 1967.

Better Homes & Gardens New Cook Book. New York: Meredith, 1962.

Betty Crocker's Picture Cook Book. New York: McGraw-Hill Book Company and General Mills, 1950.

Borella, Mr. *The Court and Country Confectioner: Or, the House-Keeper's Guide.* 1770. Reprint, London: printed for G. Riley . . . J. Bell . . . J. Wheble . . . and C. Etherington, 1772.

Bracken, Peg. *The I Hate to Cook Book.* Greenwich, CT: Fawcett Publications, 1960.

Bradley, Alice. *Electric Refrigerator Menus and Recipes: Recipes prepared especially for the General Electric Refrigerator.* Cleveland, OH: General Electric, 1927.

Briggs, Richard. *The New Art of Cookery.* Philadelphia: W. Spotswood, R. Campbell, and B. Johnson, 1792.

Brillat-Savarin, Jean Anthelme. *The Physiology of Taste.* San Francisco: North Point Press, 1986.

Brown, Peter B., and Ivan Day. *Pleasures of the Table: Ritual and Display in the European Dining Room, 1600–1900.* York, U.K.: York Civic Trust, 1997.

Browne, Junius Henri. *The Great Metropolis: A Mirror of New York.* Hartford, CT: American Publishing, 1869.

Brydone, Patrick. *A Tour Through Sicily & Malta, In a series of letters to William Beckford, Esq.* London: T. Cadell and W. Davies, 1806.

Burke, Arthur D. *Practical Ice Cream Making and Practical Mix Tables*. Milwaukee, WI: Olsen, 1933.

Butko, Brian. *Klondikes, Chipped Ham & Skyscraper Cones: The Story of Isaly's*. Mechanicsburg, PA: Stackpole Books, 2001.

Capatti, Alberto, and Massimo Montanari. *Italian Cuisine: A Cultural History*. New York: Columbia University Press, 2003.

Chardin, Jean. *A Journey to Persia, Jean Chardin's Portrait of a Seventeenth-Century Empire*. Translated and edited by Ronald W. Ferrier. London: I. B. Tauris, 1996.

———. *Travels in Persia, 1673–1677*. New York: Dover, 1988.

Ciocca, Giuseppe. *Il pasticciere e confettiere moderno*. Milano: U. Hoepli, 1907.

Coan, Peter Morton. *Ellis Island Interviews*. New York: Facts on File, 1997.

Coe, Sophie D., and Michael D. Coe. *The True History of Chocolate*. London: Thames and Hudson, 1996.

Coffin, Sarah D., et al. *Feeding Desire: Design and the Tools of the Table, 1500–2005*. New York: Assouline Publishing in association with Cooper-Hewitt, National Design Museum, 2006.

Colpi, Terri. *The Italian Factor: The Italian Community in Great Britain*. Edinburgh: Mainstream, 1991.

———. *Italians Forward: A Visual History of the Italian Community in Great Britain*. Edinburgh: Mainstream, 1991.

Corrado, Vincenzo. *Il credenziere di buon gusto*. Naples: Nella Stamperia Raimondiana, 1778. Reprint, Sala Bolognese: A. Forni, 1991.

Corson, Juliet. *Miss Corson's Practical American Cookery and Household Management*. New York: Dodd, Mead, 1886.

Crosby, Alfred W., Jr. *The Columbian Exchange: Biological and Cultural Consequences of 1492*. Westport, CT: Greenwood Press, 1972.

Cummings, Richard O. *The American Ice Harvests: A Historical Study in Technology, 1800–1918*. Berkeley: University of California Press, 1949.

Dahl, Joseph Oliver. *Soda Fountain and Luncheonette Management*. New York: Harper & Brothers, 1933.

Damerow, Gail. *Ice Cream! The Whole Scoop*. Macomb, IL: Glenbridge, 1991.

David, Elizabeth. *Harvest of the Cold Months*. New York: Viking Penguin, 1995.

———. *Is There a Nutmeg in the House?* New York: Penguin Books, 2002.

Davidson, Alan. *The Oxford Companion to Food*. Oxford: Oxford University Press, 1999.

Dayton, Abram C. *Last Days of Knickerbocker Life in New York*. New York: George W. Harlan, 1882.

DeGouy, Louis P. *Ice Cream and Ice Cream Desserts*. New York: Dover, 1938.
———. *Soda Fountain and Luncheonette Drinks and Recipes*. Stamford, CT: J. O. Dahl, 1940.
Depew, Chauncey M., ed. *One Hundred Years of American Commerce*. New York: D. O. Haynes, 1895.
DeVoe, Thomas F. *The Market Assistant*. New York: Hurd and Houghton, 1867.
———. *The Market Book*. 1862. Reprint, New York: Burt Franklin, 1969.
Dickson, Paul. *The Great American Ice Cream Book*. New York: Atheneum, 1978.
Dictionnaire portatif de cuisine, d'office, et de distillation. Paris: Vincent, 1767.
Dorsey, Leslie, and Janice Devine. *Fare Thee Well: A Backward Look at Two Centuries of Historic American Hostelries, Fashionable Spas & Seaside Resorts*. New York: Crown, 1964.
Dubelle, G. H., ed. *Soda Fountain Beverages: A Practical Receipt Book for Druggists, Chemists, Confectioners, and Venders of Soda Water*. New York: Spon & Chamberlain, 1917.
Eales, Mary. *Mrs. Mary Eales's Receipts*. London: Prospect Books, 1985. Facsimile of the 1733 edition; originally published in 1718. Distributed in the United States by the University Press of Virginia.
Ellet, Elizabeth Fries. *Practical Housekeeper: A Cyclopaedia of Domestic Economy*. New York: Stringer and Townsend, 1857.
Emy, M. *L'Art de bien faire les glaces d'office*. Paris: Chez Le Clerc, 1768.
Escoffier, Auguste. *Escoffier's Cook Book of Desserts, Sweets, and Ices*. New York: Crescent Books, 1941.
Estes, Rufus. *Good Things to Eat*. Chicago: self-published, 1911.
Eustis, Célestine. *Cooking in Old Créole Days*. New York: R. H. Russell, 1904.
Evelyn, John. *The Diary of John Evelyn*. Edited by E. S. de Beer. London: Oxford University Press, 1959.
Everson, Jennie G. *Tidewater Ice of the Kennebec River*. Freeport, ME: Bond Wheelwright, for the Maine State Museum, 1970.
Farmer, Fannie Merritt. *The Boston Cooking-School Cook Book*. Boston: Little, Brown, 1896.
Felter, Harvey Wickes, MD, and John Uri Lloyd, Phr. M., PhD. *King's American Dispensatory*. Cincinnati: Ohio Valley Company, 1898.
Fierro, Alfred. *Histoire et dictionnaire de Paris*. Paris: Éditions Robert Laffont, S.A., 1996.
A 50-Year History of the Ice Cream Industry, 1905–1955. New York: Trade Paper Division, Reuben H. Donnelley Corporation, 1955.

Finley, M. I., Denis Mack Smith, and Christopher Duggan. *A History of Sicily*. New York: Viking, 1987.

Flandrin, Jean-Louis. *Food: A Culinary History from Antiquity to the Present*. New York: Columbia University Press, 1999.

Fletcher, H. Phillips. *The St. Louis Exhibition, 1904*. London: B. T. Batsford, 1905.

Foster, George G. *New York by Gas-Light and Other Urban Sketches*. Edited and with an introduction by Stuart M. Blumin. 1850. Reprint, Berkeley: University of California Press, 1990.

———. *New York in Slices: By an Experienced Carver; Being the Original Slices Published in the N.Y. Tribune*. New York: W. H. Graham, 1849.

Fox, Minnie C. *The Blue Grass Cook Book*. New York: Fox, Duffield, 1904.

Foy, Jessica, and Thomas J. Schlereth, eds. *American Home Life, 1880–1930*. Knoxville: University of Tennessee Press, 1992.

Francatelli, Charles Elmé. *Francatelli's Modern Cook*. Philadelphia: T. B. Peterson & Brothers, 1846.

———. *The Royal Confectioner: English and Foreign*. London: Chapman and Hall, 1866.

Frieda, Leonie. *Catherine de Medici*. London: Weidenfeld & Nicolson, 2003.

Frost, Sarah Annie. *The Godey's Lady's Book Receipts and Household Hints*. Philadelphia: Evans, Stoddart, 1870.

Funderburg, Anne Cooper. *Chocolate, Strawberry, and Vanilla: A History of American Ice Cream*. Bowling Green, OH: Bowling Green State University Popular Press, 1995.

———. *Sundae Best: A History of Soda Fountains*. Bowling Green, OH: Bowling Green State University Popular Press, 2002.

Garland, Sarah. *The Complete Book of Herbs & Spices*. London: Frances Lincoln, 1989.

Garrett, Theodore Francis, ed. *The Encyclopædia of Practical Cookery*. London: Upcott Gill [1890?].

Gelernter, David. *1939: The Lost World of the Fair*. New York: Free Press, 1995.

Gentile, Maria. *The Italian Cook Book*. New York: Italian Book Company, 1919.

Giedion, Siegfried. *Mechanization Takes Command*. New York: Oxford University Press, 1948.

Gilliers, Joseph. *Le Cannameliste français*. Nancy: Chez Jean-Baptiste-Hiacinthe Leclerc, 1768.

Glasse, Hannah. *The Art of Cookery Made Plain and Easy*. London, 1796. Reprint, Hamden, CT: Archon Books, 1971.

———. *The Compleat Confectioner*. Dublin: printed by John Exshaw, 1762.

Glasse, Hannah, with considerable additions and corrections by Maria Wilson. *The Complete Confectioner, or, Housekeeper's Guide*. London: printed by J. W. Meyers for West and Hughes, 1800.

Glimpses of the Louisiana Purchase Exposition and City of St. Louis. Chicago: Laird & Lee, 1904.

The Good Housekeeping Cook Book. New York: Farrar & Rinehart, 1944.

Gosnell, Mariana. *Ice: The Nature, the History, and the Uses of an Astonishing Substance*. New York: Alfred A. Knopf, 2005.

Gouffé, Jules. *Le livre de cuisine*. Paris: Librairie Hachette et Cie, 1870.

———. *The Royal Cookery Book*. Translated from the French and adapted for English use by Alphonse Gouffé. London: Sampson Low, Marston, Searle & Rivington, 1880.

Gronow, Rees Howell. *The Reminiscences and Recollections of Captain Gronow: 1810–1860*. Vols. 1 and 2. London: John C. Nimmo, 1892.

Grover, Kathryn, ed. *Dining in America: 1850–1900*. Amherst: University of Massachusetts Press, 1987.

Gunter, William. *Gunter's Confectioner's Oracle*. London: Alfred Miller, 1830.

Haber, Barbara. *From Hardtack to Home Fries*. New York: Free Press, 2002.

Haine, W. Scott. *The World of the Paris Café: Sociability among the French Working Class, 1789–1914*. Baltimore, MD: Johns Hopkins University Press, 1996.

Haines, Pamela. *Tea at Gunter's*. London: Heinemann, 1974.

Hall, Florence Howe. *Social Customs*. Boston: Estes and Lauriat, 1887.

Handy, Etta H. *Ice Cream for Small Plants*. Chicago: Hotel Monthly Press, 1937.

Harland, Marion [Mary Virginia Terhune]. *Common Sense in the Household: A Manual of Practical Housewifery*. New York: Scribner, Armstrong, 1873.

Harris, Henry G., and S. P. Borella. *All about Ices, Jellies, and Creams*. London: Kegan Paul, 2002. Reprint of the 1926 edition published in London by Maclaren & Sons.

Haswell, Chas. H. *Reminiscences of an Octogenarian of the City of New York (1816 to 1860)*. New York: Harper & Brothers, 1896.

Havens, Catherine Elizabeth. *Diary of a Little Girl in Old New York*. New York: Henry Collins Brown, 1919.

Hayes, Joanne Lamb. *Grandma's Wartime Kitchen: World War II and the Way We Cooked*. New York: St. Martin's Press, 2000.

Heatter, Maida. *Maida Heatter's Book of Great Desserts*. New York: Alfred A. Knopf, 1977.

Heimann, Jim. *Car Hops and Curb Service: A History of American Drive-In Restaurants, 1920–1960*. San Francisco: Chronicle Books, 1996.

Henderson, Mary F. *Practical Cooking and Dinner Giving*. New York: Harper & Brothers, 1876.

Herbert, Sir Thomas. *Travels in Persia, 1627–1629*. Abridged and edited by Sir William Foster. New York: Robert M. McBride, 1929.

Hess, Karen. *Martha Washington's Booke of Cookery*. New York: Columbia University Press, 1981.

Hickman, Peggy. *A Jane Austen Household Book*. Newton Abbot, U.K.: David & Charles, 1977.

Hirtzler, Victor. *The Hotel St. Francis Cook Book*. Chicago: Hotel Monthly Press, 1919.

Hiss, A. Emil. *The Standard Manual of Soda and Other Beverages: A Treatise Especially Adapted to the Requirements of Druggists and Confectioners*. Chicago: G. P. Engelhard, 1904.

Howard Johnson's Presents Old Time Ice Cream Soda Fountain Recipes, or How to Make a Soda Fountain Pay. New York: Winter House, 1971.

Jackson, Kenneth T., and David S. Dunbar, eds. *Empire City: New York through the Centuries*. New York: Columbia University Press, 2002.

Janin, Jules. *The American in Paris*. London: Longman, Brown, Green, and Longmans, 1843.

Janvier, Thomas A. *In Old New York*. New York: Harper & Brothers, 1894.

Jarrin, G. A. *The Italian Confectioner*. 1820. Reprint, London: John Harding, 1823.

———. *The Italian Confectioner*. London: William H. Ainsworth, 1827.

Jarrin, W. A. [William Alexis]. *The Italian Confectioner*. London: E. S. Ebers, 1844.

Jeanes, William. *Gunter's Modern Confectioner*. London: J. C. Hotten, 1871.

———. *The Modern Confectioner: A Practical Guide*. London: John Camden Hotten, 1861.

Jones, Joseph C., Jr. *America's Icemen*. Humble, TX: Jobeco Books, 1984.

Kander, Mrs. Simon. *The New Settlement Cook Book*. New York: Simon and Schuster, 1951.

Katz, Solomon H., ed. *Encyclopedia of Food and Culture*. New York: Charles Scribner's Sons, 2003.

Kaufman, William I. *Quick and Easy Desserts*. New York: Pyramid Publications, 1965.

Kelly, Patricia M., ed. *Luncheonette: Ice-Cream, Beverage, and Sandwich Recipes from the Golden Age of the Soda Fountain*. New York: Crown, 1989.

Kreidberg, Marjorie. *Food on the Frontier: Minnesota Cooking from 1850 to 1900, with Selected Recipes.* St. Paul: Minnesota Historical Society Press, 1975.

Kurlansky, Mark. *Salt: A World History.* New York: Walker, 2002.

Lacam, Pierre. *Le mémorial des glaces et entremets.* Paris: Chez l'Auteur, 1911.

La Chapelle, Vincent. *Le cuisinier moderne.* La Haye, Netherlands: V. La Chapelle, 1742.

———. *The Modern Cook.* London: Nicolas Prevost, 1733.

Lane, Roger. *William Dorsey's Philadelphia and Ours: On the Past and Future of the Black City in America.* New York: Oxford University Press, 1991.

Lang, Jenifer Harvey, ed. *Larousse gastronomique.* New York: Crown, 1990.

Langdon, Philip. *Orange Roofs, Golden Arches: The Architecture of American Chain Restaurants.* New York: Alfred A. Knopf, 1986.

Larson, Charles R., ed. *The Fountain Operator's Manual.* New York: Fountain Operator's Manual Division of the Syndicate Store Merchandiser, 1940.

Latini, Antonio. *Lo scalco alla moderna.* 2 vols. Napoli: Parrino & Mutii, 1692, 1694. Reprint, Milano: Appunti di Gastronomia, 1993.

La Varenne, François Pierre de. *Le vrai cuisinier françois.* Bruxelles: Chez George de Backer . . . , 1712.

Lea, Elizabeth Ellicott. *Domestic Cookery, Useful Receipts, and Hints to Young Housekeepers.* Baltimore, MD: Cushings and Bailey, 1869.

Leslie, Eliza. *Directions for Cookery in Its Various Branches.* Philadelphia: B. L. Carey & A. Hart, 1840.

———. *The Lady's Receipt-Book; a Useful Companion for Large or Small Families.* Philadelphia: Carey and Hart, 1847.

———. *Seventy-Five Receipts for Pastry, Cakes, and Sweetmeats.* 1828. Reprint, Boston: Munroe and Francis, 1832.

Levenstein, Harvey. *Revolution at the Table.* New York: Oxford University Press, 1988.

Lewis, T. Percy, and A. G. Bromley. *The Victorian Book of Cakes.* New York: Portland House, 1991.

Liddell, Caroline, and Robin Weir. *Ices: The Definitive Guide.* London: Grub Street, 1995.

Lincoln, Mrs. D. A. *Frozen Dainties.* Nashua, NH: White Mountain Freezer Company, 1889. Reprint, Bedford, MA: Applewood Books, 2001.

———. *Mrs. Lincoln's Boston Cook Book.* Boston: Roberts Brothers, 1884.

London, Anne, ed. *The Complete American-Jewish Cookbook.* Cleveland, OH: World Publishing, 1952.

The Louisiana Purchase Exposition at St. Louis, 1904. Boston: Raymond & Whitcomb, 1904.

Lovegren, Sylvia. *Fashionable Food: Seven Decades of Food Fads*. Chicago: University of Chicago Press, 2005.

Mariani, John. *America Eats Out*. New York: William Morrow, 1991.

Marsh, Dorothy B., ed. *The Good Housekeeping Cook Book*. New York: Rinehart, 1949.

Marshall, Agnes B. *The Book of Ices*. 1885. Reprint, London: Marshall's School of Cookery and Simpkin, Marshall, Hamilton, Kent, 1894.

————. *Fancy Ices*. London: Marshall's School of Cookery and Simpkin, Marshall, Hamilton, Kent, 1894.

————. *Mrs. A. B. Marshall's Cookery Book*. London: Robert Hayes [1890?].

Marshall, Ann Parks, ed. *Martha Washington's Rules for Cooking Used Everyday at Mt. Vernon*. Washington, DC: Ransdell, 1931.

Marshall, Robert T., H. Douglas Goff, and Richard W. Hartel. *Ice Cream*. New York: Kluwer Academic/Plenum, 2003.

Mason, Laura. *Sugar-Plums and Sherbet: The Prehistory of Sweets*. Devon, U.K.: Prospect Books, 2004.

Massialot, François. *Le nouveau cuisinier royal et bourgeois*. Paris: Chez Claude Prudhomme, 1734.

————. *Nouvelle instruction pour les confitures, les liqueurs, et les fruits*. Paris: Chez Claude Prudhomme, 1716.

————. *Nouvelle instruction pour les confitures, les liqueurs, et les fruits*. Amsterdam: Aux Depens de la Compagnie, 1734.

Masters, Thomas. *The Ice Book*. London: Simpkin, Marshal, 1844.

Matthew, H. C. G., and Brian Harrison, eds. *Oxford Dictionary of National Biography*. New York: Oxford University Press, 2004.

May, Robert. *The Accomplisht Cook*. London: printed for Obadiah Blagrave, 1685.

Mayer, Grace M. *Once upon a City*. New York: Macmillan, 1958.

Mayhew, Henry. *London Labor and the London Poor*. New York: Harper, 1851.

McAllister, Marvin. *White People Do Not Know How to Behave at Entertainments Designed for Ladies and Gentlemen of Colour: William Brown's African and American Theater*. Chapel Hill: University of North Carolina Press, 2003.

McCabe, James Dabney. *The Illustrated History of the Centennial Exhibition*. Philadelphia: National, 1876.

McGee, Harold. *On Food and Cooking: The Science and Lore of the Kitchen*. New York: Collier Books, 1984.

Menon, François. *The Art of Modern Cookery Displayed* [Les soupers de la cour]. London: R. Davis, 1767.

———. *The Professed Cook*. London: R. Davis, 1769.

Mentor [Nathan D. Urner]. *Never: A Hand-Book for the Uninitiated and Inexperienced Aspirants to Refined Society's Giddy Heights and Glittering Attainments*. New York: G. W. Carleton, 1883.

Meyer, Hazel. *The Complete Book of Home Freezing*. Philadelphia: J. B. Lippincott, 1964.

Michael, P. *Ices and Soda Fountain Drinks*. London: Maclaren & Sons [1925?].

Milioni, Stefano. *Columbus Menu: Italian Cuisine after the First Voyage of Christopher Columbus*. New York: Italian Trade Commission, 1992.

Miller, Mildred, and Bascha Snyder. *The Kosher Gourmet*. New York: Vantage, 1967.

Miller, Val. *Thirty-six Years an Ice Cream Maker*. Davenport, IA: n.p., 1907.

Mintz, Sidney W. *Sweetness and Power: The Place of Sugar in Modern History*. New York: Viking, 1985.

Moore, John. *A View of Society and Manners in Italy*. Vol. 3. Dublin: printed for W. Gilbert, W. Wilson, J. Moore, W. Jones, and J. Rice, 1792.

Morier, James. *The Adventures of Hajji Baba of Ispahan*. 1824. Reprint, New York: Hart, 1976.

Moura, Jean, and Paul Louvet. *Le Café Procope*. Paris: Perrin, 1929.

Murphy, Agnes. *The American Everyday Cookbook*. New York: Random House, 1955.

Musmanno, Michael A. *The Story of the Italians in America*. New York: Doubleday, 1965.

Naft, Stephen. *International Conversion Tables*. Expanded and revised by Ralph de Sola. New York: Duell, Sloan and Pearce, 1961.

Nasaw, David. *Going Out: The Rise and Fall of Public Amusements*. New York: Basic Books, 1993.

New York Herald Tribune. *America's Cook Book*. New York: Charles Scribner's Sons, 1940.

Nutt, Frederick. *The Complete Confectioner*. 4th ed. 1789. Reprint, London: Richard Scott, 1807.

An Observer. *City Cries, or, a Peep at Scenes in Town*. Philadelphia: George S. Appleton, 1850.

Official Guide Book of the New York World's Fair, 1939. New York: Exposition Publications, 1939.

Official Guide Book: The World's Fair of 1940 in New York. New York: Rogers, Kellogg, Stillson, 1940.

Oliver, Sandra L. *Saltwater Foodways*. Mystic, CT: Mystic Seaport Museum, 1995.

Palmer, Carl J. *History of the Soda Fountain Industry*. Chicago: Soda Fountain Manufacturers Association, 1947.

Parke, Charles Ross. *Dreams to Dust: A Diary of the California Gold Rush, 1849–1850*. Edited by James E. Davis. Lincoln: University of Nebraska Press, 1989.

Parkinson, Eleanor. *The Complete Confectioner, Pastry-Cook, and Baker*. 1844. Reprint, Philadelphia: J. B. Lippincott, 1864.

Parloa, Maria. *Chocolate and Cocoa Recipes*. Dorchester, MA: Walter Baker, 1911.

———. *Miss Parloa's New Cookbook: A Guide to Marketing and Cooking*. New York: C. T. Dillingham, 1882.

Picard, Liza. *Victorian London: The Tale of a City, 1840–1870*. New York: St. Martin's, 2005.

Pinkerton, John. *Recollections of Paris, in the Years 1802–3–4–5*. London: Longman, Hurst, Rees & Orme, 1806.

Plante, Ellen M. *The American Kitchen: 1700 to the Present*. New York: Facts on File, 1995.

Pope-Hennessy, Una, ed. *The Aristocratic Journey: Being the Outspoken Letters of Mrs. Basil Hall Written during a Fourteen Months' Sojourn in America, 1827–1828*. New York: G. P. Putnam's Sons, 1931.

Powell, Marilyn. *Cool: The Story of Ice Cream*. Toronto: Penguin Group, 2005.

Prentiss, Rev. George Lewis. *The Life and Letters of Elizabeth Prentiss*. London: Hodder and Stoughton, 1882.

Quennell, Peter, ed. *Mayhew's London: Being Selections from 'London Labour and the London Poor,' by Henry Mayhew*. 1851. Reprint, London: Pilot, 1949.

Raffald, Elizabeth. *The Experienced English Housekeeper*. 1769. Reprint, Lewes, U.K.: Southover Press, 1997.

Rain, Patricia. *Vanilla*. New York: Jeremy P. Tarcher/Penguin, 2004.

Randolph, Mary. *The Virginia House-Wife*. Columbia: University of South Carolina Press, 1984. Facsimile of the 1824 edition.

Ranhofer, Charles. *The Epicurean*. New York: Charles Ranhofer, 1920.

Read, George. *The Confectioner's and Pastry-Cook's Guide*. London: Dean & Son [1840?].

———. *The Guide to Trade: The Confectioner*. London: Charles Knight, 1842.

Rebora, Giovanni. *Culture of the Fork*. New York: Columbia University Press, 2001.

Riley, Gillian. *The Oxford Companion to Italian Food*. New York: Oxford University Press, 2007.

Riley, John J. *A History of the American Soft Drink Industry, Bottled Carbonated Beverages, 1807–1957*. New York: Arno, 1972.

Robertson, Helen, Sarah MacLeod, and Frances Preston. *What Do We Eat Now? A Guide to Wartime Housekeeping*. Philadelphia: J. B. Lippincott, 1942.

Rombauer, Irma S. *The Joy of Cooking*. Indianapolis: Bobbs-Merrill, 1967.

Rorer, Sarah Tyson. *Dainty Dishes for all the Year Round*. Philadelphia: North Brothers Mfg., 1905.

———. *Good Cooking*. Philadelphia: Curtis; New York: Doubleday & McClure, 1898.

———. *Ice Creams, Water Ices, Frozen Puddings, Together with Refreshments for All Social Affairs*. Philadelphia: Arnold, 1913. Reprint, Whitefish, MT: Kessinger, n.d.

———. *Mrs. Rorer's Philadelphia Cook Book*. Philadelphia: Arnold, 1886.

———. *World's Fair Souvenir Cook Book*. Philadelphia: Arnold, 1904.

Rosenzweig, Roy, and Elizabeth Blackman. *The Park and the People: A History of Central Park*. Ithaca, NY: Cornell University Press, 1992.

Rundell, Maria Eliza Ketelby. *A New System of Domestic Cookery*. Boston: W. Andrews, 1807.

Rydell, Robert W., John E. Findling, and Kimberly D. Pelle. *Fair America*. Washington, DC: Smithsonian Institution Press, 2000.

Sala, George Augustus. *Twice Round the Clock; or the Hours of the Day and Night in London*. London: Houlston and Wright, 1859.

Seely, Mrs. L. *Mrs. Seely's Cook Book*. New York: Grosset & Dunlap, 1902.

Selitzer, Ralph. *The Dairy Industry in America*. New York: Dairy & Ice Cream Field and Books for Industry, 1976.

Senn, Charles Herman. *Ices, and How to Make Them*. London: Universal Cookery and Food Association, 1900.

Shachtman, Tom. *Absolute Zero and the Conquest of Cold*. Boston: Houghton Mifflin, 1999.

Shaida, Margaret. *The Legendary Cuisine of Persia*. Henley-on-Thames, U.K.: Lieuse, 1992.

Shapiro, Laura. *Perfection Salad: Women and Cooking at the Turn of the Century*. New York: Modern Library, 2001.

———. *Something from the Oven: Reinventing Dinner in 1950s America*. New York: Viking, 2004.

Shephard, Sue. *Pickled, Potted, and Canned: How the Art and Science of Food Preserving Changed the World*. New York: Simon & Schuster, 2000.

Sherwood, Mary Elizabeth Wilson. *Manners and Social Usages*. New York: Harper & Brothers, 1887.

Shuman, Carrie V. *Favorite Dishes: A Columbian Autograph Souvenir Cookery Book*. Chicago: R. R. Donnelley & Sons, 1893.

Simeti, Mary Taylor. *Pomp and Sustenance*. New York: Alfred A. Knopf, 1989.

Smith, Andrew F., ed. *The Oxford Encyclopedia of Food and Drink in America*. New York: Oxford University Press, 2004.

Soda Fountain, the Trade Magazine, comp. *Dispenser's Formulary*. 4th ed. New York: Soda Fountain Publications, 1925.

Spurling, Hilary. *Elinor Fettiplace's Receipt Book*. New York: Viking, 1986.

Stanley, Autumn. *Mothers and Daughters of Invention*. New Brunswick, NJ: Rutgers University Press, 1995.

Stefani, Bartolomeo. *L'Arte de ben cucinare*. 1662. Reprint, Sala Bolognese, Italy: A. Forni, 1983.

Street, Julian Leonard. *Paris à la carte*. New York: John Lane, 1912.

Theophano, Janet. *Eat My Words: Reading Women's Lives through the Cookbooks They Wrote*. New York: Palgrave, 2002.

Thomas, Edith. *Mary at the Farm and Book of Recipes*. Norristown, PA: John Hartenstine, 1915.

Thomas, Lately. *Delmonico's: A Century of Splendor*. Boston: Houghton Mifflin, 1967.

Thoughts for Buffets. Boston: Houghton Mifflin, 1958.

Tuer, Andrew W. *Old London Street Cries*. London: Field & Tuer, Leadenhall Press, 1885.

Turback, Michael. *A Month of Sundaes*. New York: Red Rock Press, 2002.

Turnbow, Grover Dean, et al. *The Ice Cream Industry*. New York: John Wiley & Sons, 1947.

Twain, Mark, and Charles Dudley Warner. *The Gilded Age: A Tale of To-day*. Hartford, CT: American Publishing, 1874.

Tyree, Marion Fontaine Cabell. *Housekeeping in Old Virginia*. Richmond, VA: J. W. Randolph & English, 1878.

Vaccaro, Pamela J. *Beyond the Ice Cream Cone*. St. Louis, MO: Enid Press, 2004.

Viard, A. *Le cuisinier royal*. Paris: Gustave Barba, 1844.

Vine, Frederick T. *Ices: Plain and Decorated*. London: Offices of the British Baker and Confectioner, and Hotel Guide and Caterers' Journal [1900?].

Visser, Margaret. *Much Depends on Dinner*. New York: Grove, 1986.

Wakefield, Ruth. *Toll House Tried and True Recipes*. New York: M. Barrows, 1948.

Wansey, Henry. *The Journal of an Excursion to the United States of North America in the Summer of 1794*. New York: Johnson Reprint, 1969.

Warner-Jenkinson Manufacturing Company. *Ice Cream, Carbonated Beverages*. St. Louis, MO: Warner-Jenkinson Mfg., 1924.

Weaver, William Woys. *Thirty-five Receipts from "The Larder Invaded."* Philadelphia: Library Company of Philadelphia, 1986.

Weightman, Gavin. *The Frozen-Water Trade: A True Story*. New York: Hyperion, 2003.

Weinreb, Ben, and Chrisopher Hibbert, eds. *The London Encyclopedia*. London: Macmillan, 1983.

Weir, Robin, Peter Brears, John Deith, and Peter Barham. *Mrs. Marshall: The Greatest Victorian Ice Cream Maker*. Otley, U.K.: Smith Settle, 1998.

West Glens Falls Fire Company Ladies Auxiliary. *What's Cooking in West Glens Falls*. Mimeographed, West Glens Falls, NY, 1977.

Weygandt, Cornelius. *Philadelphia Folks: Ways and Institutions in and about the Quaker City*. New York: D. Appleton−Century, 1938.

Wheaton, Barbara Ketcham. *Savouring the Past: The French Kitchen & Table from 1300–1789*. London: Chatto & Windus, Hogarth Press, 1983.

———. *Victorian Ices & Ice Cream*. New York: Metropolitan Museum of Art, Charles Scribner's Sons, 1976.

White, E. F. *The Spatula Soda Water Guide*. Boston: Spatula Publishing, 1905.

Wilcox, Estelle Woods. *Buckeye Cookery and Practical Housekeeping: Compiled from Original Recipes*. Minneapolis, MN: Buckeye, 1877.

Williams, Jacqueline. *Wagon Wheel Kitchens: Food on the Oregon Trail*. Lawrence: University Press of Kansas, 1993.

Williams, Susan. *Savory Suppers and Fashionable Feasts: Dining in Victorian America*. New York: Pantheon, 1985.

Wilson, C. Anne. *Food and Drink in Britain*. Chicago: Academy Chicago Publishers, 1991.

Wilson, Fred A. *Some Annals of Nahant*. Boston: Old Corner Book Store, 1928.

Wolff, Joe. *Café Life Florence: A Guidebook to the Cafés & Bars of the Renaissance Treasure*. Northampton, MA: Interlink Books, 2005.

Woloson, Wendy A. *Refined Tastes: Sugar, Confectionery, and Consumers in Nineteenth-Century America*. Baltimore, MD: Johns Hopkins University Press, 2002.

Woodward, C. Vann, ed. *Mary Chestnut's Civil War*. New Haven, CT: Yale University Press, 1981.

Woody, Elizabeth. *The Pocket Cook Book*. New York: Pocket Books, 1959.

Wyman, Carolyn. *Jell-O: A Biography*. New York: Harcourt, 2001.

Young, Terence, and Robert Riley, eds. *Theme Park Landscapes: Antecedents and Variations*. Washington, DC: Dumbarton Oaks Research Library and Collection, 2002.

PERIODICALS

American Kitchen Magazine (March 1898): xiv.

American Kitchen Magazine (March 1901): xxxiv.

"A Bang-Up Finish: Peach Bombe." *McCall's* (August 1970): 56–57.

Beard, James. "Cooking with James Beard, Ice Cream." *Gourmet* (July 1970): 27, 50–52.

Cattani, Richard J. "Superior Homemade Ice Cream—a Sunday-to-Sunday Supply." *Quincy (MA) Patriot Ledger*, August 5, 1976.

Child, Theodore. "Characteristic Parisian Cafés." *Harper's New Monthly Magazine*, no. 467 (April 1889): 687–703.

Confectioners' and Bakers' Gazette. 1913–1917. Published by H. B. Winton, New York.

Confectioners' Journal. Vols. 1–4. 1874–1878. Published by Journal Publishing Company, Philadelphia.

David, Elizabeth. "Fromage Glacés and Iced Creams." *Petits Propos Culinaires* 2 (1979): 23–35. Published by Prospect Books, London.

———. "The Harvest of Cold Months." *Petits Propos Culinaires* 3 (1979): 8–15. Published by Prospect Books, London.

———. "Hunt the Ice Cream." *Petits Propos Culinaires* 1 (1979): 8–13. Published by Prospect Books, London.

———. "Savour of Ice and Roses." *Petits Propos Culinaires* 8 (1981): 7–17. Published by Prospect Books, London.

Day, Ivan. "A Natural History of the Ice Pudding." *Petits Propos Culinaires* 74 (2003): 23–38. Published by Prospect Books, London.

———. "Which Compleat Confectioner?" *Petits Propos Culinaires* 59 (1998): 44–53. Published by Prospect Books, London.

Dewey, Stoddard. "The End of Tortoni's." *Atlantic Monthly* 73, no. 440 (June 1894): 751–762.

Durfee, Stephen. "Make a Milk Chocolate and Toasted Marshmallow Ice Cream Sandwich." *Fine Cooking* (August–September 1997): 60–65.

Fabricant, Florence. "James Beard's American Favorites." *Food & Wine* (July 1981): 25–28.

"Flourishes with Food." *McCall's* (August 1970).

Grewe, Rudolph. "The Arrival of the Tomato in Spain and Italy." *Journal of Gastronomy* 3, no. 2 (Summer 1987): 67–82.

Heck, G. O. "The Future of the Ice Cream Business." *Ice Cream Field & Trade Journal* (June 1967): 70–77.

Hesser, Amanda. "Inspiration in a Tall, Cool Glass." *New York Times*, July 5, 2000.

"Hot Plate Coming Through." *Food Arts* (July–August 1998): 134.

Ice Cream Review. 1917–1942. Published by Olsen Publishing, Milwaukee, WI.

Ice Cream Trade Journal. 1937. Published by the Trade Papers Division of Reuben H. Donnelley, New York.

Idone, Christopher. "Desserts for Melting Days." *New York Times Magazine* (August 16, 1987): 59–60.

Johnnes, Daniel. "Lazy Sundaes." *Gourmet* (August 1997): 78–82.

Keller, Thomas. "The Days of Figs and Honey Are Here, Borne on a Bed of Ice Cream." *New York Times*, July 14, 1999, D5.

———. "A Savory Summer." *New York Times*, May 26, 1999.

Lauden, Rachel. "Birth of the Modern Diet." *Scientific American* (August 2000): 76–81.

———. "A Kind of Chemistry." *Petits Propos Culinaires* 62 (1999): 8–22. Published by Prospect Books, London.

Lincoln, Mary. "Ice and Ices." *New England Kitchen* 1, no. 4 (August 1894): 238–242.

Lukins, Sheila. "Scoops of Delight." *Parade Magazine* (July 28, 2002).

Marchiony, William. "You Scream, I Scream, We All Scream for Ice Cream." *National Ice Cream Retailers Association Newsletter, NICRA Bulletin* (August 1984): 3–5.

Marlowe, Jack. "Zalabia and the First Ice-Cream Cone." *Saudi Aramco World* (July–August 2003): 2–5.

Mason, Laura. "William Alexis Jarrin: An Italian Confectioner in London," *Gastronomica* (Spring 2001): 50–64.

"Masser's Self-Acting Patent Ice-Cream Freezer and Beater." *Godey's Lady's Book* (Philadelphia) 41 (August 1850): 124.

Morrison, Joseph L. "The Soda Fountain." *American Heritage Magazine* (August 1962): 1–3.

Oliver, Sandy. "Joy of Historical Cooking: Ice Cream." *Food History News* 17, no. 1 (2005): 3–8.

O'Neill, Molly. "Postcards from the Sun." *New York Times Magazine* (January 23, 1994): 49–50.

Parkinson, James W. "Ice Cream and Ice Cream Machinery, Ancient and Modern," *Confectioners' Journal* 2, no. 15 (March 1876): 11. Published by Journal Publishing Company, Philadelphia.

———. "Letter from Paris." *Confectioners' Journal* 4, no. 40 (May 1878): 19. Published by Journal Publishing Company, Philadelphia.

Parks, Mal. "Ice Cream Cones." *American Druggist Magazine* (April 1940): 36–37, 106–108.

Potter, David. "Icy Cream." *Petits Propos Culinaires* 72 (2003): 44–50. Published by Prospect Books, London.

Quinzio, Jeri. "Asparagus Ice Cream, Anyone?" *Gastronomica* (Spring 2002): 63–67.

———. "The Ice Cream Cone Conundrum." *Radcliffe Culinary Times* 10, no. 1 (Spring 2000): 6, 17.

———. "Ices in Disguise." *Radcliffe Culinary Times* 11, no. 2. (Autumn 2001): 10–11.

———. "The Triumph of Tortoni." *Radcliffe Culinary Times* 8, no. 2 (Winter 1999): 8.

Riely, Elizabeth. "I Scream, You Scream, We All Scream for Ice Cream." *Yankee Magazine* (July 1999): 78–87.

Rossant, Juliette. "The World's First Soft Drink." *Saudi Aramco World* (September–October 2005): 36–39.

Schwartz, David M. "Sippin' Soda through a Straw." *Smithsonian* (July 1986): 114–124.

"Seasonal Kitchen." *Gourmet* (November 2000): 88–94.

Simmons, Marie. "Sure-Bet Sherbets." *Cuisine* (July 1984): 44, 82–88.

Soeffing, D. Albert. "A Nineteenth-Century American Silver Flatware Service." *Antiques* (September 1999): 324–328.

Stallings, W. S., Jr. "Ice Cream and Water Ices in 17th and 18th Century England." *Petits Propos Culinaires* 3 (1979): S1–7. Published by Prospect Books, London.

Steingarten, Jeffrey. "Scoop Dreams." *Vogue* (August 2004).

Sterns, E. E., ed. *Carbonated Drinks: An Illustrated Quarterly Gazette* (New York) 1, no. 2 (October 1877) through 2, no. 4 (April 1878).

Vought, Elizabeth. "Five Ingredients: True Vanilla." *Gourmet* (July 2000): 121.

Wechsberg, Joseph. "The Historic Café Procope." *Gourmet* (September 1972): 18–71.

Weir, Caroline, and Robin Weir. "The Egg and Ice." *Ice Screamer*, no. 112 (November 2006): 3–14.

Weir, Robert J. "An 1807 Ice Cream Cone: Discovery and Evidence." *Food History News* 16, no. 2 (2004): 1–2, 6.

Willinger, Faith Heller. "Gelato: The Inside Scoop on Italian Frozen Desserts." *Gourmet* (July 1991): 94–97.

PAMPHLETS

Connecticut Light & Power's Holiday Recipe Book. Hartford, CT: Connecticut Light & Power, n.d.

Cooking with Norge Cold. Detroit, MI: Norge Division, Borg-Warner Corporation, 1941.

Coolinary Art. Schaumburg, IL: Admiral Home Appliances, 1983.

Dainty Desserts, Salads, Candies. Johnstown, NY: Knox Gelatine, Charles Knox Company [1915?].

Desserts That Make Themselves. New York: Auto Vacuum Freezer, n.d.

Frigidaire Frozen Desserts. Dayton, OH: Frigidaire, 1930.

Frigidaire Recipes. Dayton, OH: Frigidaire, 1928.

How to Freeze Foods. Cleveland, OH: General Electric, n.d.

International Harvester Refrigerator Recipes. Chicago: International Harvester, 1950.

Live Better with Your 1951 General Electric Space Maker Refrigerator. Cleveland, OH: General Electric, 1951.

Silent Hostess Treasure Book. Cleveland, OH: General Electric, 1932.

The Westinghouse Refrigerator Book. Mansfield, OH: Westinghouse, 1935.

Your Frigidaire Recipes. Dayton, OH: Frigidaire, 1938.

WEB SITES

"About Dreyer's: Dreyer's Historic Headlines." N.d. Dreyer's Grand Ice Cream, www.dreyersinc.com, accessed July 22, 2008.

Baldock, Maurita. "Eskimo Pie Corporation Records, 1921–1926, #553." 1998. Smithsonian National Museum of American History, Archives Center. Advertising, Marketing, and Commercial Imagery Collections, http://americanhistory.si .edu/archives, accessed July 23, 2008.

"Caraffa." Units and Systems of Units. 2001. Sizes, www.sizes.com/units/caraffa .htm, accessed July 21, 2008.

"Company History." 1995. Hugh Moore Dixie Cup Company Collection, 1905–1986. Compiled by Anke Voss-Hubbard. Lafayette College Libraries,

Easton, PA, ww2.lafayette.edu/~library/special/dixie/dixie.html, accessed July 22, 2008.

"The Court Dessert in Eighteenth Century France." 2003. Historic Food: The Website of Food Historian Ivan Day, http://www.historicfood.com, accessed July 23, 2008.

"Eleanor Parkinson Biography" and introduction to *The Complete Confectioner, Pastry-Cook, and Baker*. February 2005. Feeding America: The Historic American Cookbook Project. Michigan State University Library, http://digital.lib .msu.edu/projects/cookbooks/html/project.html, accessed July 23, 2008.

Feeding America: The Historic American Cookbook Project. February 2005. Michigan State University Library, http://digital.lib.msu.edu/projects/cook books/html/project.html, accessed July 23, 2008.

Gale, Jeffrey B. "Carvel Ice Cream Records, 1934–1989, #488." 1993. Smithsonian National Museum of American History, Archives Center. Advertising, Marketing, and Commercial Imagery Collections, http://americanhistory.si.edu/ archives, accessed July 23, 2008.

"Georgian Ices." 2003. Historic Food: The Website of Food Historian Ivan Day, http://www.historicfood.com, accessed July 23, 2008.

Green, Hardy. "The Man Who Brought Ice to the Masses." *Business Week Online* (February 2003), www.businessweek.com/magazine/content/03_08/b3821033 .htm, accessed July 23, 2008.

"Herrell's in the Media," quoting *Entrepreneur Magazine* (March 1987). Herrell's Ice Cream, www.herrells.com, accessed July 23, 2008.

"History." N.d. Junket Desserts, www.junketdesserts.com, accessed July 23, 2008.

"A History of Ice Cream in Philadelphia." 2008. Chilly Philly Ice Cream, www .chillyphilly.com, accessed July 23, 2008.

"Ice Cream Recipe." N.d. Thomas Jefferson's Monticello, www.monticello.org, accessed July 23, 2008.

"Ice House." N.d. Thomas Jefferson's Monticello, www.monticello.org, accessed July 23, 2008.

"I'll Take Vanilla." *Time* (May 11, 1942). Time Archive. 1923 to the Present, www .time.com/time/archive, accessed July 23, 2008.

"Industry Facts: Ice Cream." N.d. International Dairy Foods Association, www .idfa.org, accessed July 23, 2008.

"Jell-O: America's Most Famous Dessert." N.d. Duke University Libraries Digital Collections, http://library.duke.edu/digitalcollections/eaa.ck0050, accessed July 22, 2008.

Kassel, Dominique. "Tout va très bien Madame la marquise." June 2005. Ordre National des Pharmaciens. Documents de référence, Histoire et art pharmaceutique, www.ordre.pharmacien.fr, accessed July 22, 2008.

Moak, Jefferson M. "The Frozen Sucker War: Good Humor v. Popsicle." *Prologue Magazine* (Spring 2005). U.S. National Archives and Records Administration. www.archives.gov/publications/prologue/2005/spring/popsicle, accessed July 23, 2008.

Norton, Marcy. "Dairy Queen History Curls through Area." 1998. Progress '98: 300 Things That Make the Quad-Cities Great, http://qconline.com/progress98/business, accessed July 23, 2008.

"Patterns." *Time* (June 15, 1942). Time Archive. 1923 to the Present, www.time.com/time/archive, accessed July 23, 2008.

Porta, Giambattista della. *Natural Magick.* Bk. 14, chap. 11, "Of Diverse Confections of Wines." 1658, http://homepages.tscnet.com/omard1/jportac14.html #bk14X1, accessed July 23, 2008.

"Real Scoop," *Time* (April 7, 1958), Time Archive, 1923 to the Present, www.time.com/time/archive, accessed July 23, 2008.

Reynolds, Al. "IAICV Memories: The History of Ice Cream." 1998. International Association of Ice Cream Vendors, Philadelphia, www.iaicv.org, accessed July 23, 2008.

Ryan, Chris. "An Old Favorite Gets New Attention." *Fresh Cup Specialty Coffee & Tea Trade Magazine* (July 2005), www.freshcup.com, accessed July 2008.

"Sarah Tyson Rorer Biography." February 2005. Feeding America: The Historic American Cookbook Project. Michigan State University Library, http://digital.lib.msu.edu/projects/cookbooks/html/project.html, accessed July 23, 2008.

Seaburg, Carl, and Stanley Paterson. "Frederic Tudor, the Ice King." September 2003. Harvard Business School. Working Knowledge Archive, http://hbswk.hbs.edu, accessed July 23, 2008.

Sherman, Mary. "Manufacturing of Foods in the Tenements." 1906. Tenant Net: Tenants' and Renters' Rights, New York City, www.tenant.net/community/les, accessed July 23, 2008.

Skow, John. "They All Scream for It." *Time* (August 10, 1981). Time Archive. 1923 to the Present, www.time.com/time/archive, accessed July 23, 2008.

"Wafer Making." 2003. Historic Food: The Website of Food Historian Ivan Day, http://www.historicfood.com, accessed July 23, 2008.

PATENTS

Burt, H. B. Process of Making Frozen Confections, patented October 9, 1923. U.S. Patent No. 1,470,524.

Cralle, Alfred L. Ice-Cream Mold and Disher, patented February 2, 1897. U.S. Patent No. 576,395.

Johnson, Nancy M. Artificial Freezer, patented September 9, 1843. U.S. Patent No. 3,254.

Marchiony, I. Mold, patented December 15, 1903. U.S. Patent No. 746,971.

Valvona, Antonio. Apparatus for Baking Biscuit-Cups for Ice-Cream, patented June 3, 1902. U.S. Patent No. 701,776.

INDEX

absinthe, 72, 74
African Americans, pleasure gardens
  for, 83
alcohol: in ice cream, 44, 187; in ices, 3,
  44–45, 66–67, 215n3
Aldrich, Thomas Bailey: "Unguarded
  Gates," 105
Alembert, Jean Le Rond d', 11
Alexander the Great, storage of ice, 2
All about Ices, Jellies, and Creams (Harris
  and Borella), 98
Allen, Woody, xi
ambergris, 39, 42; in mousses, 34
American Kitchen Magazine, 95, 117,
  118
America's Cook Book (1940), 199
ammonia: in ice cream freezers, 162,
  176; in ice making, 92; in refrig-
  eration systems, 176
Ancient and Honorable Artillery
  Company, banquet of, 154
Anderson, Carolyn: *The Complete Book
  of Homemade Ice Cream*, 206
Anheuser-Busch (brewery), production
  of ice cream, 161
Anthimus, on cold drinks, 5
antiquity: ice storage in, 2; wafer cones
  in, 156
Arctic Ice Cream Company, 176

aristocracy, French: household organi-
  zation of, 19, 34
Armed Forces, U.S.: ice cream consumption in, 194–95
artichokes, in ice cream, 39
Artusi, Pellegrino: *La scienza in cucina*,
  27, 101
Associated Confectioners of New York,
  price-fixing by, 99
Athenaeus, on underground
  refrigeration, 2
Audiger, Nicolas, x; career of, 17–18;
  flavored drinks of, 19; freezing
  technique of, 19–20; gifts to Louis
  XIV, 18, 217n35; ice cream of, 21,
  30; ice pyramids of, 21–22; ices of,
  18; lemonade recipe of, 20;
  liqueurs of, 17, 18, 19; *La maison
  réglée*, 17, 19
automobiles: eating in, 191; in postwar
  era, 199–200

Babette, Aunt: *"Aunt Babette's" Cook
  Book*, 134, 135, 145; Nesselrode
  pudding of, 147; presentation
  suggestions of, 150
baby boom, postwar, 200
Baer, A. C., 165
baked Alaskas, 149–50, 202

261

Baldini, Filippo: *De sorbetti*, 50, 51–52; on health benefits, 51

Balzac, Honoré de: *Splendeurs et misères des courtisanes*, 72, 221n47

Barberini, Cardinal Antonio, 10

Basic Seven Foods Chart, ice cream in, 193

Baskin, Burton, 205

Baskin-Robbins company, 204–5

bastani-e gol-o bolbol (Iranian ice cream), 216n19

Beard, James, 139, 205

Beecher, Catharine: on ice cream freezers, 132; *Miss Beecher's Domestic Receipt Book*, 93, 133; Philadelphia ice cream of, 144

beet sugar, 94

Ben & Jerry's, 206

Bent Spoon (ice cream shop), 213

Berner, Ed, 127

bicarbonate of soda, 122

biscuits: American, 146; de Savoy, 76; Rorer's, 146; Tortoni's, 72–74

Bladen, Thomas, 75

Bobo, William, 83

bombs, English, 54, 70, 71

bootleggers, ice cream, 182–83

Borella, Mr.: borrowing by, 59; *The Court and Country Confectioner*, 43, 57; flavorings of, 58; ice creams of, 57–58; muscadine ice of, 68, 69

Boston Cooking School, 134, 142

Bracken, Peg: *I Hate to Cook Book*, 203

Bradley, Alice: chocolate ice cream recipe, 184; *Electric Refrigerator Menus and Recipes*, 183–84

Brancone, Cherubino, 52

brewers, American: manufacturing of ice cream, 161

brewing, ice for, 90

Briggs, Richard: *The English Art of Cookery*, 77

Brillat-Savarin, Jean Anthelme: *The Physiology of Taste*, 79

Bromo Caffeine, 124

Buckeye Cookery, 137, 141; frozen puddings in, 146; ice preparation in, 135; molded ice cream in, 149

Burke, Arthur D.: *Practical Ice Cream Making*, 169–70, 188

Burt, Harry, 174

butter churners, 97

butterfat, in ice cream, 166, 167, 170, 195, 203, 206

cafés, Parisian, 16, 17. *See also* Le Procope; Tortoni's Café

candying, Massialot on, 28

cannelon (mold), 218n9

Capatti, Alberto: *Italian Cuisine*, x, 101

Carbonated Drinks (trade magazine), 126

carbonated waters, medicinal, 121. *See also* soda waters

Carbone, Gabrielle, 213

Carême, Marie Antoine, 63

Caribbean, sugar cultivation in, 94

Carillo Salcedo, Don Stefano, 9

Carré, Ferdinand, 91–92

Carson, Jack, 175

Carvel, Tom, 192, 200

Catherine de Medici, x

caves (ice storage), 38, 115; portable, 154

Cavour, Count Camillo Benso di, 69

celebrations, American: ice cream in, 153–54

Centennial Exposition (Philadelphia, 1876), 123

Champagne water ices, 67
Chardin, Jean, 7
Charles I (king of England), xi
Charles II (king of England), xi
Charles II (king of Spain), 1
"cheeses," frozen, 30–32
cherries: candied, 127; Emy's use of, 40–41; sour, 15, 216n19; on sundaes, 179
China, ices in, ix–x
chocolate: in French ice cream, 39, 41–42; in ices, 42; in seventeenth century, 14, 41; in Spanish drinks, 14
chopine (measurement), 21
Christmas, ice cream at, 154, 172
cinnamon: in homemade ice cream, 142; in ices, 15; popularity in Italy, 54
Ciocca, Giuseppe: *Il pasticciere e confettiere moderno*, 101
Civil War: ice shipping during, 89, 91; industrialization following, 131
clam frappé, 143
Coca-Cola, 124
Coe, Sophie and Michael: *The True History of Chocolate*, 14
coffee: in French ices, 42–43; in ice cream, 41–42, 43, 67; Middle Eastern, 217n31; Persian, 16; in seventeenth-century France, 15–16, 41; Voltaire's use of, 61
coffee shops, 209
Cohen, Ben, 206
Cold Fusion Gelato (Newport, RI), 213
Cold Stone Creamery, 210
college sodas, 128
Collet, Captain, 79
Collot, Monsieur, 83
colorings: for homemade ice cream, 143–44; for ices, 46; saffron, 46
Colpi, Terri, 107

Coltelli, Francesco Procopio dei, 16–17
Comédie Française, 17, 217n31
cones, wafer: in antiquity, 156; Italian, 159
Coney Island, ice cream at, 160, 161
confectioners, American, 79–80; ice bricks of, 116; influence on home cooks, 149; of Philadelphia, 83, 101
confectioners, English, 55–61; in America, 59, 79; *bombe* of, 54; cookbooks of, 61; on street peddlers, 111–12; study on continent, 60
confectioners, European: in America, 211; American influence on, 101; in England, 59, 211
confectioners, French, 18, 26–45; effect of French Revolution on, 59; influence on Italians, 52
confectioners, Italian, 52–55; French influence on, 52; Neapolitan, 1
Confectioners' and Bakers' Gazette: ice cream parties in, 172; molded ice cream in, 178; on nineteenth-century confectioners, 175
Confectioners' Journal, 80, 120; advice to newcomers, 102; on ice cream bricks, 117; ice cream freezers in, 98; importance of, 121; on Philadelphia confectioners, 101
Continental Divide, ice cream making at, 153
Conversations on Chemistry, on soda water, 123–24
cookbooks: American, 77, 221n9; community, 131; eighteenth-century, 26, 55; frugality in, 131; plagiarism in, 59; of postwar era, 201–2; for women, 55–56, 130–31; of World War II, 196–97, 198, 199

Gunter's Tea Shop (London), 60–61; service to carriages, 191

Häagen-Dazs Company, 205, 206; *dulce de leche* flavor of, 211
Haines, Pamela: *Tea at Gunter's*, 61
Hall, Mrs. Basil, 152
Hallauer, George, 127
Hamwi, Ernest, 159
Harland, Marion: *Common Sense in the Household*, 135–37; freezing technique of, 136–37
Hayward, Art, 203
health benefits of ice cream, 50–52, 188
Heinz, Edward, 120
Henderson, Mary F.: *Practical Cooking and Dinner Giving*, 148, 150
Hendlers Ice Cream Company, 188
Hennerich, George, 196
Henry III (king of France), x
Henry, Thomas, 123
Herbert, Thomas, 6; on coffee, 16
Herrell, Steve, 206, 210, 213; experiments of, 214
Hippocras (wine), 157
Hippocrates, 4, 5
hocus-pocus, 111
Hokeypokey (song and dance), 112–13
hokeypokeys, 111–17, 211; cost of, 114; etymology of, 111; ingredients of, 113, 114, 116; paper coverings of, 117; pejorative associations of, 111, 112
holidays, American: ice cream at, 153–54, 172, 187
home economics, 131
Horton, James, 100
houacaca (spice mixture), 39

households, aristocratic: *officiers* of, 19, 34
housekeeping, scientific approach to, 130
Howard Johnson's restaurants, 180–81, 185; ice cream cones of, 189; orange roofs of, 191, 192; in postwar era, 200; twenty-eight flavors of, 191
humors, doctrine of, 4–5

ice: bricks, 114–17; serving pieces made of, 151–52
ice, artificial: distrust of, 97; oil in, 92; for Southern states, 91–92. *See also* ice-making plants
ice, natural: availability in U.S., 75, 79, 86; for brewing, 90. *See also* ice harvesting; ice storage
iceboxes, eighteenth-century, 38
icebreakers, mechanical, 135
ice cream: chocolate, 39, 41–42, 184; chocolate-covered, 172–73; chocolate curry, 213; creation myths of, ix–xi; *dulce de leche*, 211; eighteenth-century, 24, 25, 33–38, 40–41, 43, 45, 55–61, 170–71; flash-frozen, 211; in fruit shells, 150; glossaries of, 144; health benefits of, 50–52, 188; Indian, 212; Iranian, 216n19; junket, 169, 233n48; medical opinion on, xi–xii, 24; Mexican-style, 212; with orange flower water, 21, 23, 30, 33, 56, 66; painted, 46, 175; peach, ix, 78, 139; pistachio, 58, 120; precursors of, 6; scientists' contribution to, xii, 210; seasonal, 44, 170–75, 213; shipping of, 162, 210; substitutions in, 140–41, 167–68, 197; tableware for, 152; on transatlantic steamships,

ice cream (*continued*)
100; in twenty-first century, 208–14; Voltaire on, 17; wholesale operations in, 98–102; during World War II, 193–99

ice cream, American: alcohol in, 187; availability of, 129; in Basic Seven Foods Chart, 193; bootlegged, 182–83; for breakfast, 187–88; butterfat content of, 166, 167, 170, 195, 203, 206; in celebrations, 153–54, 172; celebrity consumption of, 190; chocolate-covered, 172–73; in colonial era, 75–76; cream contents of, 165; in early U.S., 77–83; federal standards for, 164–65, 166, 168, 204; fillers in, 164, 167; flavors of, 81; formulas for, 165; gourmet, 206–7; during Great Depression, xii, 181, 182–83, 187–90; home delivery of, 187; Jefferson's recipes for, 75–76; kosher, 192; local ingredients in, 213; low-fat/low-calorie, 209; marshmallow, 197–98; mix-ins for, 210; molded, 175, 178; national distribution of, 162; of 1920s, 176–79; novelties, 189–90, 194; peach, 78; per capita consumption of, 160–61, 179, 181, 190, 200, 208; Philadelphia-style, 80, 140, 141, 164; in postwar era, 199–207; powders for, 168–69, 209–10; presentation of, 148–53; quality of, 103, 203–5; railway shipment of, 162; retail price of, 189; at roadside stands, 185–86, 190–91; Rocky Road, 197; saloons for, 85–86; seasonal, 170–75; soft-serve, 141, 192–93, 200; states' regulation of, 165; superpremium,

206, 208; taste tests of, 170; as wartime essential, 168; during World War II, 194–99, 203. *See also* ice cream, homemade; ice cream industry, American

ice cream, commercial, xii, 98; additives in, 204; advances in, 177; corporations, xiii, 208, 209; cost of ingredients in, 170; formulas for, 165, 166, 170; mechanized packing of, 177; mixtures for, 169, 186–87, 194–95, 209–10; overrun in, 163, 203; paper containers for, 177; quality of, 102; refrigerated shipping of, 203; at soda fountains, 188–89; from supermarkets, 201, 202–3, 209. *See also* ice cream industry

ice cream, English: Borella's, 57–58; brown bread in, 41, 66; coffee, 67; cookies in, 66; eighteenth-century, 24, 55–61; Gunter's, 62; homemade, 141–42; hygiene measures for, 109; nineteenth-century, 61–71; nuts in, 66; with preserves, 65; seventeenth-century, xi, 23; at tea, 188; tea in, 67; with vegetable fat, 202; during World War I, 168; during World War II, 193

ice cream, French: alcohol in, 44–45; almond, 41; artichoke, 39; Audiger's, 21; chocolate, 39, 41–42; compromises in, 43–45; cookies in, 41; Emy's, 33–38, 40–41, 43–44; "frozen cheese," 30–33; Massialot's, 26, 30–32; Menon's, 32–33, 41; nuts in, 40–41; painted, 46; preserves in, 44; seasonal, 44; serving glasses for, 47; tea in, 43; truffles in, 39; uncooked, 44; vocabulary of, 30, 31–32

ice cream making (*continued*)
science, 210. *See also* freezing
techniques; ice cream, homemade;
ice cream plants
Ice Cream Merchandising Institute, 196
ice cream peddlers, Italian, 104–8; in
England, 104, 105, 109; during Great
Depression, 182; hygiene of, 110–11,
182; ice cream sandwiches of, 117, 118;
licensing of, 110; Neapolitan ices of,
113, 114; nicknames for, 111; penny
licks of, 108–9, 113; profits of, 110–11
ice cream plants: automated, 203;
capacity of, 163; conveyer systems in,
177; hardening rooms in, 163;
refrigeration systems of, 176. *See also*
ice cream industry
Ice Cream Review, 187; on chocolate-
coated ice cream, 173; Eskimo Pie in,
172; on formulas, 165; on homemade ice cream, 183; on shipping,
162; on sugar contents, 168; on
winter sales, 171; during World War
II, 196
ice cream sandwiches, 117–19, 211;
invention of, 117, 118; popularity of,
118; round, 192; wafers covering, 118
ice cream socials, 154
ice cream sodas: invention of, 125–26;
recipes for, 126; at soda fountains,
126–27. *See also* soda waters
ice cream sundaes, 127–28; *coupes*,
202–3; homemade, 178; of 1920s,
178; origin of, 221n47; at soda
fountains, 127; specialty, 188, 196;
toppings for, 128; during World War
II, 196
Ice Cream Trade Journal, 163–64; on
counter freezers, 186; on federal

standards, 165; Five Cent Bricks
recipe, 115; on frozen salads, 185
ice cream trucks, ix, 174–75, 189
iced drinks: eighteenth-century, 7;
prejudice against, 5
ice harvesting, 86–93; cessation of, 93;
extent of, 90, 92; in Maine, 91; tools
for, 89, 90
icehouses: aboveground, 3; American,
78, 86–87, 88, 91, 137; commercial,
91; communal, 87; effectiveness of,
89; Jeanes on, 87. *See also* ice
storage
ice-making plants, 92
ice pyramids, 4; Audiger's, 21–22
ices: Chinese, ix–x; between dinner
courses, 151, 207; eighteenth-
century, 25; "essences" for, 7, 65;
health benefits of, 50–52; Marco
Polo's knowledge of, ix–x; medical
opinion on, xi–xii, 4–5; precursors
of, 6; punch water, 66–67; stabilizers for, 168; standards for, 169; stirring of, 14; sugar/liquid ratio in, 13.
See also sherbets; sorbets; *sorbetti*,
Italian
ices, English: alcohol in, 66–67;
bombs, 54, 70, 71; with elderflower,
68–69; molded, 67; muscadine, 68–
69; with preserves, 58
ices, French: alcohol in, 44–45; as
centerpieces, 21–22; chocolate, 42;
coffee, 42–43; colorings for, 45–46;
edible containers for, 47; Emy's, 30,
34–35; Massialot's, 29–30; painted,
45–46; Parisian, 17, 18; pineapple,
39; seasonal, 35, 44; strawberry, 40;
trompe l'oeil presentation of, 47–49,
50, 207; vocabulary of, 30

ices, Italian: as centerpieces, 15; chocolate, 14–15; cinnamon, 15; consistency of, 13; of eighteenth century, 50–55; with fruit, 4; Neapolitan, 1, 113, 114; paeans to, 50–51; vocabulary of, 30

ices, molded: English, 67; presentation of, 46–47

ice sculptures: French, x, 21–22; Italian, 15

ice shipping, 87–90, 162; during Civil War, 89, 91; to India, 89, 91; innovations in, 88; to London, 89–90, 97; for medicinal purposes, 90; from Norway, 100; to West Indies, 88

ice-spoons, 152

ice storage: in antiquity, 2; depots for, 90–91; in eighteenth century, 26–27, 38; underground, 2–3; in U.S., 86–87. *See also* icehouses

immigrants, following Civil War, 131

immigrants, Italian: children, 107, 111; to England, 106–8; ice cream shops of, 116; living conditions of, 109; under *padrone* system, 105–6; prejudice against, 105, 111; working conditions of, 107. *See also* ice cream peddlers, Italian

Immigration Act (U.S., 1924), 105

India, ice shipments to, 89, 91

International Association of Ice Cream Manufacturers, 194

International Exhibition (London, 1862), ice making at, 91

Italian Immigration Bureau (New York), 105–6

Italy: confectioners of, 1, 52–55; cost of salt in, 27. *See also* ice cream, Italian; ices, Italian; immigrants, Italian; Naples

jams, sugar in, 28

Janin, Jules, 72

Janvier, Thomas A.: *In Old New York,* 82

Jarrin, William, 59; *bomba* ice of, 70; confectionery business of, 62–63; death of, 63; freezing techniques of, 64, 65; grape water ices of, 68; *The Italian Confectioner,* 61, 62–63; punch water ices of, 66; on wafers, 158

Jeanes, William: freezing techniques of, 64, 65; frozen pudding of, 69–71; on Jarrin, 63–64; *The Modern Confectioner,* 61, 62, 63, 87, 120; *plombière* of, 70; punch water ices of, 66–67

Jefferson, Thomas: ice cream recipes of, 75–76; icehouse of, 86–87

Jell-O Company, ice cream powders of, 169

jelly, pokeberry, 143

J. M. Horton Ice Cream Company, 100

Johnson, Howard Deering, 180–81, 189; restaurant franchise of, 185, 191–92

Johnson, Nancy M., xii; artificial freezer of, 95–96, 134

The Joy of Cooking, ice cream recipes in, 201

Junket ice cream, 169, 233n48

Keller, Thomas, 207

Kelvinator refrigerators, 176

khulfee (Indian ice cream), 212

Kindervater, G. G., 181

King's American Dispensatory, 121

kitchen utensils, mass-produced, 132–33
Kleen Kup (paper cup), 189
Klondike bars, 189
knives, for molded ice cream, 152
Kopfer, Torrance, 213

Ladies Home Journal, 130
landscapes, picturesque, 84
Latini, Antonio: in Barberini household, 10; chocolate ices of, 14–15; cinnamon ice of, 15; early life of, 10; lemon sorbet recipe, 12–13, 15; milk sorbet recipe of, 13–14; modern methods of, 11; readers of, 13; *Lo scalco alla moderna,* 9, 10–11, 17; *sorbetti* of, 12–13, 15, 20; use of New World foods, 12
La Varenne, Pierre de: *neiges* of, 22; *Le nouveau confiturier,* 22; *Le vrai cuisinier françois,* 22
Lea, Elizabeth Ellicott: *Domestic Cookery,* 93, 143
lemonades, 7; Audiger's, 20
Leslie, Eliza, 93; *Directions for Cookery,* 138; *The Lady's Receipt-Book,* 139; *Seventy-five Receipts for Pastry, Cakes, and Sweetmeats,* 138–39
Lincoln, Mary: on fillers, 164; *Frozen Dainties,* 134, 141, 150; on frozen puddings, 146; on ice cream molds, 149; ice cream recipes of, 141, 144; *Mrs. Lincoln's Boston Cook Book,* 133, 140, 144; *The Peerless Cook-Book,* 134; on sherbet, 145
Lippincott, Charles, 123
liqueurs: Audiger's, 17, 18, 19; Noyau, 70; orange, 81
liquid nitrogen, in ice cream freezing, 142, 211

London: Gunter's Tea Shop, 60–61, 191; ice cream hygiene in, 109; ice cream peddlers of, 104, 105. *See also* ice cream, English
Longworth's American Almanac, soda fountains in, 122
Louisiana Purchase Exposition. *See* Saint Louis World's Fair

MacLeod, Sarah, 197
Maine, ice harvest in, 91
mallobet, strawberry, 198
Maolis (pleasure garden, Nahant, MA), 90
Marchiony, Italo, 159
Marchiony, William, 159
Marco Polo, knowledge of ices, ix–x
Marie Antoinette (queen of France), 95
Marshall, Agnes B.: *The Book of Ices,* 68, 141–42; cinnamon ice cream recipe, 142; ice cream cones of, 142, 158–59; ice serving pieces of, 152; innovations of, 142; on liquid nitrogen freezing, 211; on presentation of ices, 151
marshmallows, in ice cream, 197–98
Martinique, ice shipping to, 88
Masser's Self-Acting Patent Ice-Cream Freezer, 129
Massialot, François: on candying, 28; on cooking sugar, 27–29; *Le cuisinier roïal et bourgeois,* 26; "English cheese" recipe, 31, 32; ice cream of, 26, 30–32; ices of, 29–30; *Nouvelle instruction pour les confitures,* 26, 27, 156; on quality ingredients, 27, 28; raspberry water ice of, 29–30; wafer recipe of, 156
Masters, Thomas: *The Ice Book,* 96–97
Mattus, Reuben and Rose, 205

May, Robert: *The Accomplisht Cook,* 8–9
Mayhew, Henry, 104
McCabe, James Dabney: *The Illustrated History of the Centennial Exhibition,* 123
McCall's magazine, ice cream freezers in, 205
McCreary, Mrs. Governor J. B., 146
McCullough, Alex, 192–93
McCullough, J. F., 192–93
measurements, 217n38, 219n5; *chopine,* 21; *demi-setier,* 21; standard, 132–33; for sugar, 65
Mel-O-Rols, 190
Menon, François, 55; ice creams of, 32–33, 41; on painted ices, 45; *Les soupers de la cour,* 32
meringue, 157; browned, 146, 150; egg-shaped, 47, 150; in mousses, 73; as stabilizer, 8
Michael, P.: on gelatin, 115; *Ices and Soda Fountain Drinks,* 109, 167; on Italian ice cream, 116; on Neapolitan ices, 114
Michigan State University, American cookbooks of, 221n9
Middle Ages, custards of, 7–8
Middle East: coffees of, 217n31; sherbets of, 6–7, 19, 216n19
milk: safety of, 108, 109–10; shipping of, 165; in *sorbetti,* 13–14, 52; types of, 52. *See also* butterfat
Miller, Amy, 212–13, 214
Miller, Val: *Thirty-six Years an Ice Cream Maker,* 115–16, 173
mixtures, ice cream: commercial, 186–87, 209–10; patent, 169; during World War II, 194–95, 199
Mojonnier Brothers Company, 177

molasses, 94
molds: *cannelon,* 218n9; for homemade ice cream, 148–49; lead, 69, 217n39; mass-produced, 178; removable centerpieces in, 149. *See also* ice cream, molded
molinillo (wooden beater), 14
Montaigne, Michel de: on cold drinks, 5
Montanari, Massimo, x, 101
monzu, 26
Moore, John, 48–49
Morier, James, 6
mousses: chocolate, 14, 21; Emy's, 34; flavors for, 34
Mouy, M., 70
muscadine, in ices, 68–69

Naples: food specialties of, 11; *sorbetti* of, 1, 2, 12, 53
Napoleon III (king of France), 69
National Dairy Council, 194
nature, imitation of, 45
nectarines, Emy's use of, 40
Negri, Domenic, 60, 62
neiges, La Varenne's, 22
Nelson, Christian K., 173–74
Nero (emperor of Rome), ix
Nesselrode, Karl Vasilyevich, 70
Nestlé (corporation), xiii, 208
New England Kitchen (magazine), 92, 134
New World, food products of, 1–2, 9, 11–12, 24
New York: food safety in, 110–11; ice cream saloons of, 85; Italian Immigration Bureau, 105; pleasure gardens of, 81–85
Ninkotu (emperor of Japan), 2

cookbooks of, 196–97, 198, 199; English ice cream during, 202; ice cream mixes during, 194–95, 199; ice cream quality during, 203; ice cream ships of, 194; Japanese ice cream consumption during, 193; rationing during, 196–97, 200; soda fountains during, 195

Wyeth, Nathaniel, 89

zabaglione, 70; frozen and unfrozen, 54
zalabia (wafers), 159, 160

CALIFORNIA STUDIES IN FOOD AND CULTURE

DARRA GOLDSTEIN, EDITOR

TEXT: 11.5/13.5 VENDETTA MEDIUM
DISPLAY: SACKERS GOTHIC; DALLIANCE ROMAN; VENDETTA
COMPOSITOR: BINGHAMTON VALLEY COMPOSITION, LLC
PRINTER AND BINDER: MAPLE-VAIL BOOK MANUFACTURING GROUP